# Essentials

# Autodesk®
## Vault Professional 2018

July 2017

Published by
ASCENT Center for Technical Knowledge
630 Peter Jefferson Parkway, Suite 175
Charlottesville, VA 22911

866-527-2368

www.ascented.com

# Contents

# Introduction

Welcome to the *Autodesk® Vault Professional 2018 Essentials* learning guide for use in Authorized Training Center (ATC®) locations, corporate training settings, and other classroom settings.

Although this guide is designed for instructor-led courses, you can also use it for self-paced learning.

This introduction covers the following topics:

- Course objectives
- Prerequisites
- Using this guide
- Notes, tips, and warnings
- Feedback
- Free Autodesk Software for Students and Educators

Refer to **Course and Classroom Setup** section for installing the practice files and restoring the backup.

This guide is complementary to the software documentation. For detailed explanations of features and functionality, refer to the Help in the software.

## Course Objectives

This guide covers the following topics:

- Introduction to Autodesk Vault Professional
- Working with Items
- Managing Change
- Working with Bills of Materials
- Administering Autodesk Vault Professional
- Reporting
- Working with AutoCAD® Civil 3D
- Working with Autodesk® Revit®
- Thin Client
- Replication

## Prerequisites

This learning guide is designed to teach new users the essential elements of using Autodesk Vault Professional 2018.

It is recommended that you have a working knowledge of Autodesk Vault and one or more of the following products:

- Microsoft® Office
- Autodesk® Inventor®
- AutoCAD®
- AutoCAD Civil 3D
- Autodesk Revit

## Using This Guide

The lessons are independent of each other. However, it is recommended that you complete these lessons in the order that they are presented unless you are familiar with the concepts and functionality described in those lessons.

Each chapter contains:

- Lessons: Usually two or more lessons in each chapter.
- Exercises: Practical, real-world examples for you to practice using the functionality you have just learned. Each exercise contains step-by-step procedures and graphics to help you complete the exercise successfully.

## Notes, Tips, and Warnings Feedback

Throughout this guide, notes, tips, and warnings are called out for special attention.

Notes contain guidelines, constraints, and other explanatory information.

Tips provide information to enhance your productivity.

Warnings provide information about actions that might result in the loss of data, system failures, or other serious consequences.

## Feedback

Autodesk understands the importance of offering you the best learning experience possible. If you have comments, suggestions, or general inquiries about Autodesk Learning, please contact us at learningtools@autodesk.com.

As a result of the feedback we receive from you, we hope to validate and append to our current research on how to create a better learning experience for our customers.

### Free Autodesk Software for Students and Educators

The Autodesk Education Community is an online resource with more than five million members that enables educators and students to download for free the same software used by professionals worldwide (see website for terms and conditions). You can also access additional tools and materials to help you design, visualize, and simulate ideas. Connect with other learners to stay current with the latest industry trends and get the most out of your designs.

Get started today. Register at the Autodesk Education Community (www.autodesk.com/joinedu) and download one of the many available Autodesk software applications.

**Note:** Free products are subject to the terms and conditions of the end-user license and services agreement that accompanies the software. The software is for personal use for education purposes only and is not intended for classroom or lab use.

# Course and Classroom Setup

### Classroom Environment

The courseware is intended for use in an instructor-led environment. If you plan to use the courseware on your own in a non-classroom environment, you must set up Autodesk Vault correctly. Before you set up your system, you should be aware of the following:

- Do not use a production vault for the exercises. It is recommended that you set up a separate vault on a separate vault server.
- If you plan to repeat an exercise, you must remove any files that were added to the vault when you previously completed the exercise. It is recommended that you delete the entire vault and start again with a new vault.
- Do not attempt these exercises on a production vault server until you are familiar with the procedures that are covered.

 If you have installed AutoCAD or AutoCAD-based products after installing Autodesk Vault, you might need to Uninstall/Change the Autodesk Vault Client installation and select Add or Remove Features to select the appropriate Add-In software.

You must install and run this courseware from individual computers. You cannot run the courseware from a shared server. **DO NOT install the courseware on a computer that stores working vault data.**

### Overview of Installing the Courseware

The following steps describe how to install the courseware.

1. Install Autodesk Vault Professional Client and Autodesk Vault Professional Server on each computer.
2. Install the course data sets on each computer.
3. If Autodesk Vault has been previously used on the computer, restore default settings for the user interface.

## Installing Autodesk Vault

Install both Autodesk Vault Professional Client and Autodesk Vault Professional Server on each computer. See the Autodesk Vault installation help for installation instructions.

If you are using any of the following Autodesk® software applications in conjunction with Autodesk Vault, they must be installed before installing Autodesk Vault:

- Autodesk Inventor
- AutoCAD
- AutoCAD® Mechanical
- AutoCAD® Electrical
- AutoCAD®Civil 3D
- Autodesk Revit

## Installing the Practice Files

To install the data files for the exercises:

1. Download the Practice Files zip file using the link provided on the Practice Files page in the learning guide.
2. Unzip the zip file to the C: drive. An AOTG VAULT Professional folder is created and contains all the files that you will need. The path for all the files should be *C:\AOTG VAULT Professional\*.
3. The remaining files are required to restore the database. The instructions for this are detailed below.

**WARNING - The following procedure will overwrite the current datasets and file stores in your current Vault. Backup any necessary Vaults that might be required at a later time.**

## Restore the Backup

1. Click Start>All Programs>Autodesk>Autodesk Data Management>Autodesk Data Management Server Console 2018.
2. In the Log In dialog box:
- For User Name, enter **administrator**.
- Leave Password blank.
- Click OK.
- The Autodesk Data Management Server Console displays.
3. Select Tools>Backup and Restore.
4. Click Restore and click Next.

5. In the Backup and Restore Wizard dialog box, in Select backup directory for restore, navigate to the location on your local C: drive where the zip file was extracted (*C:\AOTG VAULT Professional*).

- In the Database data location, select Default Restore Location.
- In the File Store location, select Original Restore Location.

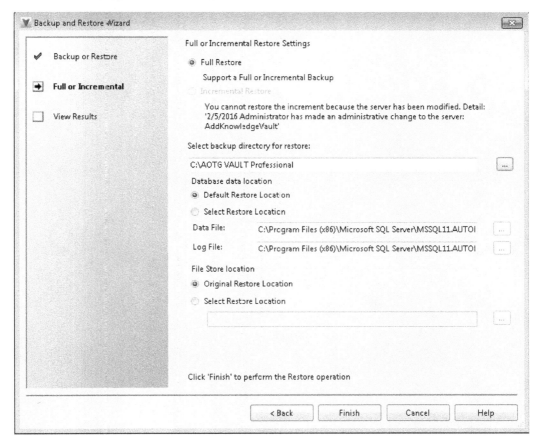

6. Click Finish.

7. In the Autodesk Data Management Server Console dialog box, click the Yes button to delete the current Datasets and File Stores.

8. The Restore Progress dialog box displays the restoring database progress.

9. In the Backup and Restore Wizard dialog box, click Close.

10. In the Autodesk Data Management Server Console dialog box, select File>Exit.

# Practice Files

To download the practice files for this learning guide, use the following steps:

1. Type the URL shown below into the address bar of your Internet browser. The URL must be typed **exactly as shown**. If you are using an ASCENT ebook, you can click on the link to download the file.

2. Press <Enter> to download the .ZIP file that contains the Practice Files.

3. Once the download is complete, unzip the file to a local folder. The unzipped file contains an .EXE file.

4. Double-click on the .EXE file and follow the instructions to automatically install the Practice Files on the C:\ drive of your computer.

   **Do not** change the location in which the Practice Files folder is installed. Doing so can cause errors when completing the practices in this learning guide.

**http://www.ascented.com/getfile?id=labefacto**

# Introduction to Autodesk Vault Professional

This chapter gives an overview of Autodesk® Vault Professional software, its features, functions, and benefits, and the Autodesk Vault Professional user interface.

## Objectives

After completing this chapter, you will be able to:

- Describe Autodesk Vault Professional features.
- Identify the user interface elements and navigate the user interface.

# Lesson: Autodesk Vault Professional Overview

## Overview

In this lesson, you learn about the basic features and functionalities of Vault Professional, and its advantages as a design data management system.

With Vault Professional, you can implement an automated release and change management process with complete tracking of bills of materials (BOMs) and related design information.

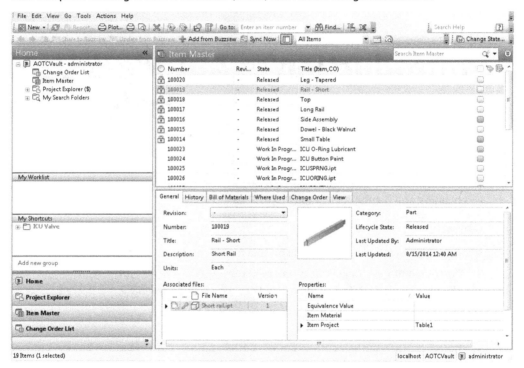

### Objectives

After completing this lesson, you will be able to:

- Describe Vault Professional.
- Explain the roles of Vault Professional in lifecycle management and change management.
- List some of the roles users can be assigned in Vault Professional.
- Describe Vault Professional integration with other design applications.

# About Autodesk Vault Professional

Autodesk Vault Professional is an integral part of the Autodesk data management solution. It uses vault files as item data, making vault files available to an extended design team that can include personnel from departments outside of engineering.

Autodesk Vault Professional helps you manage your vault data by creating and tracking change orders, managing bills of materials, and working with item revisions and lifecycles to oversee files throughout the design and manufacturing process.

## Benefits of Autodesk Vault Professional

When designers and engineers place their data files in a vault, Autodesk Vault Professional connects these files to item numbers that can integrate with ERP systems. Thus Autodesk Vault Professional is a gateway connecting two different parts of a company: the design/engineering team and the extended product team.

## Example of How to Use Autodesk Vault Professional

With Autodesk Vault Professional, more users can connect directly to the files in the vault, assign items to these files, enable other users in a larger team to work with the items, view items using visualization files, and manage these items as they move through their lifecycle from design to manufacturing to completion.

# Autodesk Vault Professional Functions

Autodesk Vault Professional automates the release management process by managing engineering changes and bills of materials. You use Autodesk Vault Professional to manage items throughout their lifecycle.

## Manage Items

| Function | Description |
|---|---|
| Create Items | With Autodesk Vault Professional, you can create items by assigning items to data files or by creating new items. |
| Delete Items | When an item has reached the end of its lifecycle and is no longer used, you can delete it from the Item Master. |
| Organize Items | Using the Item Master list, you can quickly search, sort, and filter items, and customize how the item list is viewed. |
| Add User-Defined Properties to Items | In addition to the default properties for each item, you can add user-defined properties (fields) to item records. |
| Where Used | You can analyze where items are used and check item dependencies before editing an item or requesting an engineering change order. |
| Track Item Revisions | A flexible revision numbering scheme keeps track of the history of items. You can use a predefined number of letter schemes, or use the ASME Y14.35M scheme. You can use secondary and tertiary schemes to track data with even more detail. |

## Bill of Materials (BOM)

| Function | Description |
| --- | --- |
| Link Items | A BOM is built automatically when an assembly file in the vault is assigned an item.<br><br>You can also link items together to create your own BOM that includes newly created items. |
| Edit BOMs | You can edit materials and quantities for any design. You can override quantities in a BOM. |
| Units of Measure | Autodesk Vault Professional and Autodesk® Inventor® support the same units of measure, so any units of measure used in Inventor are automatically transferred to Autodesk Vault Professional BOMs. You can also specify the base measure of items, including mass, volume, quantity, and length. |
| Property Mapping | You can map CAD properties in design files in Autodesk Vault to item properties. These CAD properties are carried over to corresponding items in Autodesk Vault Professional that can be used in the Item Master list and in the BOM. |

## Engineering Change Orders (ECOs)

| Function | Description |
| --- | --- |
| Manage ECOs | You can create ECOs and send them to members of the team. You can also attach notes and red-lined drawings to ECOs.<br><br>ECOs are reviewed and tracked by members of the team then can be rejected, approved, or withdrawn. The status of these ECOs is shown graphically and can be tracked to ensure that change orders are not forgotten or misplaced. |
| Set Up Routes | You can set up routing lists with email support. You can use these lists to ensure that the right team members are notified of changes. |

## Item Lifecycle

Every item is tracked with indicators that show the state of the item (Work in Progress, Released, In Review, and Obsolete). Revisions increment automatically in some cases when an item changes state. This process ensures that correct revision control is used. Generally, items are in a Work in Progress state when edited and in a Released state when released to manufacturing.

## Manage Security

Users receive system access based on their departments, positions, and roles. Security features prevent inadvertent changes and enable only authorized users to access or edit data. Certain functions, such as creating new numbering schemes, mapping CAD properties to item properties, and editing users, are restricted to administrators.

### Example of Linking Design Data

The design work on an ICU valve is nearing completion and released by the design team. As part of managing the valve data, you need to set up the packaged product. You add an item representing the final packaged assembly, an item representing the packaging itself, and another item representing the product specification sheet. You link these items to the assembly design data to form a BOM for all the components then release the items to manufacturing.

Based on an ECO, a new revision of the ICU valve packaged assembly has spare O-rings, and the ICU valve buttons are no longer painted.

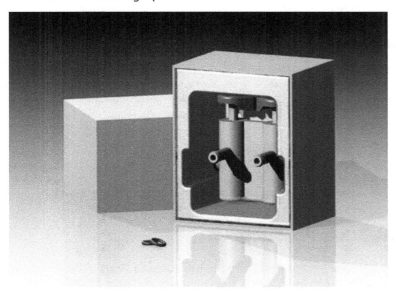

# Security and Users in Autodesk Vault Professional

You can control who has access to certain features in Autodesk Vault Professional by assigning users different roles and permissions.

### Add Users

As a Vault Professional administrator, you can add, modify, and remove users from the system. You can group users with similar roles and manage permissions and roles for both groups and individual users.

You can also add users from a domain.

### Specify Roles

In addition to the Administrator, Content Center, and Document roles, Autodesk Vault Professional has the following predefined roles: Change Order Editor (Levels 1 and 2), ERP Manager, Item Editor (Levels 1 and 2), Item Reviewer, Custom Object Consumer, Custom Object Editor (Levels 1 and 2), and Custom Object Manager (Levels 1 and 2). Users can be assigned roles based on their required level of access in the company.

 When you add a new user, you should include their email address so that they can receive automatic notification of ECOs.

### Role-Based Permissions

Users are assigned Vault Professional task permissions based on the role they are assigned by an administrator. Administrators can also create Access Control lists for any folder in a vault. Folder permissions such as Full Access and Read-Only can be assigned to groups or individual users.

### Example

New employees join the company and require access to design data in the vault. The administrator adds new users and sets their roles based on their required access to vault and Vault Professional data. However, because the new employees are training during the first two weeks, the administrator sets their access to certain sensitive folders as read-only until they have finished training.

# Integration with Other Products

The Autodesk Vault Professional software is a web services-based application. The application interfaces with files located in a vault file store and database. The file store and database were created during installation or migrated from another Autodesk Vault release.

Vault Professional integrates with the applications that produced the files in the vault. You can access the vault from the design application or open files created by these applications in Vault Professional.

### Autodesk Inventor

Vault Professional integrates with Autodesk Inventor. Vault Professional reads Autodesk® Inventor® files and the relationships amongst these files. The items' type and BOM information is built on this data.

- Inventor can control BOM data. By assigning BOM structure properties to components, such as phantom or inseparable, Inventor influences how the Vault Professional application reads and builds its BOMs for those items.
- You can transfer custom properties between Inventor and Vault Professional.
- Vault Professional fully supports all units of measure used by Inventor.

## AutoCAD-Based Products

Autodesk Vault Professional integrates with other design applications and reads data in AutoCAD® drawing (DWG™) files. The following list outlines how AutoCAD-based applications work with Autodesk Vault Professional.

- External references (xrefs) are added as attachments to items in Vault Professional when the parent drawings are assigned items.
- Vault Professional can read drawing files and map their properties to item properties.
- Vault Professional can read projects, drawings, and properties from AutoCAD® Civil 3D® drawing files, and it can map their properties to item properties. Vault Professional also provides AutoCAD Civil 3D software users with additional project management functionality by displaying a Project tree in the Prospector tab. This enables the AutoCAD Civil 3D software users to safely share their drawing files and individual AEC objects with other team members.
- Vault Professional reads BOM data in AutoCAD® Mechanical drawing files. It uses this data to create BOM data and determine object types.
- If the vault is set to enforce file locking, you cannot check out a drawing from the vault unless its lifecycle state is set to Work in Progress.

## Autodesk Revit

The Autodesk Vault Professional software with Revit Vault Add-in offers Autodesk Revit users with file security, version control, and multi-user support. Autodesk Vault integrates with Autodesk® Revit® Architecture, Autodesk® Revit® MEP, and Autodesk® Revit® Structure.

# Lesson: User Interface

## Overview

This lesson describes the features of the Vault Professional user interface.

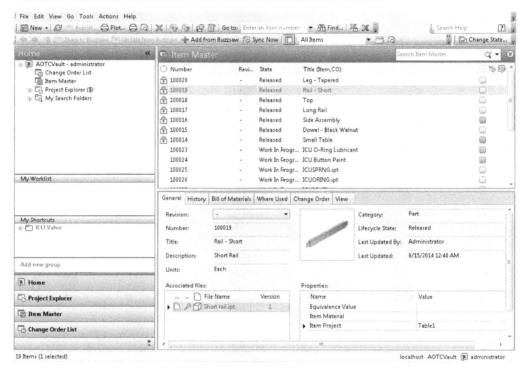

## Objectives

After completing this lesson, you will be able to:

- Identify the user interface elements in Vault Professional.
- Describe the three main areas of the user interface.
- Use the main pane in Vault Professional to show a list of objects that can be files in the vault, items, or engineering change orders (ECOs).
- Navigate the user interface.

# User Interface Elements

With the user interface elements in Autodesk Vault Professional, you can work quickly and efficiently with data.

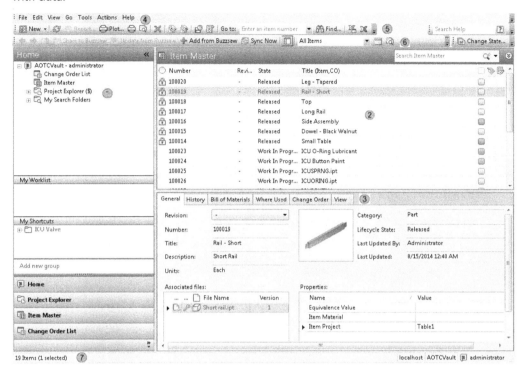

① Navigation pane – Contains folders and subfolders for different environments, shortcuts for searches, and filters. The work environment (All Folders, Item Master, Change Order List, or Vault Explorer) is determined by the selection in the navigation pane.

② Main pane – Contains the primary list of data, which changes based on the current work environment. It can be a list of items, a list of files in the vault, or a list of ECOs. Depending on the type of environment, the records for these lists can be selected, previewed in more detail, and edited

③ Preview pane – Shows a preview of the selected record in the main pane. The different tabs are logically organized views of details of the record and change, depending on the environment.

④ Main menu – Contains the commands used in Vault Professional.

⑤ Standard toolbar – The Standard toolbar provides quick access to common commands depending on the environment

⑥ Secondary toolbars – An Advanced and Behavior toolbar provides quick access to other common commands depending on the environment.

⑦ Status bar – Shows information such as the number of records in the main pane, the number of records selected, the user name, and the name of the vault in which the user is logged.

### Example of the Autodesk Vault Professional User Interface

In Autodesk Vault Professional, you normally begin in the navigation pane. This pane contains one or more objects that essentially behave as folders, because they contain other objects.

When you select one of these folders, the data in the selected folder displays in the main pane. You then work in the main pane.

When a record in the main pane is selected, it is previewed in the Preview pane.

# About the Navigation Pane

The navigation pane is the starting point in the Autodesk Vault Professional user interface. Use the navigation pane to go directly to required data.

Using the main workflows, you can work efficiently with Autodesk Vault Professional and quickly locate the data you require.

### Navigation Pane Areas

| Screen Element | Description |
|---|---|
| Home | The upper part of the navigation pane shows the folders you can click. These folders can be filtered so that only the Item Master or only Project Explorer is visible. |
| | In the following illustration the Home view is shown, where all possible folders for navigation are visible. |
| | |
| | Three major work environments exist in Vault Professional: |
| | ▪ Items |
| | ▪ Change orders |
| | ▪ Project Explorer |
| | By clicking the folders, you change the work environment displayed, which affects the main pane and the Preview pane. |
| My Search Folders | In the previous illustration, saved searches are also visible. |
| | These saved searches are environment specific. For example, if you create a search in the Item Master for the word Valve then save this search, it displays under My Search Folders. Clicking this Valve folder brings up the Item Master work environment and displays the filtered items containing the word Valve. |

| | |
|---|---|
| My Work list | ECOs requiring your attention or action are listed under My Worklist together with the due date. Clicking the listed item brings up the Change Order list work environment with the ECO highlighted.<br><br>My Worklist<br>📝 ECO-000001 (4/20/2010) |
| My Shortcuts | You can create group folders in the My Shortcuts area. You can fill these folders with shortcuts to items, documents, files in the vault, and ECO. Clicking these links takes you to the selected objects immediately.<br><br>My Shortcuts<br>   Trailer Hitch Ball<br>   Helical Spring Lock<br>  ICU Valve<br>     End Cap<br>     Housing<br><br>Add new group |
| Navigation Pane Buttons | Buttons in the navigation pane, located in the lower-left corner of the main interface screen, filter the folders at the top of the navigation pane. For example, clicking Project Explorer removes all folders except those displayed in Project Explorer.<br><br>▣ Home<br>🗗 Project Explorer<br>🗓 Item Master<br>🗓 Change Order List<br>&raquo;<br><br>**Tip:** Use these buttons to filter the folders saved under My Search Folders. In the main pane, you see the results of searches for all work environments. However, when you click a button such as Project Explorer, only search results for the Project Explorer environment display. |

### Example of the Navigation Pane

In the following illustration, Home is selected in the lower-left corner of the user interface. The Item Master is selected in the navigation pane. The contents of this folder (Item Master) display in the main pane.

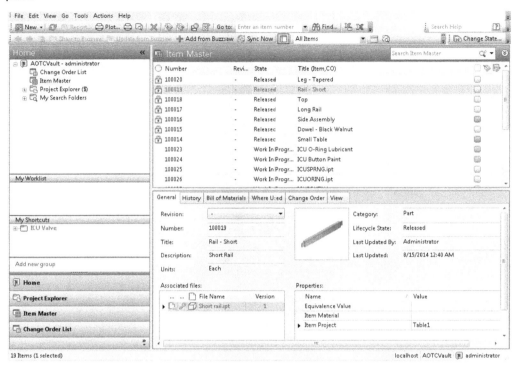

# About the Main Pane

The main pane changes based on the work environment and how the view is customized. Use the main pane to sort, filter, and view records in the list.

The main pane lists records of objects. These objects can be items, files in the vault, or ECOs, based on the work environment.

You can customize the main pane to show different fields and to filter the list based on different criteria. You can also use Find to quickly search a list.

## Example of Item Master

When working with items, the main pane shows the Item Master.

## Example of the Change Order List

ECOs are listed in the Change Order list.

## Example of Files in a Vault Folder

Files and their properties are listed when a vault folder is selected in the navigation pane.

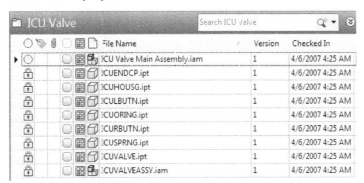

# About the Item Record Dialog Box

Along with the major interface panes, one of the most commonly used interface elements in Vault Professional is the Item Record dialog box. Use the Item Record dialog box to view (Open) or edit (Edit) items and their BOMs, and to attach and detach files. Items must be in the Work In Progress state in order to open them for editing. Otherwise they can be opened read-only for viewing. This feature is helpful when the item has a lot of details or when you want to view the associated files.

Using the Item Record interface, you can edit an item's properties, including the item's BOM, attach and detach files, and view change orders associated with that item.

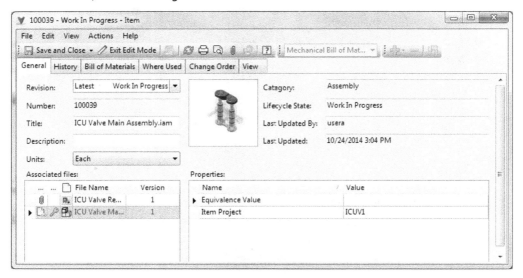

## Example of the Item Record Interface

You create a new item such as lubricant in the Item Master. In the Item Master, you double-click an item representing an assembly to open it and click Edit for editing. You add the lubricant item in the assembly item's BOM. When you have completed the task, you click Save and Close to save the changes and exit the Edit Item Record dialog box.

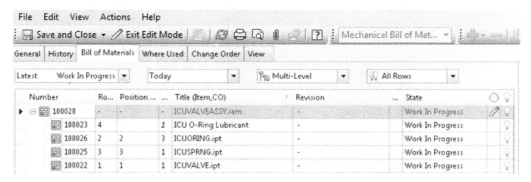

# Chapter Summary

Autodesk Vault Professional extends provides product management to your manufacturing designs. A common interface provides access to files, items, BOMs, and change orders.

Having completed this chapter, you can:

- Describe Autodesk Vault Professional features.
- Identify the user interface elements and navigate the user interface.

# Working with Items

This chapter describes how to create and manage items in Autodesk® Vault Professional. You can assign items to CAD files in the vault, or create new items for products not specifically modeled in CAD.

Items are used to represent the design data but a large collection of items can be difficult to manage in the vault. By using customized views and filters, you can sort or filter the item list based on item properties to manage the items effectively.

## Objectives

After completing this chapter, you will be able to:

- Create, modify, and delete items, use filters to view items, and add and remove file attachments.
- Create, modify, and delete custom views, use filters to view items, and find items.
- Work with default item properties and user-defined properties, including item numbers.
- Export item data.

# Lesson: Creating Items

## Overview

In this lesson you learn how to create, modify, and delete items, use filters to view items, and add and remove file attachments.

Use items to help manage your vault data and make that data available to the extended design team.

## Objectives

After completing this lesson, you will be able to:

- Create items by assigning items to selected design data from Autodesk® Vault.
- Work with the Item Master.
- Assign items to files in a vault, and create new items from scratch.
- Attach engineering documents such as specifications, design and product data sheets, and regulatory documents to items.
- Use automatic attachments to expedite assigning items to files in the vault.

# About Items

Working with items is a crucial part of automating the data management process and maintaining control of your design data. When a new design is added to the vault, each part or assembly can be assigned an item so it can be clearly identified.

You create items by assigning them to design data from the vault or by creating a new item directly in the Item Master.

## Definition of Items

Items represent physical elements that a company uses to produce the products it manufactures. Common items include parts and assemblies, documents, consumable goods such as grease, paint, fluids, and lubricants, and even artwork. Some items are purchased while others are manufactured by the company.

An item is identified by a unique identifier (the item number). This number is used to identify the item in change orders, product lists, bills of materials, and ERP systems.

| | Number | Revision | State | | Title (Item,CO) | |
|---|---|---|---|---|---|---|
| | 100019 | - | Released | | Long Rail | |

## Example of Assigning Items

As part of a new design, a new part is added to the vault. You assign an item to the part. The new item has a unique item number, which can be as simple as a six number sequence (Part 100352) or a complex set of text and numbers (Part RD-100-0152).

This item number normally follows company standards and is used to help identify the item. The application uses this number to track the item through its lifecycle.

# Item Master

To manage and track the lifecycle of items used in product development, users are required to access a list of items where they can preview, create, modify, and delete items as required. The Item Master is where this list of items is found.

## About the Item Master

The Item Master contains a complete list of all items in the Vault. These items usually represent design data in the vault.

Items in the Item Master are identified by unique identifiers (item numbers). Each item has a number of system and user-defined properties.

## Using the Item Master

Using the Item Master, you can:

- List all items in the system and define custom views to filter the list.
- Add or remove columns (fields) in the list, change column order and width, and sort by any column.
- Group items by column headings.
- Preview comments automatically.
- Go to a specific item.
- Find an item or items, and optionally save the search.
- Change column text alignment.
- Create new items.
- Edit items.
- Preview items in the Preview pane.

## Example of the Item Master

As new designs are added to the vault and assigned items, the Item Master list grows.

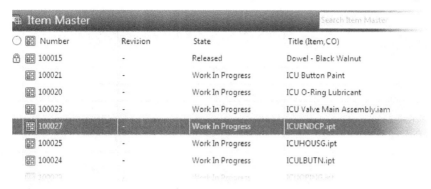

| | | Number | Revision | State | Title (Item,CO) |
|---|---|---|---|---|---|
| ○ | 🔲 | Number | Revision | State | Title (Item,CO) |
| 🔒 | 🔲 | 100015 | - | Released | Dowel - Black Walnut |
| | 🔲 | 100021 | - | Work In Progress | ICU Button Paint |
| | 🔲 | 100020 | - | Work In Progress | ICU O-Ring Lubricant |
| | 🔲 | 100023 | - | Work In Progress | ICU Valve Main Assembly.iam |
| | 🔲 | 100027 | - | Work In Progress | ICUENDCP.ipt |
| | 🔲 | 100025 | - | Work In Progress | ICUHOUSG.ipt |
| | 🔲 | 100024 | - | Work In Progress | ICULBUTN.ipt |

# Creating Items

Typically when you create items you assign them to data files in the vault. In some cases, you need to create an item that is not modeled in the design. Examples include purchased items or items that are typically not modeled such as lubricants, paint, artwork, or packaging. You can include these items in the Item Master by creating new items. Another example would be when you follow a "BOM first" workflow. You create a list of items in the Item Master based on what you know about the BOM structure and then fill it in with CAD data at a later time.

Items can be created in the following ways:

- Use the New item command in the Item Master to create an item from scratch.
- Assign an item to a file using the Assign Item command.
- Drag and Drop files into the Item Master tab.
- Drag and Drop files into the Item Master node in the browser.

If an item is in read-only mode, you can use File>Save As to copy the item's properties, BOM rows, and attachments to a new item. The new item is automatically added to the Item Master and opened in read-only mode. Note that file links are not copied to the new item. For this reason, CAD rows are copied over as manual rows.

### Procedure: Creating New Items

The following steps describe how to create new items using the New item command.

1. Click Item Master.
2. On the Standard toolbar, click New.
3. If the administrator has granted you permission to assign item categories, select a category and click OK to continue to the new item record.
4. Review the item properties. If required, add or change the units and add a title and description.
5. Click Save and Close. The new item is created. Note that you can change item numbers using Actions>Change Number.

### Procedure: Assigning Items to Files in Vault

The following steps describe how to assign items to files in Vault Professional using the Assign/Update Item command.

1. Ensure that all files to which you want to assign an item are checked into the vault.

2. Click Project Explorer.

3. In the main pane, right-click on one or more files in the main pane and select Assign/Update Item. A new item is created for each of the files selected and for the related files.

4. If you assign an item to a single file, the item record automatically opens for editing. Begin making changes, if required.

5. If you select multiple files and assign an item, an item icon displays in the Item Column. However, you must right-click on a file and select Open Item to view the item record. Select Edit on the item record toolbar to begin editing.

   **Note:** Item Numbering is automatically applied based on the default numbering scheme. However, if the numbering scheme requires user input, the Item Number dialog opens. Enter the required values and click OK to continue.

6. Click Save and Close when you are finished.

7. The item master is updated with the new items. If items were assigned to Autodesk Inventor assembly files, any associated drawing (.IDW) and presentation (.IPN) files are linked to the items. If items were assigned to Inventor part files, the associated drawing (.IDW) files are linked to the items.

 When you assign an item to an assembly file, all parts and subassemblies in that assembly must have items assigned as well. Items are assigned automatically to all the required files if they do not have items assigned already.

# Attaching and Detaching Files

When you create an item from a file in the vault, the vault file is automatically attached to the item. You can manually attach additional supporting files such as documents or images. You can add attachments such as drawings for a purchased part, product specification sheets, assembly instructions, regulatory documents, material safety data sheets, rendered images of the product, and so on.

You attach and detach files by editing items. By default, the latest version of an attached file displays when an item is updated.

In some cases you might want to maintain a specific version of an attached file by pinning the attached file. When pinned, the version of the file specified when the file was originally attached remains when the file or item is updated. This is useful in legacy data where an older part might be specified by a previous version of a now updated specification.

### Procedure: Manage File Attachments

The following steps describe how to attach files to items, or detach files from items.

1. Right-click on an item and select Attachments. The current Attachments for the item display.

2. To attach files, click Attach and browse to the location of the file or click Search to find files in the vault. Select one or more files and click Open. The most recent version of the attached file displays in the Attachments dialog box. An additional method to attach files to an item is to open an item, change to Edit mode then drag and drop a file from Vault into the item's attachments window.

   **Note:** The item must be in a Work in Progress state to modify attachments.

3. Modify the way an Item Update operates on the attached files. By default, attached files update to the most recent version each time the item is updated. You can pin a particular version of the file to the item so that it references that version instead of the newest version during item updates.

   a. Select the Version Number field and select the version of the file you want to pin from the drop-down list.

   b. Select the Pin checkbox to pin the file to the specified version. During an update, the file version specified at the time of attachment remains attached to the item and the item is updated with the most current information from that file version.

4. To detach a file, select the file, and click Detach.

5. Click OK to save your changes and close the dialog box.

# Automatic Attachments

Some files are associated automatically with the parent file when the parent file is promoted to an item.

### Definition of Automatic Attachments

When you add CAD files to a vault, the relationships and links between files are maintained. For example, the links between an assembly file, its part, and subassembly files are maintained by the vault. These linked files are automatically promoted to items when the assembly is promoted. In a similar way, cross-reference links between drawings in AutoCAD®, AutoCAD® Mechanical, AutoCAD® Electrical, or AutoCAD® Civil 3D® are also maintained in Vault.

### Example of Automatic Attachments

An Inventor drawing is created from an Inventor part, and both are checked in to the vault. In Project Explorer, the two files are visible.

After assigning an item to the Grip.ipt part, the Grip.idw file also shows a link to an item in Project Explorer.

After assigning an item to the Grip.ipt part, the item also shows a link to both the files in the Associated files list on the General tab. Note that the key icon indicates the item's primary associated file.

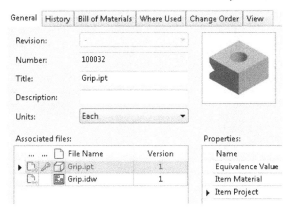

# Exercise: Assign Items to Vault Files

In this exercise, you create a custom view for Vault Explorer, assign an item to a part and an assembly, and attach files to an item.

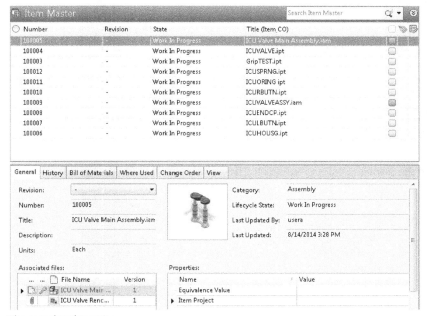

The completed exercise

## Create a Custom View

1. Start Autodesk Vault Professional. Log in using the following information:
   - User Name: **usera**
   - Password: **vault**
   - Vault: AOTCVault

2. In the navigation pane, click Home and expand AOTCVault. Expand Project Explorer.

3. Navigate to the *Designs\ICU Valve* folder.

**4.** From the Advanced toolbar, click Define custom views from the toolbar drop-down list.

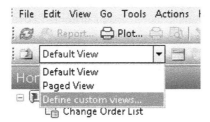

**5.** In the Manage Custom Views dialog box, do the following:

- Click New.
- Under View Name, enter **Thumbnails**.
- Click OK.

**6.** In the Manage Custom Views dialog box, select the Thumbnails view. Click Modify.

**7.** Click Fields.

**8.** In the Customize Fields dialog box, do the following:

- In the Select available fields from drop-down list, select Any.
- In the Available fields list, multi-select Attachments, Checked In, Created By, and Thumbnail. Click Add.
- Under Show these fields in this order, select Thumbnail. Click Move Up until Thumbnail displays above Name. Order the fields as shown in the following image.

- Click OK.

**9.** Click Close twice to close the other dialog boxes. The main pane displays thumbnails (generated from the visualization files) of the files.

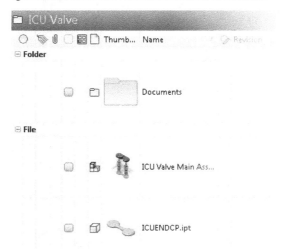

**10.** To adjust the size of the thumbnails, resize the Thumbnail column.

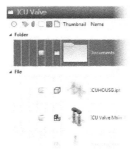

## Assign an Item

**1.** From the Advanced toolbar, click Default View from the toolbar drop-down list.

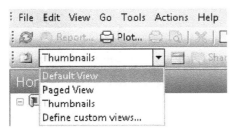

**2.** In the main pane, right-click ICUVALVE.ipt.

**3.**  Right-click Assign / Update Item.

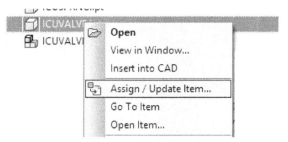

**4.**  The Item is created for ICUVALVE.ipt displaying the General tab information.

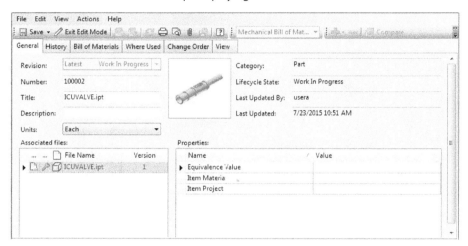

**5.**  On the toolbar, click Save and Close to save the item and close the window.

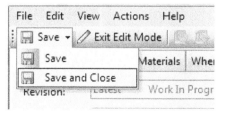

**6.**  In the main window, place the pointer on the item icon located in the last grid column. The Go to Item tooltip displays.

**7.** Hold <Ctrl> and click the item icon to display the item in the Preview pane. In the Preview pane, click the View tab. Under Attached Files, click ICUVALVE.ipt.

**8.** Click the Version 1 thumbnail.

**9.** Note the warning. In the View tab, click Update to update the view. Ensure that the Designs.ipj in the root folder ($) is set as the Inventor project file.

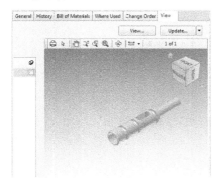

**10.** Under Home, click *Designs\ICU Valve*.

**11.** In the main pane, drag ICU Valve Main Assembly.iam onto the Item Master node in the Navigation pane. A new Item is created for the assembly.

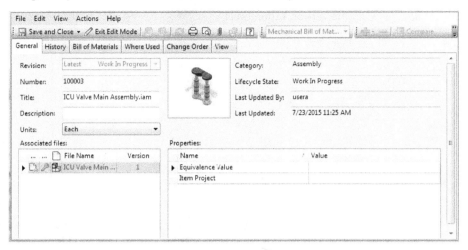

**12.** On the toolbar, click Save and Close.

**13.** An item icon displays next to all files in the ICU Valve folder.

Note that when you assign an item to an assembly file, it automatically assigns items to all subassemblies and parts used in the assembly. Without these extra items, the bill of materials is incomplete.

**14.** Under Home, click Item Master. If required, from the Advanced toolbar drop-down list, click All Items. The list is updated with the new items.

## Attach Files to an Item

**1.** In the Item Master window, select ICU Valve Main Assembly.iam.

**2.** In the preview pane, select the General tab.

Only one file is associated with the item in the main assembly.

**3.** In the Item Master, double-click ICU Valve Main Assembly.iam.

**4.** Click Edit to edit the item.

**5.** On the toolbar, click Attachments.

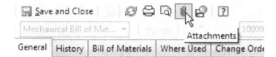

**6.** In the Attachments dialog box, click Attach.

**7.** Navigate to the *Designs\ICU Valve\Documents* folder. Do the following:

- Select ICU Valve Rendering.png.
- Click Open.

**8.** In the Attachments dialog box, click OK. The attached files are listed under the associated files.

**9.** On the toolbar, click Save and Close.

# Exercise: Create New Items

In this exercise, you create new items to represent physical objects not modeled in the vault.

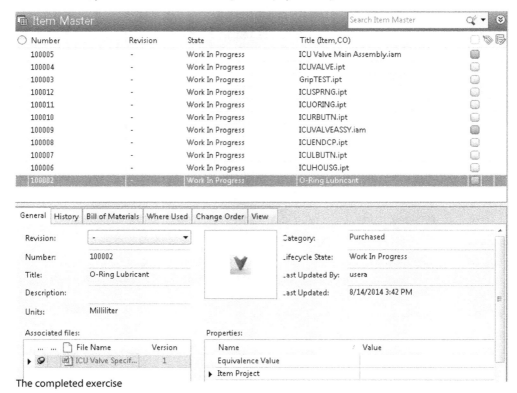

The completed exercise

1.      Start Autodesk Vault Professional. Log in using the following information:
   - User Name: **usera**
   - Password: **vault**
   - Vault: AOTCVault

2.      Under Home, click Item Master. Do the following:
   - Right-click on Item Master.
   - Click New Item.

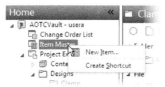

**3.** In the New Item – Select Category dialog box, select Purchased and then click OK.

**4.** In the Edit Item dialog box, do the following:

- For Title, enter **O-Ring Lubricant.**
- For Units, select Milliliter.
- Click Save and Close.

**5.** The new item displays in the Item Master.

**6.** In the Item Master, right-click on the O-Ring lubricant and select Attachments.

**7.** In the Attachments dialog box, click Attach.

**8.** Navigate to the *Designs\ICU Valve\Documents* folder. Select ICU Valve Specification Sheet - Grease doc. Click Open.

**9.** In the document row, in the Pinned icon column, select the checkbox.

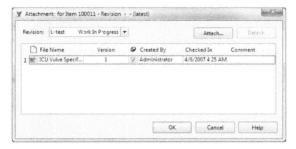

**10.** Click OK.

# Lesson: Working with Items

## Overview

In this lesson you learn how to create, modify, and delete customized views, use filters to view items, and work with item properties.

You can also export items for use with other applications or to create reports.

Use items to index and manage products in manufacturing. You also use items in the creation of Bills of Materials (BOMs) in Autodesk Vault Professional and in tracking change orders.

### Objectives

After completing this lesson, you will be able to:

- View specific items and files attached to the item.
- Use the Where Used tab to show item dependencies in the vault.
- Define custom filters to view and work with items.
- Use the Item Master to view, search, and filter items.
- Find items using Go To, shortcuts, and saved searches.

# Using the Item Preview Pane to View Items

The extended design team requires access to design data. Because many team members outside the engineering team do not use CAD, items cannot be viewed directly in the native CAD application.

Visualization files are the main tools used for viewing items. Visualization files can be of different file formats but the most common are DWF™ and DWFx files. Visualization files can be published automatically when files are checked in to the vault, thereby making viewing items in the vault easier and faster. With 3D visualization files, users can pan, zoom, and orbit 3D Autodesk® Inventor® models. Individual components in an assembly can be shown, hidden, or isolated. With 2D visualization files, users can print and view drawings and mark them up to provide feedback.

Use the View tab in the preview pane to view an item's associated vault files.

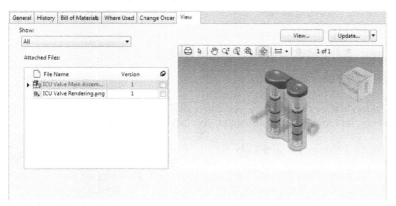

## Viewing Revision History

You can view revisions on the History tab. Vault Professional provides thumbnail images of the different revisions to the file.

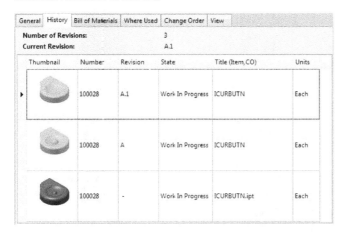

### Procedure: Viewing an Item

The following steps describe how to view an item's associated files.

1. In the Item Master window, select the item.

2. In the Preview pane, click the View tab.

### Procedure: Viewing Data in Separate Dialog box

The following steps describe how to view data that opens in a separate dialog box.

1. In the Item Master window, select the item.

2. In the Preview pane, click the View tab.

3. Click View to open the file in the Viewer.

4. Click Maximize in the upper right corner to view in full screen mode.

## Using the Where Used Tab

With the Where Used tab in the Preview pane, you can analyze where items are included in the vault. By detecting dependencies before making changes, you can avoid costly mistakes.

### Example of Using the Where Used Tab

In the following illustration, the Where Used tab shows that the ICUVALVE part is used in the ICUVALVEASSY assembly. In turn, the assembly is used in the ICU Valve Main Assembly file. The part is used directly in one assembly (it has one direct parent) and is used in a total of two assemblies (total number of parents).

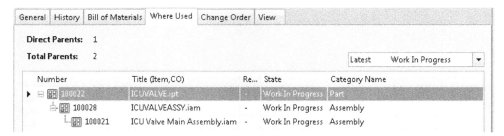

## How to Define Custom Filters to View Items

The number of items in the system can grow quite rapidly, and finding items in the list can be difficult. Many methods are available to filter the item list. By default, a custom view is already applied to the Item Master, which shows the items that have been updated in the last seven days.

The default custom view displays on the Advanced toolbar.

It is strongly recommended that you create custom views to filter your data. Customizing helps speed up the display of item lists because only filtered item data is retrieved from the server rather than the entire item list.

### Procedure: Defining a Custom Filter in the Item Master

The following steps describe how to define a custom filter in the Item Master.

1. In the Item Master list, right-click on the heading of a column and select Customize View.
2. In the Customize View dialog box, click Custom Filters.
3. In the Custom Filters dialog box, select an item property, condition, and value required.
4. Click Add.
5. If required, select additional properties, conditions, and values then add them to the criteria list.
6. Click OK. The Item Master list is filtered. A small filter symbol displays on the right side of the Item Master title bar.

 If the Item Master list is not displaying items you expect to see, check the filter settings and ensure that it is displaying the required content.

### Procedure: Saving Custom Views

The following steps describe how to save custom views.

1. On the Advanced toolbar, from the Views list, select Define Custom Views.

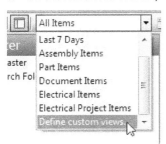

2. In the Manage Custom Views dialog box, click New.
3. In the Create Custom View dialog box, enter the required view name. Click OK.

 If a custom filter already exists (the filter icon displays on the Item Master title bar), then you might not want to edit the filter again. Skip the next four steps.

4. Click Modify.

5. In the Customize View dialog box, click Custom Filters.

6. In the Customize View dialog box, add the filter criteria.

7. Click OK to exit the Custom Filters dialog box. Click Close to exit the Customize View dialog box.

8. Click Close to exit the Manage Custom Views dialog box.

## Procedure: Managing Custom Views

The following steps describe how to manage custom views.

1. On the Advanced toolbar, from the Views list, select Define Custom Views.

2. In the Manage Custom Views dialog box, select the required view name.

3. Click Modify, Copy, Rename, or Delete, as required.

4. Close all dialog boxes.

 You cannot rename or delete the default custom views (e.g., All Items, Last 7 Days, etc.). Although not recommended, it is possible to add additional custom filter criteria to these two custom views

## Procedure: Clearing Custom Filters

The following steps describe how to clear custom filters.

1. In the Item Master window title bar, right-click Custom Filter Applied.

2. Click Clear Custom Filters.

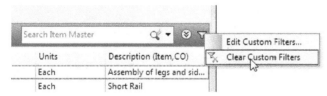

 Use the Custom View list on the Advanced toolbar to switch between custom views.

### Procedure: Enabling Filtering by Column

The following steps describe how to enable filtering by column.

1.  On the right side of the column heading, click Column Filter.

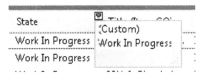

2.  Select one of the filter options. The column's values are listed, and you can filter based on these values.

    If you select (Custom), you are prompted to set up a custom auto-filter for that column.

# How to Customize Column Display in the Item Master

Columns in the Item Master list represent item properties. Many item properties are available, and you can filter the number of columns (properties) displayed in the list.

In this procedure, you customize the Item Master view by working with the list columns.

### Procedure: Removing Columns in the Item Master

The following step describes how to remove a column in the list.

1.  In the Item Master list, right-click on the column header you want to remove.

2.  Select Remove This Column.

### Procedure: Adding, Removing, and Rearranging Columns in the Item Master

The following steps describe how to add, remove, and reorder columns.

1.  In the Item Master list, right-click on a column header in the Item Master. Select Customize View.

2.  In the Customize View dialog box, click Fields.

3.  In the Customize Fields dialog box, add and remove fields as required.

4.  Customize the order of the fields by moving them up and down the list.

If you want to customize only the order of the fields (columns), drag the column headers to rearrange them in the Item Master list.

## Procedure: Group Items by Column Header

The following steps describe how to group items by column header.

1. On the Advanced toolbar, click Group By Box.

2. In Item Master, drag a column header to the location indicated. The items in the list are automatically listed in groups based on the column header value.

   In the following illustration, the items are grouped by state.

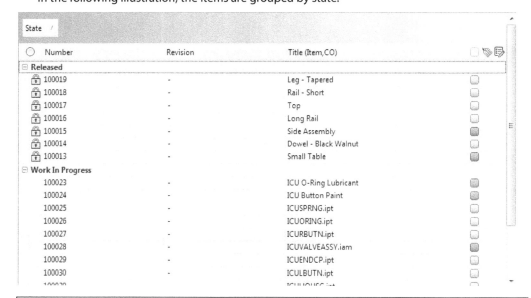

 Grouping by column header value can be useful when you work on a number of projects:
- Add a project name property to each item in the Item Master.
- Customize the view to show the Item Project field then group the items by this field.

## Procedure: Toggle Off the Group By Box Display

The following steps describe how to toggle off the Group By Box display.

1. On the Advanced toolbar, ensure that Group By Box is selected.
2. Drag the column header back to the header row.
3. On the Advanced toolbar, click Group By Box to disable the utility.

# How to Find Items

In this procedure, you find items by using the item number, using shortcuts, and searching for items.

### Search Tips

- Use Go To and go directly to an item.
- Use My Shortcuts to go to items.
- Search for items using Find.

### Procedure: Going to a Specific Item by Item Number

The following steps describe how to go to a specific item by item number.

1. On the toolbar click in the Go To box.

2. Enter an item number. Press Enter.

### Procedure: Creating and Using Shortcuts to Navigate in the Item Master

The following steps describe how to create and use shortcuts to navigate in the Item Master.

1. In the Item Master, drag an item to the My Shortcuts window in the navigation pane.

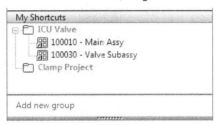

2. Under My Shortcuts, you can also add new groups (folders) to organize the shortcuts.

3. To go to an item, click the item shortcut.

## Procedure: Searching Items

The following steps describe how to search for an item or items and how to save the search.

1. In the Search box, enter the search text.

2. Click Search. The items containing the search string display.

3. To save the search, do the following:

- On the Search bar, click Show search options menu.
- Click Save Search.
- Enter a search name and click OK.

In the navigation pane under My Search Folders, the saved search displays.

# Exercise: Work with Items

In this exercise, you will create shortcuts and a saved search for the project. You will also learn how to link the ICU Button Paint item to the ICU buttons, how to delete items, and how to export the Item Master view.

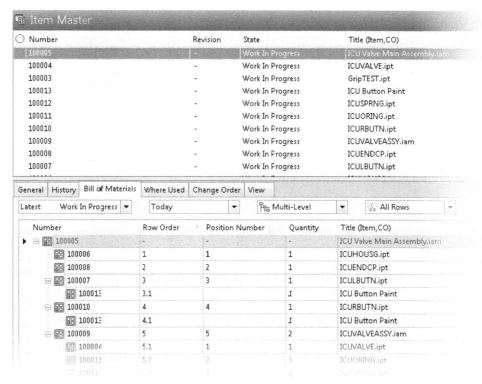

The completed exercise

## Create Shortcuts

1. Start Autodesk Vault Professional. Log in using the following information:
   - User Name: **usera**
   - Password: **vault**
   - Vault: AOTCVault

2. Under My Shortcuts, click Add new group.

3. Enter **ICU Valve**. Press Enter.

4. Under Home, click Item Master. In the Item Master, drag the ICU Valve Main Assembly.iam item to the ICU Valve shortcut group.

5. Expand the ICU Valve shortcut group.

**6.** Right-click on the shortcut to the ICU Valve Main Assembly.iam item. Select Rename.

**7.** Enter - **Main Assembly** after the item number.

**8.** Press Enter. Note that your item number might differ than the one shown in the image below.

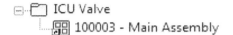

**9.** On the standard toolbar, click Find.

**10.** On the Basic tab, for Search Text, enter **\*BUTN.** Press Enter.

**11.** Click File>Save Search.

**12.** In the Save Search dialog box, for Search Name, enter **Buttons**. Click OK.

The saved search displays under My Search Folders.

**13.** Close the Find dialog box.

## Link Items

**1.** Under Home, right-click Item Master.

**2.** Click New Item.

**3.** In the New Item – Select Category dialog box, select Purchased and then click OK.

**4.** In the Edit Item dialog box, do the following:

- For Title, enter **ICU Button Paint**.
- For Description, enter **Paint**.
- Set Units to Milliliter.
- Click Save and Close.

**5.** Under My Search Folders, click Buttons.

**6.** Right-click on the ICURBUTN item and click Update to edit it.

**7.** Click the Bill of Materials tab.

**8.** Right-click on the row. Click Add Row>From Existing Item...

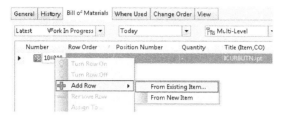

**9.** In the Find dialog box, click the Basic tab if it is not selected already. Do the following:

- For the search text, enter **Paint**.
- Click Find Now.
- Select the row displayed.
- Click OK.
- The ICU Button Paint item is linked to the ICURBUTN.ipt item.

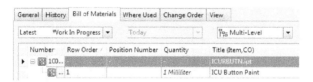

**10.** Click Save and Close. Repeat the previous steps to link the ICU Button Paint item to the Left button (ICULBUTN.ipt) item.

**11.** In the ICU Valve shortcut group, click the shortcut to the Main Assembly.

**12.** In the preview pane, click the Bill of Materials tab. Verify that the ICU Button Paint item is listed twice, under the ICU buttons.

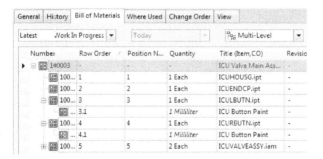

## Delete Items

1. In the Item Master, right-click on the O-Ring Lubricant item.

2. Click Change State.

3. In the Select Lifecycle dialog box, click Obsolete.

4. Click OK.

5. In the Item Master, right-click on the O-Ring Lubricant item again.

6. Click Delete.

7. Click Yes to confirm the item deletion.

 You can delete an item only if its lifecycle state is set to Obsolete.

# Lesson: Item Properties

## Overview

In this lesson, you will learn how to use item properties to search for and sort items, organize items, and filter the Item Master list. You use item properties to manage items.

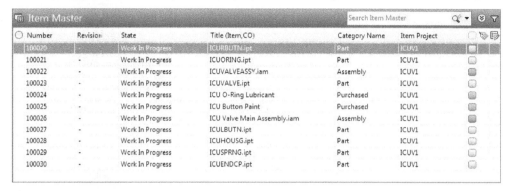

## Objectives

After completing this lesson, you will be able to:

- Describe default item properties.
- Describe the use of revisions.

# Default Item Properties

By default, each item has several properties that store and manage its number, revision lifecycle, and other associated data.

### Definition of Default Item Properties

Items have properties that apply to all items by default, called system properties. In some cases the properties are marked (Item, CO) to denote that they are unique to items and change orders.

The following list describes the main properties that display on the General tab.

| Property Name | Description | Comment or Example |
|---|---|---|
| Number | Unique item identifier | Normally a numerical sequence |
| Category | Categorization of the item. | "Part," "assembly," or "purchased" |
| Title | Brief description of item or change order | Up to 128 characters |
| Description | Secondary description of item or change order | Up to 128 characters |
| Units | Quantity | Select from a list |
| Lifecycle State | Item lifecycle state | "Work in Progress" or "Released" |
| Revision | Item revision | String or character |
| Last Updated By | Name of user who last updated item | Read-only, assigned by system |
| Last Updated | Date the item was last updated | Read-only, assigned by system |

### Example of Specifying Default Item Properties

When an item is assigned to a file the item is given a number of default properties.

The new item has a unique item number, which can be as simple as a six- number sequence (Part 100010) or as complex as a set of text sequences (Part BRD-200-0012). You can change the item number after it is assigned if required. The Title and Description can be used to help distinguish the item later on. The Units are specific to the item – for the most part the unit is 'each' but for consumables it can specify how much (volume, weight, etc.) of the item is used in the product.

The final set of properties is controlled by the system. The Lifecycle State designates the position in the product development process. You can change the lifecycle state to Released, signifying it is ready for production or Work In Progress, denoting that it is being edited. As designs evolve they are given Revisions to denote major milestones in a product development lifecycle. For example, a part can be released to manufacturing at Revision A, but later be modified based on warranty reports to Revision B to correct a defect noted by customers. The updates are tagged with the user that last updated the item (Last Updated By) and the time the update was done (Last Updated).

# User Defined Item Properties

In addition to the system properties, there are a number of predefined user defined properties that are assigned to Items as they are created. These are based on common file properties associated with the different authoring applications. For example, the property Material – designating what property the item is made of– can be set from a file property in Autodesk Inventor.

Additionally, you might want to specify some properties that are unique to your company. For example, you can have different Business Units that produce designs that you might want to identify or search on.

## Best Practices for Working with User-Defined Properties

The administrator can define additional item properties to add company-specific properties to items. You can use these properties to help arrange or find items in the vault.

It is recommended that:

- You attach user-defined properties to items or remove them from items in the vault. Properties are created and managed by the administrator using the Property Definitions dialog (found under Tools>Administration>Vault Settings>Behaviors>Properties).

- The administrator maps item properties to read values from CAD files in the vault if possible. For example, the property Material – designating what property the item is made of– can be set from a file property in Autodesk Inventor

- You begin all user-defined properties with Item (or an acceptable prefix), as shown in the following illustration. This will avoid confusion with properties in the vault or in another application. You can also scroll to the right to view the Association column which displays the entity class of the property.

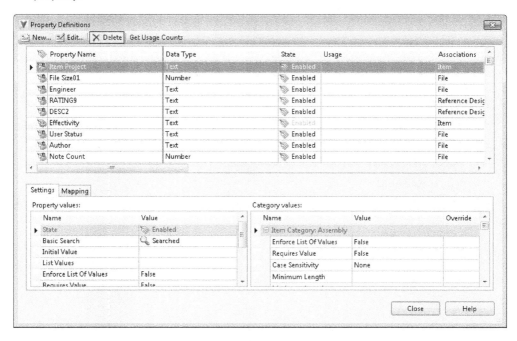

### Example of Using a User-Defined Item Property

You create an Item Project property value for a predefined Item user-defined property so that you can sort by that property or use it to search for items.

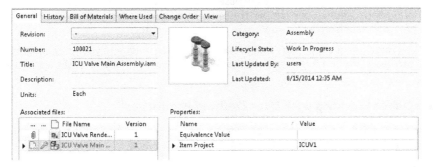

You can ask the administrator to map the user-defined item property to properties in the vault files.

 You can attach or detach properties per item by right-clicking in the Properties field and selecting Add or Remove Property.

 You can edit the properties of more than one item at a time by selecting multiple items and then selecting Edit Properties (<Ctrl>+<E>).

# Item Numbering Schemes

All items have unique item numbers that you can use to identify and track the items in different operations. These item numbers are assigned based on a numbering scheme that is created by the administrator.

### Guidelines for Item Numbers

There are two predefined numbering schemes shipped with Vault Professional. It is recommended that you use customized numbering schemes created by the administrator.

The two predefined schemes are shipped with the software by default.

- Sequential numbering

   This scheme creates item numbers in sequence and is the default. This is a simple numbering scheme that starts with 100001 and goes to 999999.

- Mapped numbering

   This scheme is selected automatically when a file property is mapped to the item number. You can choose the numbering scheme when you add new items to the vault. It can be any value up to 50 characters long.

## Custom Numbering Schemes

If you choose to use a custom numbering scheme, the scheme can follow company standards or use any identifier. It is recommended that you make this identifier as simple as possible. A six-digit numbering scheme starting with 100000 is ideal.

## Example of Using Item Numbers

The following illustration shows the use of a custom sequential scheme. Note that parts, assemblies, and purchased items are numbered from 100033 to 100043.

| | | | Number | Revision | State | Title (Item,CO) | Category Name | Units |
|---|---|---|---|---|---|---|---|---|
| ▶ | | | 100033 | A | Work In Progress | ICUVALVE.ipt | Part | Each |
| | | | 100034 | B | Released | ICU O Ring Lubricant | Purchased | Milliliter |
| | | | 100035 | B | Released | ICU Button Paint | Purchased | Milliliter |
| | | | 100036 | A | Work In Progress | ICU Valve Main Assembly.iam | Assembly | Each |
| | | | 100037 | B | Released | ICULBUTN | Part | Each |
| | | | 100038 | A | Released | ICUHOUSG.ipt | Part | Each |
| | | | 100039 | A | Released | ICUSPRNG.ipt | Part | Each |
| | | | 100040 | A | Released | ICUENDCP.ipt | Part | Each |
| | | | 100041 | C | Work In Progress | ICURBUTN | Part | Each |
| | | | 100042 | A | Work In Progress | ICUORING.ipt | Part | Each |
| | | | 100043 | A | Work In Progress | ICUVALVEASSY.iam | Assembly | Each |

Numbering schemes can include such things as company initials, a type sequence, a numeric sequence, and a manufacturing process code, as in BRD-PRT-10051-P. However, a scheme like this might be needlessly complex and require too much work to set up and use.

It is recommended that you start the item numbering with a digit other than zero since some spreadsheets eliminate the leading zeros when data is imported.

For example, the following illustration shows the use of the sequential scheme. Note that parts, assemblies, and purchased items are numbered from 000012 to 000022.

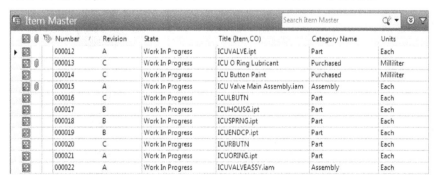

| | | | Number | Revision | State | Title (Item,CO) | Category Name | Units |
|---|---|---|---|---|---|---|---|---|
| ▶ | | | 000012 | A | Work In Progress | ICUVALVE.ipt | Part | Each |
| | | | 000013 | C | Work In Progress | ICU O Ring Lubricant | Purchased | Milliliter |
| | | | 000014 | C | Work In Progress | ICU Button Paint | Purchased | Milliliter |
| | | | 000015 | A | Work In Progress | ICU Valve Main Assembly.iam | Assembly | Each |
| | | | 000016 | C | Work In Progress | ICULBUTN | Part | Each |
| | | | 000017 | B | Work In Progress | ICUHOUSG.ipt | Part | Each |
| | | | 000018 | B | Work In Progress | ICUSPRNG.ipt | Part | Each |
| | | | 000019 | B | Work In Progress | ICUENDCP.ipt | Part | Each |
| | | | 000020 | C | Work In Progress | ICURBUTN | Part | Each |
| | | | 000021 | A | Work In Progress | ICUORING.ipt | Part | Each |
| | | | 000022 | A | Work In Progress | ICUVALVEASSY.iam | Assembly | Each |

This is poor practice. Many software programs such as spreadsheets import the item numbers without the leading zeros, so item number "000020" displays as "20", which might be undesirable when creating a report.

## Change Item Numbers

1. Right-click on one or more items in the Item Master or BOM view and select Change Number.

2. Select a numbering scheme from the drop-down list. Use Property Mapping uses mapped properties to generate the item number.

3. If a field requires user input, enter text as required.

4. Click Precheck to verify the new item number. Make any changes, if required.

5. If more than one item is in the list and you want to remove one, select the item and click Remove.

6. Click OK to accept the new item number.

# Exercise: Work with Item Properties

In this exercise, you add a new item with user-defined properties, link the item to the ICU valve assembly, display the user-defined property in the item master view, add a customized view for the current project, change the item project property, group the item master list by project, customize the view by box, and renumber items.

| Number | Revision | State | Title (Item,CO) | Item Project |
|---|---|---|---|---|
| 100021 | - | Work In Progress | ICU Valve Main Assembly.iam | ICUV1 |
| 100022 | - | Work In Progress | ICUVALVE.ipt | ICUV1 |
| 100023 | - | Work In Progress | ICU O-Ring Lubricant | ICUV1 |
| 100024 | - | Work In Progress | ICU Button Paint | ICUV1 |
| 100025 | - | Work In Progress | ICUSPRNG.ipt | ICUV1 |
| 100026 | - | Work In Progress | ICUOFING.ipt | ICUV1 |
| 100027 | - | Work In Progress | ICURBUTN.ipt | ICUV1 |
| 100028 | - | Work In Progress | ICUVALVEASSY.iam | ICUV1 |
| 100029 | - | Work In Progress | ICUENDCP.ipt | ICUV1 |
| 100030 | - | Work In Progress | ICULBUTN.ipt | ICUV1 |
| 100031 | - | Work In Progress | ICUHOUSG.ipt | ICUV1 |

The completed exercise

## Add a New Item

1.  Start Autodesk Vault Professional. Log in using the following information:
    - User Name: **usera**
    - Password: **vault**
    - Vault: AOTCVault

2.  Under Home, click Item Master to display items for the ICU valve.
    - Right-click on Item Master.
    - Click New Item.

3.  In the New item – Select Category dialog box, select Purchased and click OK.

4.  In the Edit Item dialog box:
    - For Title, enter **ICU O-Ring Lubricant**.
    - For Description, enter **Grease for subassembly**.
    - For Units, select Milliliter.

5.      Under Properties, if the Item Project user- defined item is visible, skip to Step 8.

6.      Under Properties, right-click under Name. Click Add or Remove Property.

7.      In the Add or Remove Property dialog box:

  - Select Item Project.
  - Select Add from the Action drop-down list.
  - Click OK.

8.      Under Properties, click the Value field next to Item Project. Enter **ICUV1**.

9.      On the standard toolbar, click Attachments. Click Yes to save.

10.      In the Attachments dialog box, click Attach.

11.      Navigate to the *Designs\ICU Valve\Documents* folder.

  - Select ICU Valve Specification Sheet - Grease.doc.
  - Click Open.
  - Click OK.

12.      On the standard toolbar, click Save and Close.

  The new item displays in the Item Master list.

### Link Item to the Assembly

1.      Double-click the ICUVALVEASSY.iam item to open it.

2.      On the standard toolbar, click Edit.

3.      Select the Bill of Materials tab. Right-click on the top row>Add Row>From Existing Item.

4.      In the Find dialog box, click the Basic tab if it is not selected already.

5.      Enter **Grease** as the search text. Click Find Now.

6.      Select the row displayed. Click OK.

  The ICU O-Ring Lubricant item is now linked to the ICUVALVEASSY.iam item. (Your item numbers might be different.)

7.      Click Save and Close.

## Display the User-Defined Property

1. On the Advanced toolbar, select All Items from the Custom Views list.

2. On the Advanced toolbar, select Define Custom Views from the Custom Views list.

3. In the Manage Custom Views dialog box, click New.

4. In the Create Custom View dialog box, for View Name, enter **Listing by Project**. Click OK.

5. Select Listing by Project. Click Modify.

6. In the Customize View dialog box, click Fields.

7. In the Customize Fields dialog box, for Select available fields from, select Items from the list.

8. From Available fields, select Item Project.

9. Click Add to add Item Project to the list on the right after Title (Item, CO).

Show these fields in this order:
Vault Status
Number
Revision
State
Title (Item, CO)
Item Project
Category Glyph
Property Compliance
Controlled By Change Order

10. Click OK.

11. Close the remaining dialog boxes.

12. The Item Master list now shows the Item Project column.

> The new customized view you just created lists all items in the Item Master. Because this list can be very long, you create another custom view that is based on it, but that adds a custom filter to search for "ICUV1" in the Item Project property.

## Add a Customized View

1. On the Advanced toolbar, select Define Custom Views from the Custom Views list.

2. In the Manage Custom Views dialog box, with Listing by Project selected, click Copy.

3. In the Create Custom View dialog box, for View Name, enter **ICU Valve 1 Project**. Click OK.

4. With ICU Valve 1 Project selected, click Modify.

5. Click Custom Filters.

6. In the Custom Filters dialog box, do the following:
   - For Property, select Item Project.
   - For Condition, select contains.
   - For Value, enter **ICUV1**.
   - Click Add.
   - Click OK to close the Custom Filters dialog box.

7. Close the remaining dialog boxes.

8. On the Advanced toolbar, select ICU Valve 1 Project from the Custom Views list. Only one item, the ICU O-Ring Lubricant you added, displays because none of the other ICU Valve items have ICUV1 in the Item Project property.

## Change Item Project Property

1. On the Advanced toolbar, select Listing by Project from the Custom Views list.

2. In the Item Master, double-click the ICUVALVE.ipt item. Click Edit.

3. Under Properties, click the value next to Item Project. Do the following:
   - Enter **ICUV1**.
   - Click Save and Close.

4. Repeat the previous three steps for all of the items belonging to the ICU valve.

5. Under Home, expand Project Explorer, Designs, and Table.

6. In the Table list, right-click Small Table.iam. Select Assign/Update Item.

7. Click Save and Close.

8. Under Home, click Item Master.

9. Edit each of the seven items belonging to the Table project, and enter **Table1** in the Item Project property.

10. On the Advanced toolbar, for Custom Views, select ICU Valve 1 Project from the list. Only the ICUV1 project items display.

11. For practice, add a new custom view, called Table 1 Project, which is based on the ICU Valve1 project, by searching for the Table1 Item project using the custom filters.

## Group the Listing by Project

1.  On the Advanced toolbar, select Listing by Project from the Custom Views list.

2.  In the Item Master, right-click on the Item Project header. Select Group by This Field.

3.  Click View menu>Refresh.

4.  In the Advanced toolbar, click Group by Box to toggle it off. The listed items are grouped and boxed by project. You can expand or collapse each project as you work.

 The Group by Box view does not display as expected for items that are used in more than one project. For example, an item that is used in the Table1 and ICUV1 projects might have an Item Project property of "ICUV1, Table1." This shared item lists correctly using the ICU Valve 1 Project custom view and the Table 1 custom view, but does not list correctly under the Group by Box Listing by Project View.

## Renumber Items

1.  On the Advanced toolbar, from the Custom Views list, select ICU Valve 1 Project.

    Make a note of which items are assemblies and which are purchased. In this case, items 100005 and 100009 are assemblies, and items 100002 and 100013 are purchased. (Your item numbers might be different.)

2.  In Item Master, do the following:
    - Select the first item in the list.
    - Press <Shift> and select the last item in the list.
    - Right-click anywhere over the selected items.
    - Click Change Number.

3.  In the Change Item Number dialog box, from the Select a Numbering Scheme list, select AOTC-Complex.

4.  In the Change Item Number dialog box, do the following:
    - For Type, select 200 to change the assembly item numbers.
    - For Type, select 300 to change the purchased item numbers.

**5.**    Click OK. The new item numbering scheme displays in the Item Master.

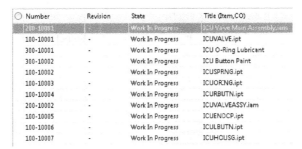

| Number | Revision | State | Title (Item,CO) |
|---|---|---|---|
| 200-10001 | - | Work In Progress | ICU Valve Main Assembly.iam |
| 100-10001 | - | Work In Progress | ICUVALVE.ipt |
| 300-10001 | - | Work In Progress | ICU O-Ring Lubricant |
| 300-10002 | - | Work In Progress | ICU Button Paint |
| 100-10002 | - | Work In Progress | ICUSPRNG.ipt |
| 100-10003 | - | Work In Progress | ICUORNG.ipt |
| 100-10004 | - | Work In Progress | ICURBUTN.ipt |
| 200-10002 | - | Work In Progress | ICUVALVEASSY.iam |
| 100-10005 | - | Work In Progress | ICUENDCP.ipt |
| 100-10006 | - | Work In Progress | ICULBUTN.ipt |
| 100-10007 | - | Work In Progress | ICUHOUSG.ipt |

**6.**    In the Advanced toolbar, click the Custom Views list. Select All Items.

**7.**    On the Advanced toolbar, from the Custom Views list, select ICU Valve 1 Project.

**8.**    In Item Master, do the following:

- Select the first item in the list.
- Press <Shift> and select the last item in the list.
- Right-click anywhere over the selected items.
- Click Change Number.

**9.**    In the Change Item Number dialog box, from the Select a Numbering Scheme list, select AOTC-Numeric. Click OK.

Note that the item numbers differ from the ones at the start of the exercise. To avoid confusion, old item numbers are not reused.

# Lesson: Exporting Items

## Overview

Other data management and analysis applications are often used along with Autodesk Vault Professional. You can export Vault Professional item properties in a range of file formats to provide engineering and product data to other applications.

### Objectives

After completing this lesson, you will be able to:

- Export item data.

# Export Items from Vault Professional

You can export item data from Autodesk Vault Professional to a variety of file formats.

## Procedure: Exporting Items

The following steps describe how to export items to a file.

1. Log in to Autodesk Vault Professional as a user assigned the ERP Manager role.

2. In the Item Master, select all the items to export. It might be useful to filter the items, or export from a saved search to restrict the items to those required.

3. Select File>Export Items.

4. Select the Released and Obsolete items only checkbox to only show items in this state.

5. Items that are checked are exported. If you do not want to export an item that is checked, toggle off the checkbox next to that item.

 If you export an assembly, its child components are automatically selected for export.

6. Click Next.

7. On the Specify File pane, under File types, click CSV (Comma Separated Values .CSV).

File types:

```
CSV (Comma Separated Values .CSV)
TDL (Tab Separated Values .TXT)
Design Web Format (DWF)
XML
```

8. Under BOM Indicator, click Level numbers.

The exported file includes a numeric indicator of the hierarchical position of the file in the item structure. For example, if the first subassembly was assigned Level 1, the first child part in the subassembly is assigned Level 1.1, the second part 1.2, and so on.

 If you se ect Parent Item for the BOM indicator, each exported item, other than the top- level items, includes the item number of its parent item.

| | A | B | C | |
|---|---|---|---|---|
| 1 | Level | Number | Title (Item,CO) | Qua |
| 2 | 1 | 100002 | Hitch Assembly | |
| 3 | 1.1 | 100012 | ISO 8678 M12 x 25 | |
| 4 | 1.2 | 100008 | Hex Thick Nut - Inch 3/4 - 10 | |
| 5 | 1.3 | 100007 | Mounting Weldment.iam | |
| 6 | 1.3.1 | 100017 | end_plate_LH.ipt | |
| 7 | 1.3.2 | 100015 | DrawBarMountTopPlate.ipt | |

9. Click Browse. Erowse to your export folder. Enter the filename. Click Save.

10. Click Next. On the Specify Attributes pane, drag field names from the Attributes list to the Export File list. To remove a field from the Export File list, drag it outside the Export list. Click Clear Mapping to remove all fields except Level.

 If you select Level Numbers as the BOM indicator, you must include the Number attribute in the Export File list.

11. Click Export. An export summary displays. On the Summary pane, you can print the report or distribute it by email.

12. Click Finish. The exported file is available for import into an ERP system or other software. An example CSV export file is shown in the following illustration.

```
Level,Number,Title,Quantity,Units,R
1,100002,Hitch Assembly,1,Each, -
1.1,100012,ISO 8678 M12 x 25,4,Eac
1.2,100008,Hex Thick Nut - Inch 3/4
1.3,100007,Mounting weldment.iam,1,
1.3.1,100017,end_plate_LH.ipt,1,Eac
1.3.2,100015,DrawBarMountTopPlate.i
1.3.3,100013,ANSI AISC 2x2x 1/4 - 1
1.3.4,100016,end_plate_RH.ipt,1,Eac
```

# Exercise: Export Items from Vault Professional

In this exercise, you change an assembly and its components to a Released lifecycle state, then export properties of the items to a CSV file.

1. Start Autodesk Vault Professional. Log in using the following information:
   - User Name: **administrator**
   - Password: leave blank
   - Vault: AOTCVault

 To export items, you must be logged in as a user with at least ERP Manager role permissions

2. Under Home, click Item Master to display the list of items in the vault.

3. On the Advanced toolbar, select Assembly Items from the Custom Views list.

4. In the main pane, right-click on the Small Table assembly item.

5. Do the following:
   - Click Change State.
   - In the Select Lifecycle dialog box, click Released.
   - Click OK.

The lifecycle state of the table assembly and each of its components is set to Released.

6. In the Main pane, click the Small Table assembly item.

7. Click File menu>Export Items.

8. For Specify File, do the following:
   - Click Next.
   - Select CSV.
   - Browse to the Desktop folder.
   - For File Name, enter **Small Table Items**.
   - Click Next.
   - Drag a few field names from the Attributes list to the Export file list.
   - Click Export.

9. Open the file in Microsoft Excel and review the data.

# Chapter Summary

All Autodesk Vault Professional users must be able to work with items, using the application's various features and functionalities.

You can assign items to CAD files in the vault or create new items for products not specifically modeled in CAD.

Items are used to represent the design data. A large collection of items in Vault Explorer can be difficult to manage. By using customized views and filters, you can sort or filter the item list based on item properties to manage the items effectively.

Having completed this chapter, you can:

- Create, modify, and delete items, use filters to view items, and add and remove file attachments.
- Create, modify, and delete custom views, use filters to view items, and find items.
- Work with default item properties and user-defined properties, including item numbers.
- Export item data.

# Managing Change

Vault Professional provides control over how new designs or design changes are released, eliminating the issues commonly involved with manual processes. Creating a change order enables you to describe the changes to a design and manage the progression of that change order as it is reviewed, approved, or rejected.

## Objectives

After completing this chapter, you will be able to:

- Create and change item lifecycles manually.
- Create and approve change orders.

# Lesson:  Revision Control

## Overview

In this lesson, you learn how to use revision control to manually control lifecycle states and how different workflows affect revision control.

In design and manufacturing, a part can go through many design iterations. Lifecycle states control the revisions of a part or assembly in this process.

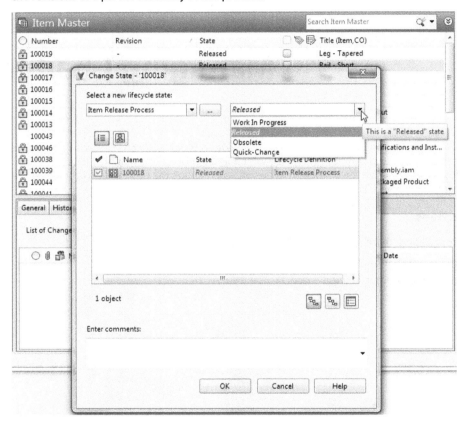

### Objectives

After completing this lesson, you will be able to:

- Define item lifecycle states.
- Control lifecycle states.
- Manually change lifecycle states.

# Item Lifecycle States

To manage design data you must control the various stages from design to manufacturing. To do this, you mark an item using one of the lifecycle states.

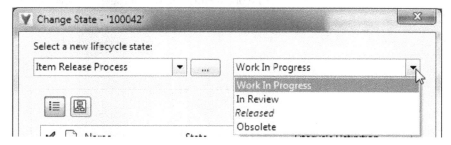

## Definition of Lifecycle States

The lifecycle state of an item indicates where it is in the design and manufacturing process. The following table describes the default states:

| Lifecycle State | Description |
| --- | --- |
| Work in Progress | The item is available for editing. Files associated with the item can be checked out and edited. The item can be updated to the latest file versions. New items are automatically assigned Work in Progress status. |
| In Review | The item is being reviewed prior to release to production. The item and its associated files cannot be edited or updated. |
| Released | The item is available for production. The item cannot be edited or updated. |
| Obsolete | The item is no longer used in production and cannot be updated. Items in the Obsolete state can be deleted. |

The actual names of the lifecycle states can be changed to reflect those used in your organization. This will be covered in a later lesson.

### How to Manually Change a State

To change a state, right-click on the item in the Item Master, then select Change State. The Change State dialog box displays the states available based on the current state of the item.

In the following illustration, the item is set to Work in Progress. You can select In Review, Released, or Obsolete.

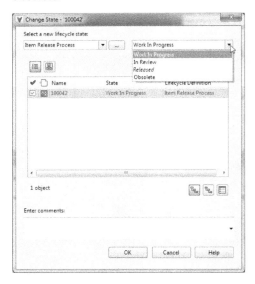

### Example of a Manual State Change

The design team has determined that a part is ready for manufacturing. During the design phase, the part has a Work in Progress lifecycle state. You set the lifecycle state to Released to indicate that the part is ready for manufacturing and distribution.

### Revisions and Lifecycle State

By default, when you change an item's state from Released to WIP, the revision automatically bumps using the primary revision bump action.

The following state changes do not bump the revision status of an item:

- WIP to Obsolete
- WIP to Released
- WIP to In Review
- Released to Obsolete
- In Review to Obsolete
- In Review to Released
- In Review to WIP
- Obsolete to In Review
- Obsolete to WIP

**Note:** Depending on your company's configuration, not all of these state changes will be available.

### Revision Formats

A user with an administrator or Item Editor (Level 2) role sets the revision sequence and can either specify one of the formats shown in the following illustration or create a custom revision scheme.

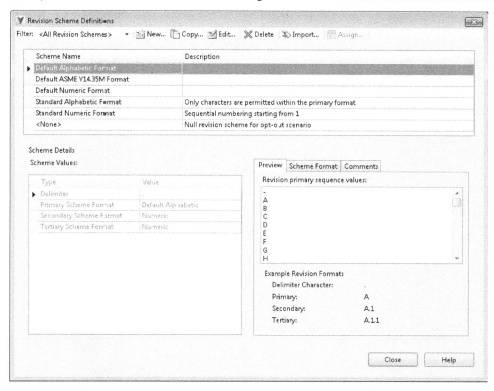

Examples of the revision format display in the Preview tab of the Revision Scheme Definitions dialog box.

# Changing States Manually

A user with an administrator or Item Editor (Level 2) role can change an item's lifecycle state manually in the Item Master.

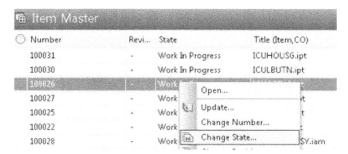

### Definition of Manually Changing Lifecycle States

You can use lifecycle states to control the release status of items by manually changing an item to Work in Progress, In Review, Released, or Obsolete.

### Changing a State

To change a state, right-click on the item in the Item Master then select Change State. The Change State dialog box displays the states and options available based on the current state of the item and your assigned role permissions.

In the following illustration, the item is currently set to Work in Progress. When the Select Lifecycle dialog displays, you can select In Review, Released, or Obsolete.

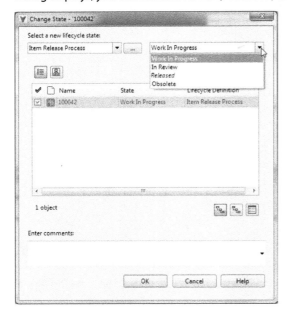

# Exercise: Change Lifecycle States Manually

In this exercise, you create an item, attach it to a change order, and manually change the lifecycle state.

The completed exercise

1.  Start Autodesk® Vault Professional. Log in using the following information:

    - User Name: **usera**
    - Password: **vault**
    - Vault: AOTCVault

2.  Click Go menu>Item Master.

3.  On the Advanced toolbar, select All Items from the Custom Views list.

4.  Click Go menu>Project Explorer.

5.  Click Tools menu>Options. Ensure that Show hidden files is selected. The DWF™ files displays.

    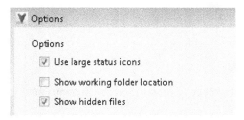

6.  Click OK.

**7.** Expand the Designs folder. Click the Clamp folder.

**8.** Right-click Handle.ipt. Select Assign/Update Item...

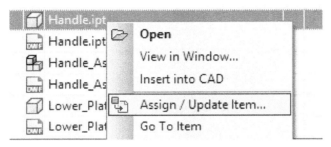

**9.** In the Edit Item window, click Save and Close. An item icon displays next to the filename.

**10.** Click Go menu>Item Master.

**11.** In the Item Master, click the Number column to sort the item numbers in descending order.

**12.** In Item Master, right-click on the new item.

**13.** Select Change State.

 Your item number might differ from the illustrations shown in this exercise. Your item should be the highest number. In this example, it is 100032.

**14.** In the Select Lifecycle dialog box, select Released.

**15.** Click OK. Note that the revision is a dash (-) and the lifecycle state is changed to Released. A lock symbol is placed beside the item.

**16.** Click Go menu>Project Explorer.

**17.** Review the part. Note the lock symbol beside the part here as well.

**18.** Click Go menu>Item Master.

**19.** Right-click on the item, then select Change State.

**20.** Select Work In Progress.

**21.** Click OK.

**22.** Review the status of the part. The Revision is now set to A. Note that the lock icon is removed from the item.

**23.** Return to Project Explorer. Note that the lock icon is removed from the part.

The company wants to create a series of revisions before releasing the part. To do this, you use secondary revisions.

**24.** Return to the Item Master.

**25.** With the Handle item highlighted, select Actions > Change Revision.

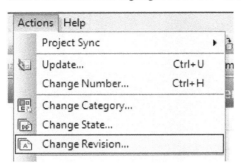

**26.** For Select next revision, select Secondary. Click OK. In this example, the revision is A.1.

The modification to the part is now complete. You select a new secondary revision.

**27.** With the Handle item highlighted, select Actions > Change Revision.

**28.** For Select next revision, select Secondary. Click OK. In this example, the revision is A.2.

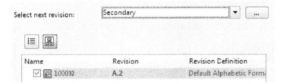

The secondary revision is now complete. The design team wants the part to be reviewed.

**29.** Right-click on the item, then select Change State.

**30.** Select In Review. Click OK. Note the lock symbol.

**31.** Right-click on the item, then select Change State.

**32.** Select Released. Click OK.

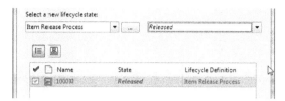

**33.** The lifecycle state is changed to Released and the revision stays at A.2. Note that the item is still locked. You decide that further work requires to be done after release.

**34.** Right-click on the item, then select Change State.

**35.** Select Work in Progress. Click OK.

**36.** The lifecycle state is changed to Work in Progress and the Revision changes to B. Note that the lock symbol has been removed.

**37.** Return to Project Explorer. Note that the part is unlocked. You can now make modifications to the part.

# Lesson:  Change Orders

## Overview

This lesson describes how to create change orders to control the release of new designs or changes to those designs.

The Change Order Editor role provides permissions to create or participate in a change order. In addition, the administrator defines appropriate change order permissions for each participant in the change order process.

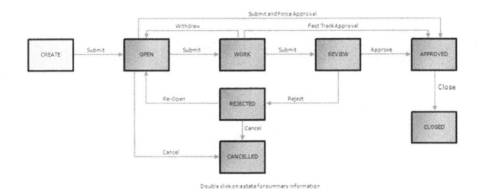

### Objectives

After completing this lesson, you will be able to:

- Review the Change Order dialog box.
- Create a change order.
- Attach an item to a change order.
- Review lifecycle states.
- Review change order routing.

# Introduction to Change Orders

When you create a revision, design changes are made and the changes are then approved by one or more people. Using the Change Order process, when you (the change requestor) modify files or items, the change is routed to the correct members in the design team before being released to production. When the change order reaches the Closed state, it will display a dialog box with the associated items and files that enables the user to manually change the states.

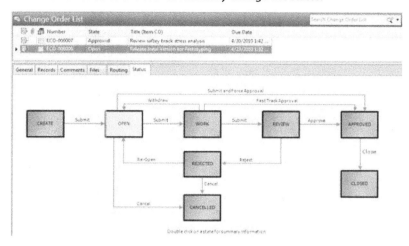

## Definition of Change Orders

You can use change orders to both describe the changes made to a design and to manage the progress of those changes through review, approval, rejection, and release to production. The Change Order dialog box provides a historical record of why, how, and when changes were made.

## Description of Change Order Workflow

The Status tab in the Change Order dialog box displays a workflow chart of all possible combinations of state progressions.

**Note:** Some companies include a Check state between Work and Review.

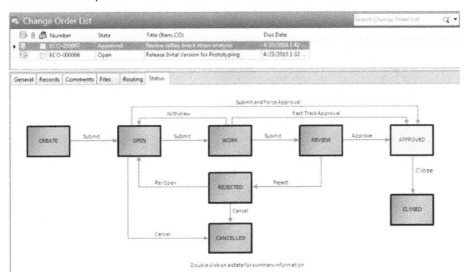

## Change Order Workflow Chart

You can also visually identify the current status of the change order by clicking the Status tab on the respective Change Order dialog box. Double-clicking a state gives you summary information about that state.

| State | Description |
|---|---|
| OPEN | After a user has created and submitted the change order, the change order enters the Open state. In the Open state, the Change Administrator can edit the title, edit the value of a user-defined property, and change the attachments.

The Change Administrator can perform the same editing tasks in the open state as in the state when the change order is first being created with one exception: The specified numbering scheme cannot be changed.

Change the lifecycle state of an item by using the change state command in the context menu of a selected item. |
| WORK | As soon as the change order enters the Work state, the Responsible Engineer is notified that there is a change order requiring attention, then the following occurs:
- The change order number is added to each participant's work list.
- An email message is sent to each person on the routing list if they have subscribed to email notification for change order events.

Anyone can view the status.

A reviewer can view, add, and reply to change order comments.

The Responsible Engineer can edit the change order, make any required revisions, and then submit the change order for review. |

| | |
|---|---|
| **REVIEW** | As soon as the change order enters the Review state, routing participants are notified that there is a change order requiring attention, then the following occurs:<br><br>■ The change order number is added to each participant's work list.<br>■ An email message is sent to each person on the routing list if they have subscribed to email notification for change order events.<br><br>A reviewer can view, add, and reply to change order comments.<br><br>Anyone can view the status. |
| **APPROVED** | A participant with approver status can approve a change order.<br><br>The Change Administrator can change the life cycle state of the item by selecting an item and selecting Change State from the context menu. |
| **REJECTED** | When a participant with Approver status rejects a change order, the change order enters into the Rejected state.<br><br>As a Change Administrator, you can do the following:<br><br>■ Cancel the change order.<br>■ Reopen the change order. |
| **CANCELLED** | In the Cancelled state no action can be taken by anyone. |
| **CLOSED** | In the Closed state no action can be taken by anyone. |

# Create a Change Order

Use the Change Order dialog box to create change orders. A change requestor initiates the process and adds comments, attaches files, and selects the routing participants.

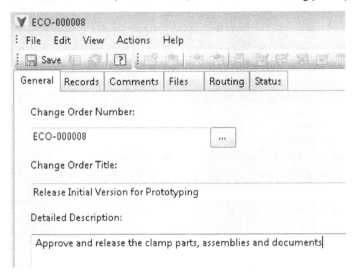

## Change Order Options

The tab functions in the Change Order dialog box are described in the following table.

| Options | Description |
|---------|-------------|
| General | Contains the change order attributes. |
| Records | Displays the list of files and items associated with the change order. The record details for each file or item include a title, description, revision, and state. |
| Comments | Summarizes the decisions for the change order in the form of comments, attachments, and markups. You can also customize email notifications. |
| Files | Lists all files and associated items for the change order. Attachments and markups are also listed. |
| Routing | Lists the participants involved with the current change order. |
| Status | Contains a graphical representation of the current status of the change order. |

## Procedure: Creating a Change Order

The following steps describe how to create a change order. You must have Administrator or Change Order Editor Perm ssions to create or participate in a change order.

1. You can right-click on items in the Item Master or file in the Project Explorer view to display the context menu. Select Add To Change Order>To New.

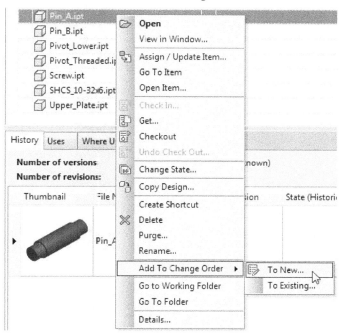

2. The Change Order dialog box displays.

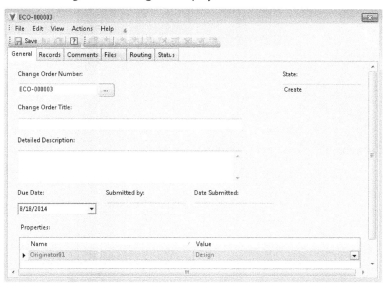

3.  Click the button next to Change Order Number […] to display the Change Order Numbering Schemes dialog box. Select a numbering scheme from the list.

 The numbering scheme cannot be changed after the change order has been created and has entered the Open state.

4.  Enter a title under Change Order Title and enter a detailed description. Under Due Date, select a date when the change order is to be completed.

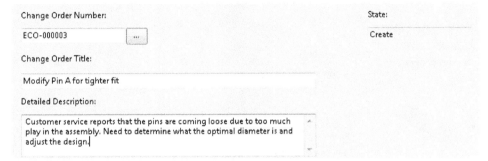

5.  Click the Records tab. The file selected in step 1 displays.

You can use Add to attach other files or items to the change order.

6. Select the Comments tab then click Add Comment to add information about the required design change, etc.

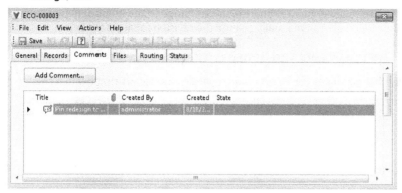

7. Click the Routing tab. Select a routing list.

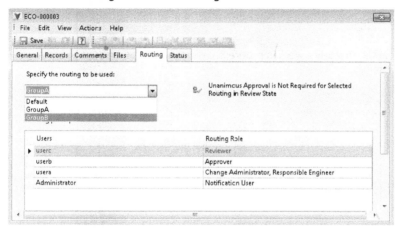

An example of a routing list and what it represents is shown in the Example of Change Order Routing section.

8. Click Save to create the change order.

# Change Orders and Revisions

The lifecycle state change generates a primary revision change to the items or files included in a change order. A qualified user can manually change the revision for any item or file.

## Definition of Change Orders and Item Revisions

You can manually change an item or files revision regardless of its participation in a change order.

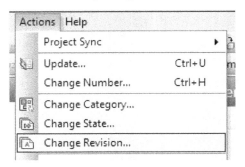

For example, if a part is currently a work in progress, a department can create a secondary revision to indicate a design change.

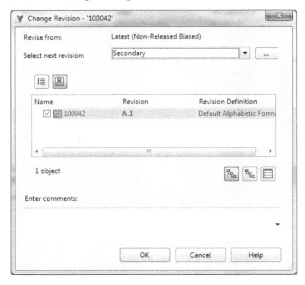

By default, items are locked and only the Change Administrator or Responsible Engineer can make them editable. If an item in the Released state is added to a change order and editing is enabled, the item's state changes to Work in Progress. A new revision is automatically created unless the bump revision action is set to None in the Lifecycle Rules dialog box.

### Example of a Revision Change

In the following example, the part file Grip.ipt is released and has a revision -. When you use the Change State option to change the item state to Work in Progress, the revision changes from - to A and the part is now editable.

# Change Orders and Lifecycle States

### Example of a Change Order

Engineering has been notified that a part has had a higher-than-expected failure rate under certain conditions and must be redesigned. When you create the change order for the existing item, the part can be modified and the change routed through the design team for approval.

When the item is not included in an active change order, you can manually change the state of the item.

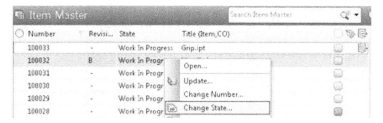

When an item is attached to a change order, the functionality is disabled at the item level and transferred into the Change Order while in the Edit mode.

## Rules for Using Change Orders with Files

### General Rules

- Only users with Administrator or Change Order Editor security permissions can affect change orders.
- A file can only be associated with one active change order at a time. Once a change order has been closed or cancelled, the file can be associated with a new or a currently active change order.
- Change orders do not drive file state changes. However, a change order will prevent certain lifecycle state changes for the file depending on the change order's state and if linked to change order is added as a criteria in the file's lifecycle transition.

### Rules for Closing a Change Order

- The change order must be in the Approved state.

### Rules for Releasing Files with Relationships

- Releasing an assembly on a change order that has unreleased children (not on a change order), releases the children. Effectivity is immediate.
- If a previously unreleased child is on another change order, the change order containing the parent item cannot be closed until the change order associated with the child item is either closed or cancelled.

### Best Practices

- As a best practice, you should add all children to a change order with an assembly. Reviewers and Approvers are notified of all affected files.
- In general, you should add all files affected by a design change to the change order. For example, in Autodesk Inventor, changing a part also charges the parent assembly.

## Rules for Using Change Orders with Items

Certain rules apply to using change orders with items and lifecycle states, closing a change order, or releasing items with relationships. Follow these rules and best practices for using change orders with items.

### General Rules

- To alter change orders, you must have Administrator or Change Order Editor security permissions.
- An item can only be associated with one active change order at a time. Once a change order has been closed or cancelled, the item can be associated with a new or active change order.
- The Change Order Administrator can make an item editable in all states except Canceled and Closed. The Responsible Engineer can make an item editable in the Work State, changing the lifecycle state.
- When an item is in the Work in Progress state and associated with a change order, an Item Editor Level 2 can edit the item, but cannot use the following commands:
  - Change State
  - New Change Order

### Rules for Using Change Orders with Items and Lifecycle States

- If a released item is added to a change order and the Change Order Administrator changes the state of the item to Work in Progress, the item changes to Work in Progress and a new revision is created according to the Bump revision action specified in the Lifecycles rules dialog box. If the Bump revision action is set to None, a new revision is not created.
- The state of an item does not change when it is attached to a change order.
- After a new revision is created, the Change Order Administrator can change the lifecycle state of the item to make the item editable or non-editable. To do this, use the Change State command available from the context menu.

### Rules for Closing a Change Order

- In order to close a change order, it must be in the Approved state.
- When you close a change order, a Change State dialog displays asking whether you want to change the state for associated items. You can modify the item states before closing the change order, or simply close the change order without making any changes.

### Rules for Releasing Items with Relationships

- Releasing an assembly on a change order that has unreleased children (not on a change order), releases the children. Effectivity is immediate.
- If a previously unreleased child is on another change order, the change order containing the parent item cannot be closed until the change order associated with the child item is either closed or cancelled.

### Best Practices

- As a best practice, you should add all children to a change order with an assembly. Reviewers and Approvers are notified of all affected items.
- In general, you should add all items affected by a design change to the change order. For example, in Autodesk Inventor, changing a part also changes the parent assembly.

# Roll Back the Lifecycle State of a File

Return a file to a previous lifecycle state with the Roll Back Lifecycle State Change command.

When a file is rolled back, it:

- Returns to the file version associated with the rolled-back state.
- Returns to the security, lifecycle definition, and revisions scheme associated with the rolled-back state.
- Retains any property definitions associated with the current version.
- Deletes the current version of the file.

### Rules for Rolling Back a File Lifecycle State

The lifecycle of a file can be rolled back if:

- The file is currently checked in.
- No parent versions consume the current child version that you want to roll back.
- The previous lifecycle state has not been deleted.
- The file is not in <null> definition.
- There is no label on the current version of the file.
- The administrator has not enabled the Restrict File and Item Lifecycle State Changes to Change Orders option.

### Roll Back a File's Lifecycle State

You must be a Document Manager Level 2 or Administrator to roll back a file's lifecycle state.

1. Select a file in the main view and select Actions>Roll Back Lifecycle State Change.
2. A dialog displays describing to which state the file will be rolled back.
3. Click Continue to complete the lifecycle state rol back.

# Roll Back the Lifecycle State of an Item

Return an item to a previous lifecycle state with the Roll Back Lifecycle State Change command.

When an item is rolled back, it:

- Returns to the item version associated with the rolled-back state.
- Returns to the security, lifecycle definition, and revisions scheme associated with the rolled-back state.
- Retains any property definitions associated with the current version being rolled back.
- Deletes the current version of the file.

### Rules for Rolling Back an Item Lifecycle State

You can roll back an item from any state to another state as long as:

- The rolled back state has not been deleted.
- The current lifecycle state is not <null> and the rolled back state is not <null>.
- The rolled back state is not controlled by purge settings.
- There are no ECO restrictions on state change.
- The rolled back state did not exist before the ECO was created.
- The ECO is not closed.

**Note:** If the ECO was canceled, you can still roll back to the last state in the ECO.

There are no component link restrictions.

For example, if rolling back to the previous state would link the item to a component that is only permitted one link and the component is already linked to another item, then the roll back is not permitted.

Only users with Item Editor Level 2, ERP Manager, or Administrator roles can change the state on an item.

### Roll Back the Lifecycle State of an Item

1.   Select an item in the Item Master, and then select Actions >Roll Back Lifecycle State Change.

2.   Click Continue to complete the lifecycle state rollback.

## Clear Item and Change Order Locks

Occasionally, it is required to remove the item and change order locks reserved to you. Use the Clear Item and CO Locks command to clear all of the locked items, change orders, and return them to read-only mode.

**Note:** This command releases locks for items and change orders that are reserved to the user performing the command. Changes to the items or change orders are not saved.

### Clear Item and Change Order Locks

1.   In the Vault Client, select Actions>Clear Item and CO Locks.

2.   Verify that you want to clear the locks.

3.   All locked items and change orders are returned to read-only state. Changes are not saved.

## Identifying Change Order Participants

When you create a change order, you specify a routing list of participants with predefined roles and specific permissions and responsibilities. Participants are notified that a change order requires their attention. The change requestor and approver roles control the progression of the change order. The reviewer role can only view, add, and reply to comments.

## Example of Change Order Routing

The administrator creates routing participant lists in the Global settings dialog (Tools menu> Administration>Global Settings>Change Orders tab) dialog box, as shown in the following illustration.

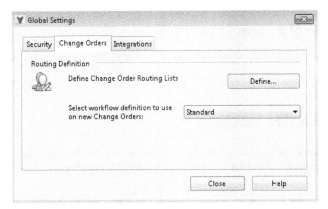

Lists can contain any number of users, but you must specify at least one Approver, one Responsible Engineer, and one Change Administrator in order to create a routing list. A checker must also be included if the Check state is enabled.

Routing participants:

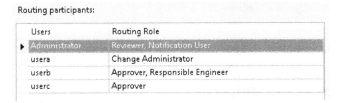

To set the routing, the administrator can select Unanimous Approval for Review State Required in the Routing Settings dialog box.

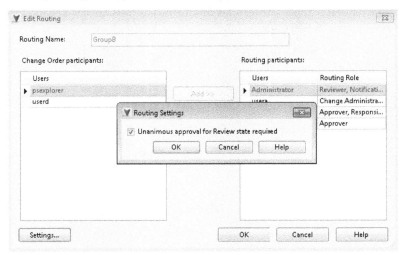

## Routing Editing Rules

The following rules apply to editing the routing after the change order has been created:

- Depending on the state of the change order, anyone on the routing can add another reviewer, except for the Notification User.
- The Administrator, Change Administrator, and Responsible Engineer can add or remove approvers and Change Administrators.
- Only the Administrator, Change Administrator, and Responsible Engineer can remove a reviewer.
- Change order activities can only be performed by the routing participants.

## Notification

A user on the routing list is notified when the change order enters a state that requires their attention. There are three notification methods:

- My Worklist: In the navigation pane when Home or Change Order List displays. The change order number and due date display on this list. Clicking on a change order in this list will change the main pane to Change Orders with that change order selected.
- Pop-up alert: Displays briefly in the lower right hand corner when a change order is added to the user's work list. This pop-up message can be toggled off or on. By default, the pop-up notification is on. To change the setting, click View menu>Notification Display.

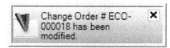

- E-mail notification: The administrator must configure Autodesk Data Management Server for email notification and Vault Professional users must have valid e-mail addresses in their user profiles.

### Routing participants are notified

- The change order number displays on each Routing participant's 'My Worklist' depending on the state of the change order. For example, the Responsible Engineer is notified when the change order enters the Work state, but the Approver does not get notified until it enters the Review state.
- Following the same logic, an email message is sent to each person on the routing list depending on the state of the change order. For example, the Reviewer is notified by an e-mail when the change order enters the Review state.
- Vault Professional includes a role called Notification Users in the ECO Routing tab. This user is notified when a change order is closed, usually indicating that a new revision of items or documents is now available.
- If Vault Professional is running but inactive, a pop-up alert displays momentarily on the user's screen in the lower right corner when the change order is added to his or her work list.

## Participants and Change Order Roles

The following steps describe the typical workflow for creating a change order as well as the roles of participants at each step in the process.

1. A user creates a change order. This user can be any member of the design team as long as they have a Change Order Editor role. The following actions occur:

- They are added to the routing list as a Change Requestor.
- The change order enters the Create state.
- The Change Requestor or the Change Administrator submits to the Open state.
- The change Administrator is notified if the change order is submitted to the Open state.

2. In the Open State the Change Administrator reviews the order and determines whether to add comments, markups, or additional properties. In the Open state, it is the Change Administrator's task to determine whether the change order should be processed. It can be canceled for a request that is unfulfillable.

- The Change Administrator selects the items in the Records tab of the change order and changes state to put them in Work In Progress.
- The Change Administrator submits the change order to the work state.
- The Responsible Engineer is notified.

3. If the Change Administrator did not put the items into the Work In Progress state the Responsible Engineer can at this point. The Responsible Engineer checks out the files from the vault and modifies them with regards to the change order. The files are checked back in to the vault and the items are updated and the State is changed to In Review.

4. The Responsible Engineer submits the change order and it enters the Review state.

5. The Reviewers and Approvers are notified. They can review the design changes, add comments and markups. The Approvers can, at any time, accept the change order. If the administrator has selected the Unanimous Approval for Review State Required in the Routing Settings dialog box, all Approvers must review and submit their acceptance of the change order. The change order is now set to Approved.

6. The Change Administrator is once again notified. Any Work In Progress or In Review items on the change order are set to Released.

7. The change order is now closed. All Notification Users are notified by e-mail (if configured), indicating new items are ready for production.

# Exercise: Create and Approve Change Orders

In this exercise, you create two change orders. You submit and approve the first. For the second, three routing participants must approve the change order because unanimous approval is required.

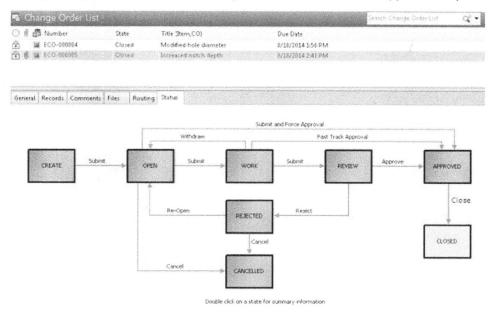

The completed exercise

## Create and Approve Change Orders

1.  Start Autodesk Vault Professional. Log in using the following information:
    - User Name: **usera**
    - Password: **vault**
    - Vault: AOTCVault

2.  In Project Explorer, expand the Designs folder.

3.  Click the Clamp folder.

4.  Right-click Grip.ipt. Select Assign/Update Item.

---

**5.** In the Edit Item window, select Save and Close.

An icon displays next to the part name and the associated drawing. After the item has been created, it is recommended to right-click on the file and select Go To Item to quickly change to the Item Master view with the particular item selected.

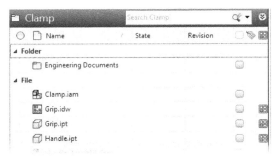

**6.** Switch to the Item Master. Right-click on the new item, then select Add To Change Order>To New.

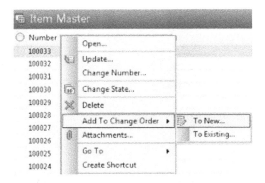

**7.** In the Change Order dialog box, General tab, for Change Order Title, enter **Modified hole diameter**.

**8.** For Detailed Description, enter **Increased hole diameter to 7.92 mm**.

**9.** Click Save. Close the Change Order dialog box.

**10.** An icon displays next to items controlled by a change order.

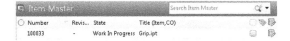

**Note:** Your item and change order numbers might differ from the illustrations in this exercise.

**11.** Switch to the Change Order list by selecting Change Order List. It is recommended to right-click on the item and select Go To>Go To Change Order.

**12.** In the Change Order list, right-click on the new change order. Do the following:
- Select Respond>Submit.
- Click OK to dismiss the Submit – Add Comment dialog box.

The status of the change order is set to Open.

**13.** In the Change Order list, right-click on the new change order. Do the following:
- Select Respond>Submit and Force Approval.
- Click OK.

**Note:** Usera is a Change Administrator and can force the approval of a change order.

**14.** Select the change order.

**15.** Click the Status tab to display the workflow chart. Do the following:
- Double-click the Approved state icon to display summary information about the state.
- Close the Summary dialog box.

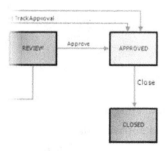

**16.** In the Change Order list, right-click on the new change order. Do the following:
- Select Respond>Close Change Order.
- Click OK.
- Select Released.
- Click OK.

**17.** Review the status. Because the effectivity was set to immediate, the status is now closed.

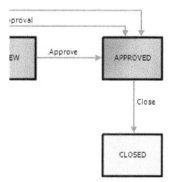

18. Switch to the Item Master.

19. Select the item.

20. In the preview pane, note that the lifecycle state is set to Released.

## Create a New Change Order

1. In the Item Master, right-click on the item created in the previous section of the exercise. Do the following:

   - Select Change State>Work in Progress.
   - Click OK.

   A revision is created. In this example, the new revision is A.

   Right-click on the item, then select Add to Change Order>To New. Do the following:

   - For Change Order Title, enter **Increased notch depth**.
   - For Detailed Description, enter **Notch depth increased to 3.18 mm**.

2. Under Properties, Value column, click Design. Select Manufacturing from the list.

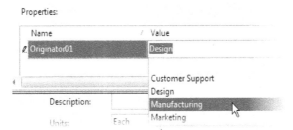

3. Select the Files tab. In the Attached Files list, select Grip.idw.

**4.** Do the following:

- On the top view, zoom in to the notch feature.
- Click the arrow next to the Rectangle callout.
- Click Rectangle callout, revision cloud.

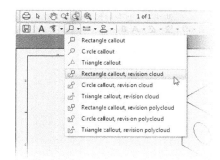

**5.** Click and drag to create a markup around the notch.

**6.** In the text box, enter **Notch depth increased to 3.18 mm**.

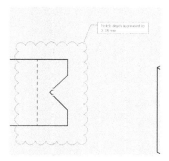

**7.** Click Fit to Window.

**8.** Click the down arrow next to Stamps. Do the following:

- Select the For Review stamp.
- Click in the sheet to place the stamp.

9. On the toolbar above the DWF window, click Save. Do the following:

- In the Save As dialog box, navigate to the Clamp folder.
- Enter the filename **clamp_markup**.
- Click Save to add the markup file to the vault.

10. In the Add Comment dialog box, do the following:

- For Title, enter **Notch depth increased to 3.18 mm**.
- For Comments, enter **Due to a number of failures in the field, the notch depth has been increased**.
- Click OK.

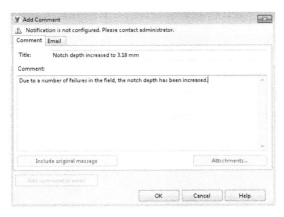

11. Click the Routing tab. From the list, select GroupB.

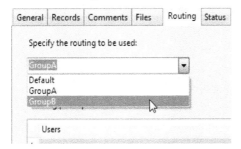

12. Review the Routing participants. usera, userb, and userc are part of this group.

- usera is the Change Administrator. Since usera is creating the change order he will also be the Change Requestor for this change order.
- userb is an Approver and the Responsible Engineer.
- userc is an Approver.

The administrator created this list with unanimous approval required for a change order.

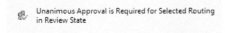

**13.** Click the Status tab. The workflow chart shows that the change order is set to Create.

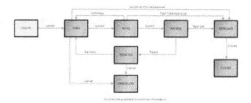

**14.** Click Save. Close the Change Order dialog box. It is recommended to NOT save the change order until this step. Saving beforehand will remove the user's ability to set the routing choice as shown in step 15.

**15.** In the Change Order list, right-click on the new change order. Do the following:

- Select Respond>Submit.
- Click OK to dismiss the Submit – Add Comment dialog box. Note that by default a title is entered indicating the ECO is submitted to the Open state.

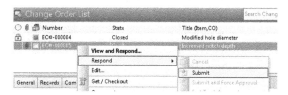

**16.** In the Change Order list, select the new change order. Click the Status tab to display the workflow chart.

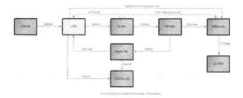

**17.** In the Status diagram, double-click the Open state to display the summary information about the state. Close the Summary dialog box.

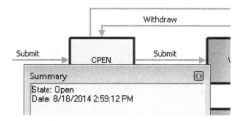

usera submits the change order again to change the status to Work.

**18.** In the Change Order list, right-click on the new change order. Do the following:

- Select Respond>Submit.
- Click OK in the Submit – Add Comment dialog box, again accepting the default comment.

Note the new state of the change order in the Status tab.

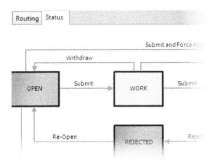

You now log in as userb, the Responsible Engineer.

**19.** Click File menu>Log Out.

**20.** Click Log In.

**21.** Log in using the following information:

- User Name: **userb**
- Password: **vault**
- Vault: AOTCVault

**22.** Review My Worklist. The ECO is listed.

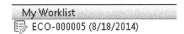

Clicking on the ECO in your worklist will take you directly to the Change Order list with the change order selected.

**23.** Click the Comments tab. Review the comments. Note that the details in the comment titled Notch depth increased to 3.18mm. Right-click on this comment and view the attachment. Close the attachments window.

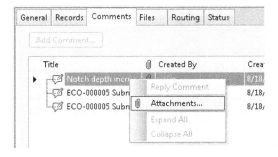

**24.** Select the Files tab and click the attached markup file clamp_markup.dwf in the Attached files list.

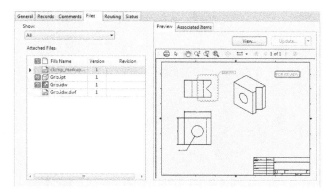

**25.** In the Change Order list, right-click on the new change order. Do the following:

- Select Respond>Submit. This will move the change order to the next state Review.
- The Submit – Add Comment dialog box displays. In the Comments field, enter **Reviewed by the responsible engineer. The new design is correct.**
- Click OK.

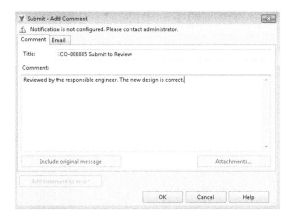

**26.** Note that the change order still displays in My Worklist. The change order requires unanimous approval from all reviewers. In addition to being the Responsible Engineer, userb is also a Reviewer. userb must also approve the change order.

**27.** In the Change Order list, right-click on the new change order. Do the following:

- Select Respond>Approve.
- In the Approve – Add Comment dialog box, enter **The design has been reviewed and is correct. Ready for re-release.**
- Click OK.

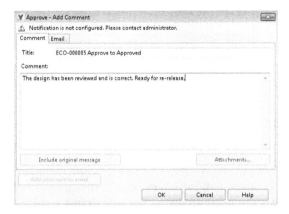

**28.** Select the Status tab. Note that the change order state is still Review. Double-click on the State to review the status. The change order requires unanimous approval from all reviewers.

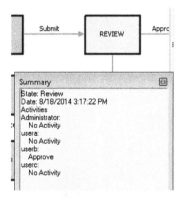

userc must also approve the change order.

**29.** Click File menu>Log Out.

**30.** Click Log In.

**31.** Log in using the following information:

- User Name: **userc**
- Password: **vault**
- Vault: AOTCVault

**32.** Note that the change order is in My Worklist. Select on the change order to switch to the Change Order list with the change order selected.

**33.** Double-click on the change order to open it for review.

**34.** Select the Comments tab and review the comments.

**35.** In the Respond toolbar, note that there are two possible icons enabled – Reject and Approve. Select Approve.

**36.** In the Approve – Add Comments dialog box, in the Comment section, enter **Agreed – ready for immediate re-release.**

**37.** Select OK to exit the dialog box.

**38.** Close the Change Order dialog box.

**39.** Click the Status tab. Because all three participants have approved the change, the state is set to Approved.

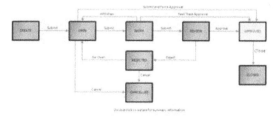

The Change Administrator is responsible for Closing the change order by setting the effectivity of the items on the change order. In this scenario usera is the Change Administrator.

**40.** Log in as usera using the data provided earlier in this lesson.

**41.** Note once again that the change order displays in My Worklist. Select it to go to the change order.

**42.** In the Change Order list, right-click on the new change order. Do the following:

- Select Respond>Close Change Order.
- Click OK.
- Select Released.
- Click OK.

**43.** In the Change Order list, review the status of the change order. Note that it is now closed.

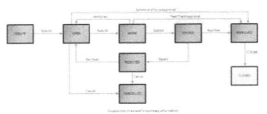

**44.** Select the Records tab and note the Revision and State (Historical) of the item. It has been now released at Revision A.

# Chapter Summary

In this chapter, you learned how to use Autodesk Vault Professional to assign items to a part and then create a new change order using the item.

Having completed this chapter, you can:

- Create and change item lifecycle states manually.
- Create and approve change orders.

# Working with Bills of Materials

This chapter describes how to use bills of materials in Autodesk® Vault Professional. You learn how these BOMs are integrated with other applications, including Autodesk® Inventor® and Autodesk® Vault.

## Objectives

After completing this chapter, you will be able to:

- Manage bills of materials (BOMs).
- Describe the integration of Inventor, Vault, and Vault Professional and the relationship between an Inventor bill of materials (BOM) and the associated Vault Professional item BOM.

# Lesson: Bills of Materials

## Overview

This lesson describes how to manage and use bills of materials (BOMs).

As an essential element in the design or manufacture of products, a BOM, in its simplest form, can be a list of components and the quantity of each required. It can, however, describe much more. BOMs can indicate which parts are manufactured and which are purchased, the materials, part numbers, and stock numbers of each part, and how the parts are structured and assembled.

Use the Bill of Materials tab in the Edit Item Record dialog box or in the Preview pane to work with the items BOM.

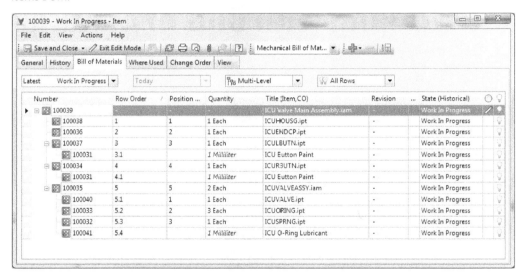

### Objectives

After completing this lesson, you will be able to:

- View part BOMs.
- Edit BOMs to add, delete, and reorder items, and change item quantities.
- Format, print, and export BOMs.

# About Bill of Materials

You can manage and track components of an assembly by using a BOM that lists all its parts and subassemblies. When you link purchased items to an assembly, the items become part of the BOM list as well. Although you typically associate a BOM with an assembly, all items have a bill of materials. You can view the BOM for any item by clicking the Bill of Materials tab.

## Part and Assembly Bill of Materials

A part BOM contains information related to a single item. The item can represent an Autodesk Inventor part, a purchased part, or another item added to the Item Master. If the item is linked to other items as part of a larger group, you might not be able to edit some of its properties, such as the quantity. You can add rows of other items to a part BOM. For example, you can include an existing document item that provides process or materials information on the part.

Unlike a part BOM, an assembly BOM contains multiple rows of item data that are linked directly or indirectly to the assembly item. Because these linked items are required for an assembly, some industries refer to this list as a recipe or formula. An assembly BOM does not require an actual modeled assembly. You can create a new item for non-modeled assemblies and add rows of other items to this new items BOM.

## Examples of Part Bill of Materials

The following illustration shows a BOM for an ICUSPRNG part. Standard modeled parts are usually measured in units of one (each). Note that the quantity field for this item is edited in its parent BOM.

The following illustration shows a BOM listing for a non-modeled part (lubricant). Its unit of measurement is set to milliliter.

## Examples of Assembly Bill of Materials

The following illustration shows the BOM for an ICU valve main assembly, including parts, subassemblies, and non-modeled items such as paint and lubricant.

Note that when viewing the BOM in Vault Professional, the Row Order column indicates the order of the items. Each subassembly listed in the BOM displays its own numbering scheme, starting at 1. The parent rows increment by one and the children rows increment by tenths. For example, if a parent row is 4, then the first child starts with 4.1.

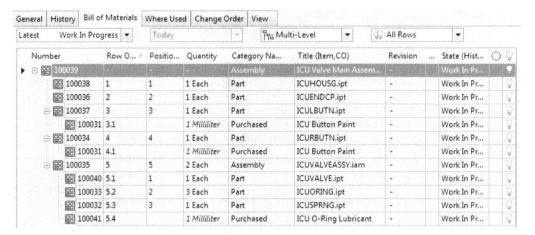

The following illustration shows the BOM for an ICU valve left button. Note that another item (button paint) is linked to the button part, making it an assembly.

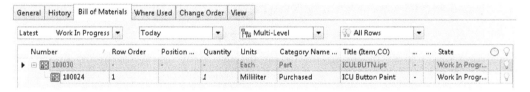

## Viewing a Bill of Materials

You can change your view of an item's Bill of Materials based on item revision/lifecycle state, date, BOM structure, or BOM row on/off status.

## By Revision/Lifecycle State

Select the required revision/lifecycle state. Depending on the current item state, not all items will be displayed. Items in the Obsolete state only display the latest revision:

- Latest – The current BOM. There can be items in any state in the BOM.

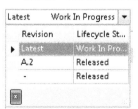

- Prior Revisions – Past released BOMs. Views of past released BOMs are read-only, even if the item record is in edit mode.

## By Date

Select a date from the Date drop-down. The last date before a later revision was released is now displayed in the Date drop-down. Change this date to reflect the released child item revisions for that specific date. The date selected must be on or after the date that the revision was released. The selected child revision BOM displays as of the selected date.

## By Bill of Materials Structure

You can select from three types of BOM structures:

- **Multilevel**: A hierarchical list of all child items in the current BOM. BOM rows can only be modified when the BOM is in Multi-Level view.

- **First Level:** This displays only the top-level child items of the current item.
- **Parts Only:** Items for parts only. The BOM is flattened to a single level. No subassembly items display.

## By Bill of Materials Row Display

You can filter whether all BOM rows are displayed, or only those rows that are toggled on or toggled off using the BOM Rows drop-down list.

- All Rows – All BOM rows display regardless of whether they are toggled on for the BOM.
- On Rows Only – Only rows that have been toggled on for the BOM display.
- Off Rows Only – Only rows that are toggled off display.

**Note:** When Parts Only view is selected, the row filter is automatically set to On Rows Only and cannot be changed.

# Editing a Bill of Materials

You can view an items BOM on the BOM tab in the Item Master. You must use the Item Editor to make changes to the BOM. The item must be in a Work in Progress state.

To edit an item, double-click it in the Item Master and select Edit from the toolbar. The Edit Item dialog box displays.

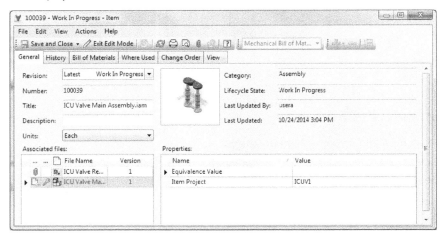

Click the Bill of Materials tab to access the BOM data.

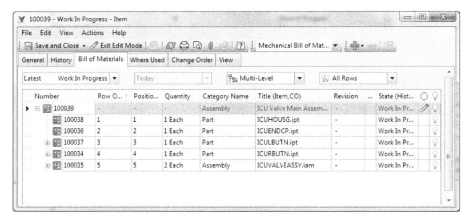

## Procedure: Adding Item Rows to an Item Bill of Materials

The following steps describe how to add item rows to an item BOM.

1. In the Item Master window, click the Bill of Materials tab. Right-click on the top row of the BOM.

2. Click Add Row>From Existing Item (or From New Item).

3. If you selected From Existing Item, enter the item number or search for the item in the list.

4. Click OK. The new item row displays in the BOM list.

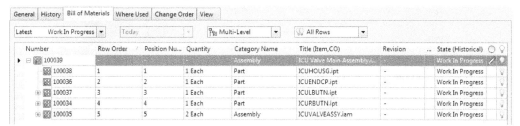

5. If you selected From New Item, new items added to the BOM in Vault Professional are appended to the end of the order. New items added to the BOM from a CAD add-in are appended to the end of the order when an update is performed.

 You can edit a BOM only if it displays in the Multi-level view (BOM tree view) that shows the relationships between the items. You cannot edit a BOM if it displays in the First Level or Parts Only list views (the flat BOM view). Any row that you add to the top level item becomes a first-level child item of the top-level item. To add items to a subassembly, you edit that item and add the item rows there.

## Procedure: Deleting Item Rows from an Item Bill of Materials

The following steps describe how to delete item rows from an item BOM. When you delete an item from a BOM it is not removed from the Item Master, but rather it is removed from the Item BOM.

1. In the Item Master, click the Bill of Materials tab. Right-click on the item row to be removed.

2. Click Remove Row. The item row is removed. When an item is removed from the BOM, a gap occurs in the numbering sequence. To update the order, drag-and-drop rows to reset the numbers. Only the top-level children in an item's BOM can be renumbered.

 CAUTION: You receive no warning that the row will be removed. Ensure that you are removing the correct row. You can remove only item rows that are first level children of the top-level item. To remove items in subassemblies, you must edit the subassembly item

## Procedure: Reordering Item Rows in an Item Bill of Materials

Items listed in the BOM can be reordered by dragging and dropping items in the BOM. The items can be returned to the last saved order by clicking Restore Saved Order  on the toolbar. The following steps describe how to reorder item rows in an item BOM:

1. In the Item Master, double-click the item to edit and click the Bill of Materials tab.

2. Click the any column header to sort first-level child items by the values in the column. Click the same header to invert the sort order.

3. You can also reorder individual rows if there are multiple items with the same value in the column controlling the sort order. To reorder one or more rows, you select and then drag the rows to their new position.

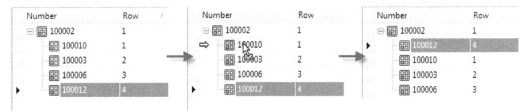

4. On the BOM Item toolbar, click Save and Close to save the changed order, or click File>Exit to close the item record without saving the new BOM order.

5. To restore the previous saved BOM order, select Restore Saved Order from the Edit toolbar.

 You can also reorder the BOM based on the values in a specific column. Click a BOM column header to sort the rows based on the values in that column. Click the same header to reverse the sort order

## Procedure: Changing Bill of Materials Item Quantities

The correct quantities of modeled items are calculated by default. Vault Professional works with the Inventor BOM structure, uses the same units of measure, and automatically adjusts for phantom, reference, or inseparable assemblies.

The quantity of any item can be changed in the BOM. For example, you can change the quantity of items that were added to the BOM from scratch, or of parts that are modeled once but are reused throughout the design (such as bolts). When adding non-CAD items to a BOM, you must include a quantity because there is no CAD data to determine the quantity automatically. Item quantity can only be edited on the Bill of Materials tab in an item record.

The BOM can only be edited when it is in multi-level view. Quantities can only be edited for the direct children of the host item. To edit a quantity in a subassembly listed in the BOM, open the subassembly from the item master.

The item quantity can be either static or calculated. A calculated quantity is derived from the source CAD file and updates accordingly. A static quantity overrides the quantity specified in the linked CAD file, which means that the original quantity contained in the CAD design is no longer reflected in the BOM.

A different font is used to identify whether a quantity is static or calculated. An Italic font is used for static quantities.

You can change any quantity in the BOM, including calculated numbers. The following steps describe how to change BOM item quantities.

1. In the Item record, click Edit and click the Bill of Materials tab.

2. Select a row in the BOM.

3. Click the quantity for the row.

4. Enter a new number for the quantity.

5. Press Enter.

 When you change the quantity of an item, you override the quantity derived from the linked CAD file by default. The original quantity contained in the CAD design is no longer reflected in the BOM, and the BOM does not update if the quantity is changed in the source file.

### Override the Current Quantity

Right-click on the quantity and then select Static Quantity. The quantity no longer reflects the value in the linked CAD file and does not update when the quantity is changed in the source file.

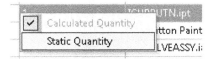

### Revert the Quantity to the CAD Value

Right-click on the quantity and select Calculated Quantity. The quantity reflects the value in the linked CAD file.

# Bill of Materials Output

You can view item BOMs in either tree or list view. Both views can be printed or exported to a Microsoft Excel spreadsheet, a tab-delimited text file, or an HTML page.

You can customize the setup for printing BOMs from the File menu or the toolbar in the Edit Item Record dialog box.

The following illustration shows the use of Print Preview to display the form to be printed.

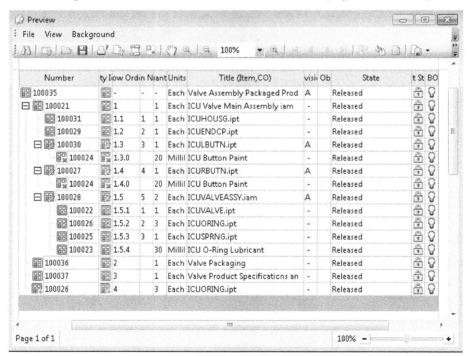

## Procedure: Formatting and Printing Bill of Materials

The following steps outline how to prepare and print a bill of materials.

1.  In the Open or Edit Item dialog box or in the Preview pane, click the Bill of Materials tab.

2.  Select the BOM Revision/Lifecycle State for the selected item.

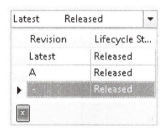

3.  Select the BOM format from the Structure list.

4.  Click File menu>Print Preview or click Print Preview icon.

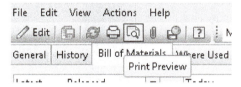

5.  In the Print Preview dialog box, click Customize.

6.  In the Printable Component Editor, select format and behavior settings to customize the print out. Click OK.

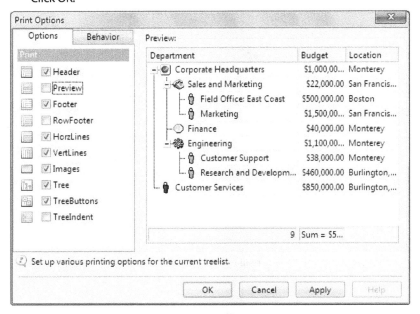

7.  In the Print Preview dialog box, on the toolbar, click Header and Footer or Page Setup to further customize the report.

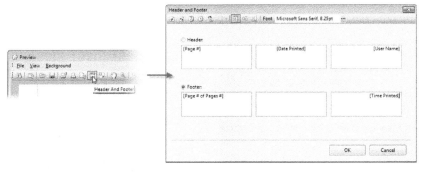

8.  Click Print or Print Direct.

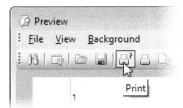

## Procedure: Exporting Bill of Materials

The following steps outline how to export a BOM in a variety of file formats.

1.  In the Item Master window, right-click on an item. Click Open.

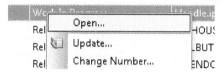

2.  In the Item Record dialog box, click Edit and click the Bill of Materials tab.

3.  Select the BOM format from the Structure list. In this example, print the Parts Only list of the BOM.

4.  In the File menu, click Save BOM View, or click the Save BOM View icon on the Standard toolbar.

5.  Select the file format for the export. Enter a filename. Click Save to save the BOM to a file.

# Exercise: Work with an Assembly Bill of Materials

In this exercise, you manage and edit a product's BOM. You learn to:

- Change BOM quantities.
- Add new items and link items in the BOM.
- Reorder BOM rows.
- View BOMs.
- Redesign the Valve Assembly Packaged Product.
- Save BOM View.

## Change BOM Quantities

1. Start Autodesk Vault Professional. Log in using the following information:
   - User Name: **usera**
   - Password: **vault**
   - Vault: AOTCVault

2. In the Item Master, double-click the ICUVALVEASSY.iam item and click Edit in the toolbar. Click the Bill of Materials tab.

3. On the Bill of Materials tab, right-click on one of the column headers then select Customize View.

4. Click Reset to reset the fields to their default state.

5. In the Customize View dialog box, click Fields.

6. Do the following:
   - For Select available fields from, select Item Fields.
   - Under Available fields, select Units and Entity Icon. Click Add.
   - Under Show these fields in this order, select Units.
   - Click Move Up until it displays below Quantity.
   - Move Entity Icon below Number.
   - Click OK.

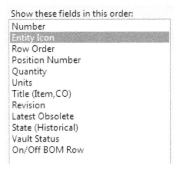

---

7. In the Customize View dialog box, click Close.

8. On the Bill of Materials tab, select the ICU O-Ring Lubricant item. Do the following:
   - For Quantity, enter **30**.
   - Press Enter.
   - Click Save and Close.

9. In the Item Master, double-click the ICULBUTN.ipt item and click Edit in the toolbar.

10. On the Bill of Materials tab, for the quantity of the ICU Button Paint, enter **20**. Click Save and Close.

11. Repeat the previous two steps for the ICURBUTN.ipt item.

## Add New Items and Link Items in the BOM

1. Under Home, right-click Item Master.

2. Click New Item.

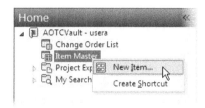

3. For Category, select Product.

4. For Title, enter **Valve Assembly Packaged Product**.

5. To complete the information for the new item, do the following:
   - For Units, verify that Each is selected.
   - Under Item Properties, select the Item Project row.
   - For Value, enter **ICUV1**.
   - Click Save and Close.

6. Under Home, right-click Item Master.

7. Click New Item.

8. For Category, select Purchased.

9.     Enter the following information for the new item:

- For Title, enter **Valve Packaging.**
- For Description, enter **Product Box**.

10.    To complete the information for the new item, do the following:

- For Units, verify that Each is selected.
- Under Properties, select the Item Project row.
- For Value, enter **ICUV1**.
- Click Save and Close.

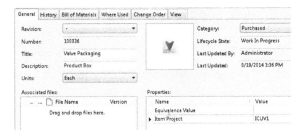

11.    Under Home, right-click Item Master.

12.    Click New Item.

13.    For Category, select Document.

14.    Enter the following information for the new item:

- For Title, enter **Valve Product Specifications and Instructions Sheet**.
- For Description, enter **Product Spec**.

15.    To complete the information for the new item, do the following:

- For Units, verify that Each is selected.
- Under Properties, select the Item Project row.
- For Value, enter **ICUV1**.
- Click Save and Close.

16.    In the Item Master, double-click the Valve Assembly Packaged Product item and click Edit. Click the Bill of Materials tab.

17.    Right-click Valve Assembly Packaged Product. Click Add Row>From Existing Item.

18.    In the Find dialog box, click the Basic tab if it is not selected already. Do the following:

- For Search Text, enter **valve**.
- Click Find Now.

**19.** Select the following items in the Found list:

- ICU Valve Main Assembly.iam.
- Valve Product Specification and Instructions Sheet.
- Valve Packaging.
- Click OK.

**20.** In the Bill of Materials, select the ICU Valve Main Assembly row. Press * on the numeric keypad to expand the view to its children. Your BOM should look like the following illustration.

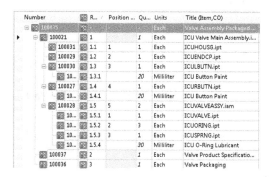

## Reorder BOM Rows

**1.** Review the rows in the BOM. Company policy requires the packaging to be the last item in the BOM.

**2.** Click the (-) symbol to close the ICU Valve Main Assembly.iam tree view.

**3.** Drag the Valve Packaging row to the bottom of the list if required.

**4.** Drag the Valve Product Specifications and Instructions Sheet down to the last row.

5. Click Save and Close. The Valve Assembly Package is complete.

6. In the Item Master, right-click Valve Assembly Packaged Product then select Change State.

7. In the Select Lifecycle dialog box, select Released. Click OK.

   Note that all the children (the components) of the Valve Assembly Package were also released.

## View BOMs

1. In the Item Master, select the Valve Assembly Packaged Product if it is not selected already.

2. In the preview pane, click the Bill of Materials tab. Review the BOM rows. Note that the quantity of the O-ring lubricant is 30 milliliters in the ICUVALVEASSY item. (There are two ICUVALVEASSY items.)

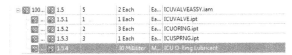

3. For Structure, select Parts Only. Note the quantity of the ICU O-ring lubricant (60 milliliters). This value is the correct total because there are two ICUVALVEASSY items with 30 milliliters of lubricant each.

4. For Structure, select First Level. The three items you linked to the Valve Assembly Packaged Product display.

5. For Structure, select Multi-Level to return to the structured BOM list.

## Redesign the Valve Assembly Package

1. In the Item Master, right-click on the ICULBUTN.ipt item. Click Change State.

2. In the Select Lifecycle dialog box, select Work in Progress. Click OK.

3. Repeat steps 1 and 2 to change the lifecycle state to Work in Progress for the ICURBUTN.ipt, ICUVALVEASSY.iam, and Valve Assembly Packaged Product items.

4. Double-click ICURBUTN.ipt item and click Edit. On the Bill of Materials tab, do the following:

   ▪ Select the ICU Button Paint row.
   ▪ Right-click on the selected row.
   ▪ Click Remove Row.
   ▪ Click Save and Close.

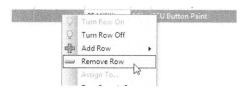

5. Repeat the previous step to remove the ICU Button Paint row from the ICULBUTN.ipt item.

6. In the Item Master, double-click the Valve Assembly Packaged Product item and click Edit. Click the Bill of Materials tab.

7. Select and right-click on the top row. Click Add Row>From Existing Item.

8. In the Find dialog box, do the following:

   ▪ Click the Basic tab if it is not selected already.
   ▪ Under Search Text, enter **ICU\*.**
   ▪ Click Find Now. A number of items are returned in the search results.
   ▪ Select the ICUORING.ipt row.
   ▪ Click OK.

9. The ICUORING.ipt item is added to the BOM. Do the following:

   ▪ Change its quantity to 3.
   ▪ Click Save and Close.

10. In the Item Master, change the lifecycle state of the Valve Assembly Packaged Product item to Released. If prompted to confirm the state change for children, click Yes.

## Save BOM View

**1.** In the Item Master, double-click the Valve Assembly Packaged Product item. Click the Bill of Materials tab and select File>Save BOM View.

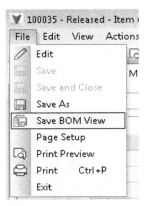

**2.** For File Name, enter **ICU Product BOM - Rev B**. Click Save.

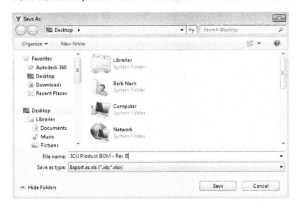

**3.** Open Microsoft Excel. Open ICU Product BOM - Rev B.XLS.

**4.** Close Vault Professional and Excel.

# Lesson: Integration with Autodesk Inventor

## Overview

This lesson describes how to use Autodesk Vault Professional with other applications. The primary focus is the relationship between Autodesk Inventor and Vault Professional BOMs. The lesson also covers working with Vault Professional and Autodesk Vault, AutoCAD®, AutoCAD® Mechanical, and AutoCAD® Electrical.

### Objectives

After completing this lesson, you will be able to:

- Describe the integration of Inventor with Vault Professional.
- Describe the relationship between an Inventor bill of materials (BOM) and the associated Vault Professional item BOM.
- Work with Autodesk Inventor virtual components.
- Customize content center library components to use with Vault Professional.
- Describe how Vault and Vault Professional work with drawing files.

# About Autodesk Inventor and Integration with Vault Professional

Autodesk Vault integrates with Autodesk Inventor software using an Autodesk Inventor add-in. Users can use Vault Professional to assign item numbers to vaulted parts and assemblies. You can edit assembly BOMs in both Autodesk Inventor and Vault Professional, and coordinate property information between Autodesk Inventor, Autodesk Vault, and Autodesk Vault Professional.

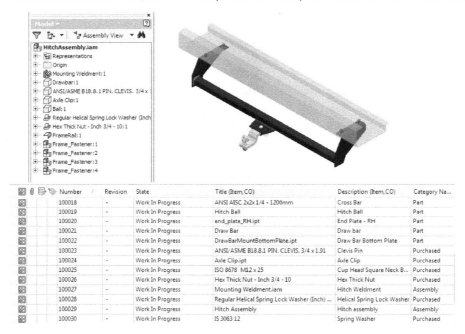

| Number | Revision | State | Title (Item, CO) | Description (Item, CO) | Category Na... |
|--------|----------|-------|------------------|------------------------|---------------|
| 100018 | - | Work In Progress | ANSI AISC 2x2x1/4 - 1200mm | Cross Bar | Part |
| 100019 | - | Work In Progress | Hitch Ball | Hitch Ball | Part |
| 100020 | - | Work In Progress | end_plate_RH.ipt | End Plate - RH | Part |
| 100021 | - | Work In Progress | Draw Bar | Draw bar | Part |
| 100022 | - | Work In Progress | DrawBarMountBottomPlate.ipt | Draw Bar Bottom Plate | Part |
| 100023 | - | Work In Progress | ANSI/ASME B18.8.1 PIN. CLEVIS. 3/4 x 1.91 | Clevis Pin | Purchased |
| 100024 | - | Work In Progress | Axle Clip.ipt | Axle Clip | Purchased |
| 100025 | - | Work In Progress | ISO 8678 M12 x 25 | Cup Head Square Neck B... | Purchased |
| 100026 | - | Work In Progress | Hex Thick Nut - Inch 3/4 - 10 | Hex Thick Nut | Purchased |
| 100027 | - | Work In Progress | Mounting Weldment.iam | Hitch Weldment | Assembly |
| 100028 | - | Work In Progress | Regular Helical Spring Lock Washer (Inch) ... | Helical Spring Lock Washer | Purchased |
| 100029 | - | Work In Progress | Hitch Assembly | Hitch assembly | Assembly |
| 100030 | - | Work In Progress | IS 3063 12 | Spring Washer | Purchased |

## Application Overviews

Autodesk Inventor is a 3D parametric CAD application. You can combine individual part models in a hierarchy of assemblies to create a complete digital design. You supply values for intrinsic document properties and can add custom properties to any part or assembly.

Use Autodesk Vault to provide work-in-progress version control for Inventor models and other documents. A vault stores versions of documents, file relationships between documents, and property data associated with each version. You check files out of the vault to modify them in Inventor and check in the new versions to share with your design team.

When you use Autodesk Vault Professional to assign items to these files, users outside the engineering department can also access property and bill of materials data from the files stored in a vault.

## Working with Autodesk Vault Professional and Autodesk Vault

Autodesk Vault Professional is an external application that adds manufacturing and release data to documents in the vault. You create an Autodesk Vault Professional item when you assign an item number to a file stored in the vault. Initial property values for the item are extracted from the property information stored in the vault. After it is created, the item is connected to the file in the vault, but property values are largely independent. You can add Autodesk Vault Professional items without associating them to a vault file.

You need to understand how actions in Autodesk Vault Professional affect the associated files in Autodesk Vault because a number of tasks can be completed only when files are checked in to the vault and lifecycle state changes can affect the state of the associated files in Autodesk Vault.

### Autodesk Vault Professional and Autodesk Vault

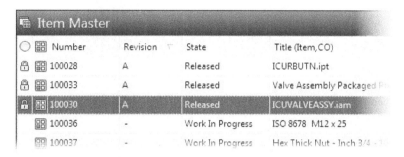

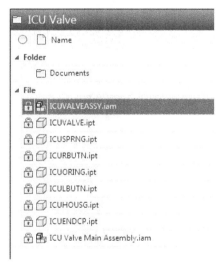

All of the associated files of a released item in Vault Professional are locked in the vault.

## Working with Autodesk Vault Professional and Autodesk Inventor

When you create an item from a part or assembly stored in a vault, Autodesk Vault Professional extracts property information from Autodesk Vault. The property values are typically assigned in Autodesk Inventor, but you can edit values for existing properties in Autodesk Vault. Item properties can be mapped back to the properties in the associated Autodesk Inventor part or assembly document. If you understand the relationship between properties in all three applications, you can effectively integrate Autodesk Vault Professional into an Autodesk Inventor design environment.

An Autodesk Inventor assembly BOM maps information to the BOM in the associated item in Autodesk Vault Professional. Your understanding of this process helps to ensure its accuracy.

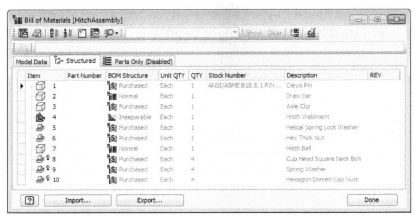

Autodesk Inventor Bill of Materials

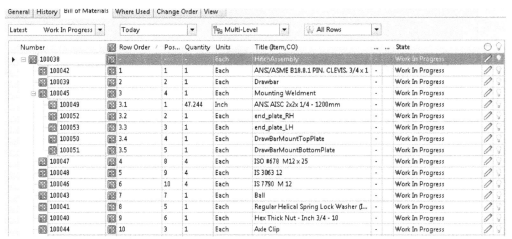

Autodesk Vault Professional Bill of Materials

## Example of Application Integration

The following example shows a workflow for a change order performed on a Released item. The associated file in the vault is locked when the item is in a Released state.

1. A Vault Professional user creates a new change order for a released part or assembly item. On submittal of the change order, the Change Administrator or Responsible Engineer changes the item status to Work in Progress creating a new item revision. This action unlocks the part or assembly the vault.

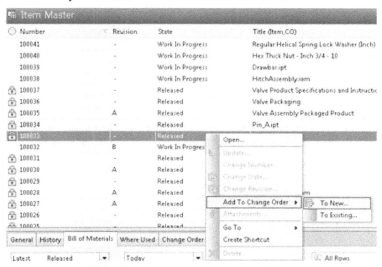

2. When the Responsible Engineer works on the change order, they can open the change order and examine the items associated with it. The items are on the Records tab. From here, the user can directly go to the item. Note that having an item associated to the change order on the Records tab causes the files associated to the item to be displayed on the Files tab. In the Work state, the Responsible Engineer can open a file directly from the Files tab and can check the file out at that time.

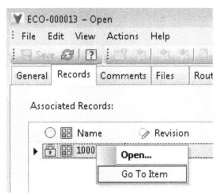

3. Looking at the item, the user can see which file is associated with what requires work and go directly to the vault folder containing the file.

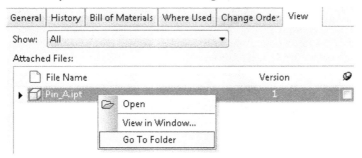

4. Not looking at the files in the vault, the user can open and check out the file.

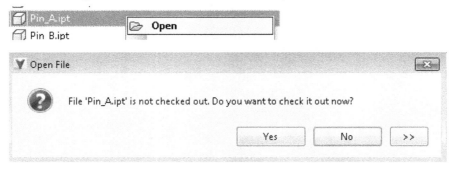

5. The Autodesk Inventor user edits the file and checks them back in to the vault.

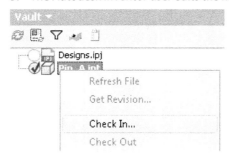

6. The Vault Professional user then updates the item to update the link to the new file version.

7. Finally, the change order is completed, returning the item to a Released state. The files are again locked in the vault.

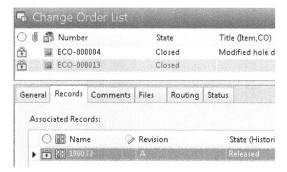

 When you check out, edit, and check in a component, you must update the associated item in Autodesk Vault Professional before you can change the lifecycle state of the item. Each item revision is associated with a specific version of the component in the vault. The change order cannot be completed unless the items have been updated.

# Autodesk Inventor BOMs

Information in Autodesk Inventor assembly BOMs is translated into the BOMs of the associated Autodesk Vault Professional items.

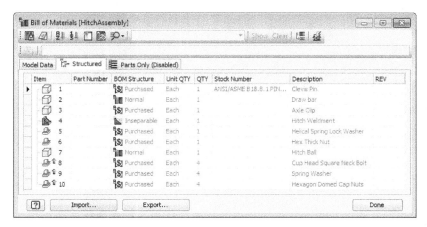

## Definition of Autodesk Inventor BOM

Autodesk Inventor assembly BOMs contain information about their hierarchy of parts, subassemblies, and virtual components and are usually displayed as structured lists of components, as shown in the following illustration:

## Parts Only BOM

You can select a Parts Only view that flattens the BOM to a single level and aggregates all parts in the assembly hierarchy as shown in the following illustration:

## BOM Structure

Each part, subassembly, and virtual component in the assembly is assigned a BOM structure that determines the status of the component in the assembly BOM.

The following table explains the display status of individual parts assigned different BOM structure types.

| Part BOM Structure | Structured BOM View Status | Parts Only BOM View Status | Notes/Example |
|---|---|---|---|
| Normal | Shown as a single line | Shown as a single line | Default BOM structure for most parts Quantity can be affected by parent BOM structure |
| Reference | Excluded from view | Excluded from view | Typically assigned to parts that provide reference for the current design |
| Phantom | Excluded from view | Excluded from view | Skeleton model parts are often assigned a Phantom structure |
| Purchased | Shown as a single line | Shown as a single line | Assigned to components that are not fabricated |
| Inseparable | Not normally assigned to parts | Not normally assigned to parts | |

The following table outlines the display status of a subassembly and its child components when it is assigned different BOM structure types.

| Subassembly BOM Structure | Structured BOM View Status | Parts Only BOM View Status | Notes/Example |
|---|---|---|---|
| Normal | Shown as a single line<br><br>Child components displayed as subcomponents in the assembly BOM | Excluded from view | Default BOM structure for most subassemblies |
| Reference | Components and all children excluded from view | Excluded from view | Typically assigned to parts or assemblies that provide reference for the current design |
| Phantom | Excluded from view<br><br>Child components promoted to Phantom subassembly level<br><br>Quantity of Phantom component affects quantity of promoted children | Excluded from view | A Phantom assembly that groups a bolt, nut, and washers and can reduce model complexity |
| Purchased | Shown as a single line<br><br>Child components displayed as subcomponents (often not shown in parts list) | Shown as a single line (treated as a part)<br><br>Child components excluded from view | Assigned to assemblies that are not fabricated |
| Inseparable | Shown as a single line<br><br>Child components displayed as subcomponents (often not shown in parts list) | Shown as a single line<br><br>(treated as a part)<br><br>Purchased child components promoted and shown<br><br>Other child components excluded from view | Assigned to assemblies that are not easily disassembled<br><br>Weldments and riveted assemblies are examples of Inseparable assemblies |

A component's BOM structure also determines how the corresponding item displays in an Autodesk Vault Professional BOM.

## Assigning a BOM Structure

Subassemblies retain their current BOM structure when you place them in a higher-level assembly. Parts are assigned Normal BOM structure when placed in an assembly.

The following illustration shows how you select the BOM structure in the Create In-Place Component dialog box.

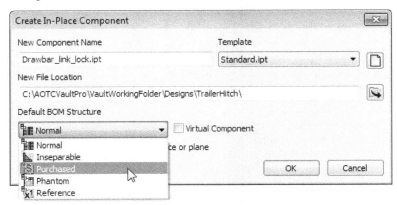

## Editing a BOM Structure

You can change the BOM structure of a component from its default setting to Reference by right-clicking the component in the browser and selecting BOM Structure>Reference. You can restore the default BOM structure using the same steps.

The following illustration shows how you can select any BOM structure for a component in the Bill of Materials dialog box. These options are not available from the browser shortcut menu.

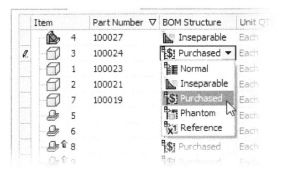

### Example of BOM Structure

You can assign Inseparable BOM structure to the welded frame assembly, as shown in the following illustration. The assembly itself can contain a skeleton part model (Phantom BOM structure), multiple frame members (Normal BOM structure), and purchased components, such as lifting shackles (Normal or Purchased BOM structure).

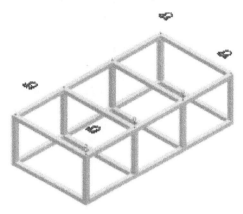

# Virtual Components

You add virtual (non-geometric) components to assemblies to represent engineering components that cannot be easily modeled.

### Definition of Virtual Components

You create virtual components in place in Inventor assemblies. They have no geometry and are not saved as separate files when you save the parent assemblies. Lubricants, glue, and other engineering materials are often represented by virtual parts. You can add any number of virtual components to an assembly.

## Virtual Components and Autodesk Vault Professional Items

From a BOM perspective, virtual components are similar to user-created items in Vault Professional. You can add a user-created item to the BOM of another item. Similarly, when you add a virtual component to an assembly, it is automatically added to the BOM of the assembly.

When you assign item numbers to an assembly containing virtual components in Autodesk Vault Professional, each virtual component with Normal, Purchase, or Inseparable BOM structure is assigned a separate item number.

Your company's practices determine whether you should represent something as a virtual component in Inventor, or ignore it in Inventor and add a user-defined item in Vault Professional. You can add key engineering components to Inventor assemblies in the engineering environment. You can add common non-modeled components as items in Vault Professional. As with other items in a Vault Professional BOM, you can override quantity and other values for the item you create from the virtual component.

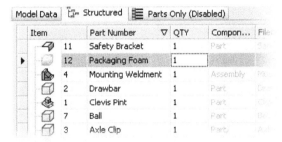

Autodesk Inventor BOM with virtual component

Autodesk Vault Professional BOM with virtual component

## Creating Virtual Components

You must create virtual components in place in an assembly. The following steps describe how to create virtual components.

1.  On the Assemble panel, click Create Component.

2.  In the Create In-Place Component dialog box, select the Virtual Component checkbox.

3.  Under New Component Name, enter a name for the virtual component.

4.  Under Default BOM Structure, select a BOM structure from the list. Click OK.

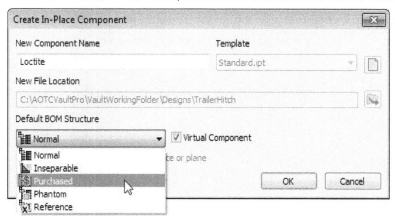

5.  The virtual component is listed in the assembly browser.

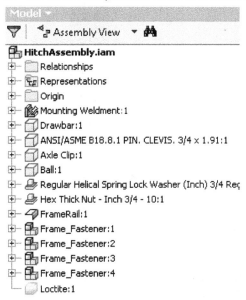

## Editing Virtual Components

Virtual components are not separate files but they contain the same properties present in other Inventor documents. You can edit both their properties and their BOM structure. You can change this setting to better reflect the component in the assembly BOM.

## Procedure: Editing a Virtual Component

The following steps describe how to change the units and quantity for a virtual component.

1.  In the browser, right-click on the virtual component. Select Component Settings.

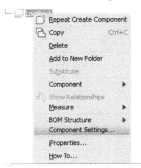

2.  In the Locktite Component Settings dialog box, click the Base Quantity drop-down list and scroll until you find the appropriate value. Select OK.

3.  In the Unit Quantity field enter the appropriate value.

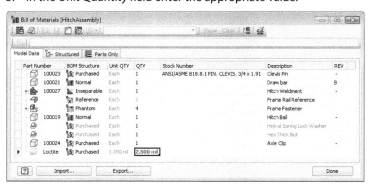

If the Base Quantity value is not in the list it can be created by editing the Parameters table and entering a new user-defined parameter. The units associated with the user parameter are assigned to the base quantity field for virtual part.

4. Override the quantity for the virtual part in the assembly BOM.

### Guidelines for Virtual Components

- Develop a company or departmental strategy for implementing virtual parts, user-created items, or combination of both.
- Virtual components are not saved as separate files, but rather are contained in assemblies.
- Virtual components with Normal, Purchased, or Inseparable BOM structures are assigned separate item numbers when their parent assemblies are assigned item numbers.
- Virtual components have the same properties as other Autodesk Inventor documents.

# Modifying Content Center Component Properties

You can customize Content Center library components to integrate them into Vault Professional.

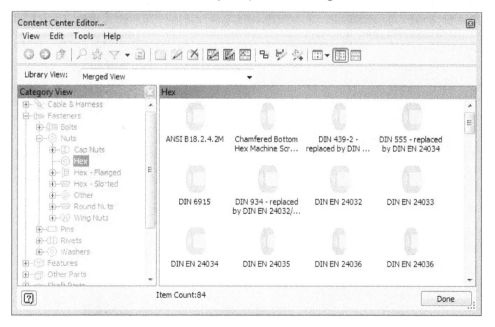

## Content Center Library Components

Many Autodesk Inventor assemblies contain components from the Content Center libraries that ship with Autodesk Inventor. These libraries contain a large number of common engineering components from a variety of standards, including ANSI, ISO, JIS, and others. You copy data from the read-only default libraries to a custom read/write library where you can customize the property information in the component family. When you assign an item to an Autodesk Inventor assembly that contains library components, those components are also assigned items.

The following illustration shows a custom read-write library added to the content center libraries.

You can also publish your own components to a custom library by creating an iPart factory that includes a table to define the variations in the part. You can include model properties as columns in the table and assign default values for each variation of the part. After you publish the iPart factory to a custom Content Center library, you can place the different versions in assemblies. Each variation retains the property values defined in the original iPart table.

See "iParts" and "Content Center" in the Autodesk Inventor Help for more information on working with and publishing your own library parts.

The following illustration shows an iPart Factory part and the iPart Author table that you use to create the different iPart member definitions.

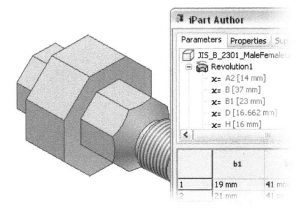

## Procedure: Modifying Properties of Content Center Components

The following steps describe how to copy data from a default read-only library to a custom read-write library and edit the properties in the library table.

1. Log in to the Autodesk Data Management Server Console as a user with at least Content Center Editor permission.

2. Expand the folders and select Libraries. Right-click and select Create Library.

3. Enter the Display Name and select a Partition based on the Inventor version you are using for the library.

4. Select OK to create the library.

5. In Autodesk Inventor, open any assembly. Click Tools ribbon and select Editor in the Content Center section. User requires a Content Center Editor role.

6. In the Content Center Editor dialog box, do the following:
- Right-click on the category or family to copy. Select Copy To.
- Click the name of a read-write library.
- Click Yes to refresh the content in the server.

7. In the read-write library, locate the part family you want to edit. On the List panel, right-click on the part family then click Family Table to display the Family Table dialog box.

8. In the Family dialog box, display the iProperties columns only. Add a new column.

9. In the Column Properties dialog box, enter a column name and column caption. Select a data type for the property.

10. Under Map to Inventor Property, select the Autodesk Inventor property to populate with the value from the new column.

11. Select the Expression checkbox. Enter a constant string or use a combination of strings and parameter names to populate the cells based on other values in the table. Click OK.

12. If required, repeat steps 5 through 8 to add other columns.

13. Optionally, delete or suppress rows in the table that are not used in your designs. You can also add rows or edit parameter values to create custom versions of the library part.

When you place parts from the table into subsequent assemblies, the property values in the library part reflect the values in the columns mapped to Inventor properties.

 Any component placed from the Content Center has a default Purchased BOM structure. You can edit this structure in the Bill of Materials dialog box.

# Working with DWG Files

You can use Autodesk Vault Professional with drawing (DWG™) files created in the AutoCAD software products such as AutoCAD, AutoCAD Mechanical, AutoCAD Electrical, and Autodesk Inventor.

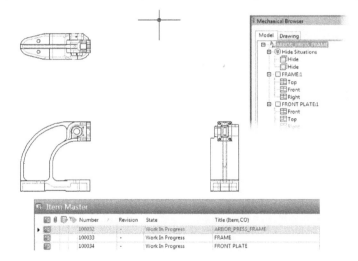

### DWG Files, Autodesk Vault, and Autodesk Vault Professional

Many companies work with a variety of Autodesk CAD software applications. Although a focus of Autodesk Vault and Autodesk Vault Professional is to work with data from Autodesk Inventor, you can manage versions and assign items to drawing files in Autodesk Vault.

Always check out and check in drawing files using the Vault ARX application inside your AutoCAD-based software. AutoCAD Electrical users must check out and check in all files in a project at the same time.

When you have checked drawing files into the vault, you can assign items to them using the same technique you use to assign items to Inventor parts and assemblies. The following illustration shows an AutoCAD Mechanical file being checked in to the vault

When you work with drawing files in Autodesk Vault Professional, consider the following:

- AutoCAD Mechanical BOM data is used to determine Category. Assembly drawing file BOM data is translated into the item BOM.

- When you assign an item to a drawing file, any externally referenced files (Xrefs) are added as attachments to the item in Autodesk Vault Professional. Always check in the drawing containing the Xrefs to maintain the file relationships.

- Property extraction and mapping between Autodesk Vault Professional and drawing files is not as robust as it is with Inventor documents. No provision exists for writing item property values back to the properties in a drawing file.

- You can control lifecycle status and changes to drawing files with Autodesk Vault Professional engineering change orders. If the vault is set to enforce file locking, you cannot check out a drawing file from the vault unless its lifecycle state is set to Work in Progress.

You can generate 2D drawings in Autodesk Inventor in either Autodesk Inventor's native format (IDW), or in DWG format. You can assign items to both of these file formats. If a drawing file does not exist in the vault when you assign an item to its associated part or assembly, you must manually attach the drawing item to its part or assembly item when the drawing is added to vault and assigned an item.

### Example of AutoCAD Files and Autodesk Vault Professional

Your design team uses AutoCAD or AutoCAD Electrical in combination with Inventor. An AutoCAD drawing contains a 2D reference layout for your Inventor assembly. AutoCAD Electrical drawing files detail electrical requirements for your design and provide pin and wire information for a harness assembly in Autodesk Inventor Professional.

You add the AutoCAD drawing file to the vault. You then attach it to your top-level Inventor assembly file and assign an item to the Inventor assembly. You add the AutoCAD Electrical drawings to the vault. You assign items to the AutoCAD Electrical drawings and use their Vault Professional bills of materials to aid the design.

# Exercise: Work with Autodesk Inventor Assemblies and BOMs

In this exercise, you examine an Inventor assembly BOM and how various BOM structure settings affect Vault Professional item creation. You work with components having Normal, Reference, Phantom, Purchased, and Inseparable BOM structures. You add a component to the assembly after assigning an item number to the assembly and examine how the new component is added to the Item Master.

| Number | Row Order | Pos... | Quantity | Units | Title (Item,CO) |
|---|---|---|---|---|---|
| ⊟ 🔲 100038 | 🔲 - | - | - | Each | HitchAssembly |
| 🔲 100042 | 🔲 1 | 1 | 1 | Each | ANSI/ASME B18.8.1 PIN. |
| 🔲 100039 | 🔲 2 | 2 | 1 | Each | Drawbar |
| ⊞ 🔲 100045 | 🔲 3 | 4 | 1 | Each | Mounting Weldment |
| 🔲 100047 | 🔲 4 | 8 | 4 | Each | ISO 8678 M12 x 25 |
| 🔲 100048 | 🔲 5 | 9 | 4 | Each | IS 3063 12 |
| 🔲 100046 | 🔲 6 | 10 | 4 | Each | IS 7790 M 12 |
| 🔲 100043 | 🔲 7 | 7 | 1 | Each | Ball |
| 🔲 100041 | 🔲 8 | 5 | 1 | Each | Regular Helical Spring Lι |
| 🔲 100040 | 🔲 9 | 6 | 1 | Each | Hex Thick Nut - Inch 3/ι |
| 🔲 100044 | 🔲 10 | 3 | 1 | Each | Axle Clip |
| ▶ 🔲 Safety Bracket | 🔲 11 | 11 | 1 | Each | Safety Bracket.ipt |

## Vault Setup

1.  Start Autodesk Vault Professional. Log in using the following information:
    - User Name: **administrator**
    - Password: leave blank
    - Vault: AOTCVault

2.  Click Go menu>Project Explorer. Click Tools menu>Options. If required, clear the Show Hidden Files checkbox. Click OK.

3.  In the browser, right-click on the Project Explorer ($) folder. Do the following:
    - Click Details...
    - The working folder should be set to *C:\AOTCVaultPro\VaultWorkingFolder*.
    - Click OK.

4.  In the browser, click the Project Explorer ($) folder. Do the following:
    - In the list, right-click Designs.ipj.
    - Click Get.
    - Click OK.

5. The Title property needs to be re-mapped in order for the item Title property to be displayed correctly. Do this:

- Select the Tools menu>Administration>Vault Settings.
- Select the Behaviors tab and then select Properties from the Properties group.
- In the Property Name column find the System property Title (Item, CO).
- On the Property Definitions toolbar select Edit.
- Select the Mapping tab.
- Find the entry for Provider: Inventor and select the file property Component Name.
- Select the up arrow in the Mapping toolbar to move this entry to the top of the list.
- Select OK to dismiss the Edit dialog.
- Select Close to dismiss the Property Definitions dialog.

6. Start Autodesk Inventor.

7. Click Projects.

8. In the Projects dialog box, click Browse.

9. Do the following:

- Browse to *C:\AOTCVaultPro\ VaultWorkingFolder*.
- Click Designs.ipj.
- Click Open.
- Click Done.

10. Click the Vault tab then select Log In in the Access group. Log in using the following information:

- User Name: **usera**
- Password: **vault**
- Database: AOTCVault

**Note:** If you have installed Inventor with separate log-ins for Vaults and Content Center libraries, select Vault Log In.

## Work with Autodesk Inventor Assemblies and BOMs

1. Click the Vault tab then Open from the Access group. Do the following:

- Navigate to the *Designs\TrailerHitch* folder.
- Click HitchAssembly.iam.
- Click Open.

**2.** If prompted to check out the assembly, click No. If prompted to get files from the vault, click Yes to All.

**3.** Examine the assembly browser. The browser is a hierarchical list of the assembly components.

The Mounting Weldment subassembly contains the black components that make up the welded portion of the hitch assembly.

Each instance of the Frame_Fastener subassembly contains one bolt, one washer, and one nut.

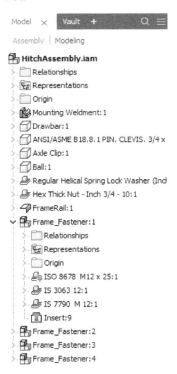

**4.** In the browser, right-click Frame_Fastener:1.

**5.** Place the cursor over BOM Structure to display the assigned structure of the Phantom assembly.

**6.** In the browser, repeat the two previous steps to examine the BOM structure of other components.

For example, the FrameRail:1 component is assigned a Reference BOM structure.

On the Assemble tab click Bill of Materials from the Manage group.

**7.** In the Bill of Materials dialog box, click the Structured tab.

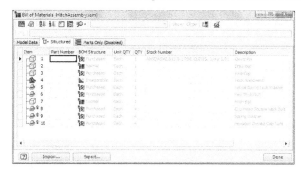

The Phantom Frame_Fastener subassemblies are not listed in the BOM. The three child components from the Frame_Fastener subassembly display as promoted items in the BOM as items 8 - 10. The QTY column displays the number of components in one subassembly (1) multiplied by the number of phantom subassemblies (4).

**8.** If a column is not visible, do the following:

- In the BOM, right-click on a column header.
- Click Runtime Column Customization.
- Drag the required column from the Customization dialog box to required location on the display.

**9.** Add the Filename column to the display if it is not visible.

**10.** All items display unavailable because they are not checked out of the vault.

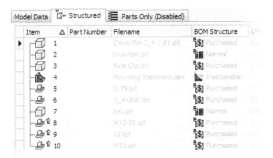

The BOM Structure column displays the assigned BOM structure for each component. The library components are shown as Purchased. The Drawbar and Ball components are Normal. The Mounting Weldment assembly is shown as Inseparable.

**11.** In the Bill of Materials dialog box, click Done. If you get prompted to check out the files select No to All.

## Assign an Item to the Assembly

**1.** Switch to Autodesk Vault Professional.

Click Go menu>Project Explorer. Expand the Designs and TrailerHitch folder.

**Note:** The components with the Reference and Phantom BOM structures are included in the vault. The BOM structure affects only items in Vault Professional

**2.** Right-click HitchAssembly.iam. Click Assign/Update Item. If the assembly is checked out, click Undo Check Out first.

**3.** In the item record window, click the Bill of Materials tab.

The Inseparable Weldment assembly and all its child items are included in the default tree view. The Reference FrameRail part and the Phantom Frame_Fastener assembly are not included in the list. The child components in the Phantom Frame_Fastener assembly are assigned item numbers.

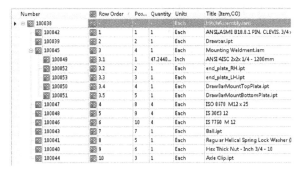

**Note:** Your item numbers and column organization might not match the previous illustration.

**4.** Select First-Level from the Structure drop-down list.

The child items of the Inseparable Weldment assembly are not displayed.

| | Number | Quantity | Title (Item,CO) | Revisi |
|---|---|---|---|---|
| ▶ | 100048 | 4 | IS 3063 12 | - |
| | 100047 | 4 | ISO 8678 M12 x 25 | - |
| | 100046 | 4 | IS 7790 M 12 | - |
| | 100045 | 1 | Mounting Weldment.iam | - |
| | 100044 | 1 | Axle Clip.ipt | - |
| | 100043 | 1 | Ball.ipt | - |
| | 100042 | 1 | ANSI/ASME B18.8.1 PIN. CLEVIS. 3/4 x 1.91 | - |
| | 100041 | 1 | Regular Helical Spring Lock Washer (Inch) 3/4 Re... | - |
| | 100040 | 1 | Hex Thick Nut - Inch 3/4 - 10 | - |
| | 100039 | 1 | Drawbar.ipt | - |

**5.** For Structure, select Multi-Level.

**6.** Click Save and Close.

**7.** Switch to Autodesk Inventor.

**8.** On the Vault tab in the Access group select Place.

**9.** In the Select File from Vault dialog box, navigate to the *$\Designs\TrailerHitch* folder. Do the following:

- Click Safety Bracket.ipt.
- Click Open.
- Click in the graphics window background.

**10.** Right-click then click OK.

**Note:** You typically position the bracket in the assembly with assembly constraints. You are not required to apply the constraints in this exercise.

**11.** Save the assembly. In the Save dialog box, click OK.

**12.** In the browser title bar, select Vault.

**13.** In the Vault browser, right-click HitchAssembly.iam.

**14.** Click Check In.

**15.** In the Check In dialog box, enter **Added safety bracket** as a comment. Click OK.

**16.** Switch to Vault Professional.

**17.** In the Item Master, right-click on the Hitch Assembly row. Click Update.

**18.** In the Item record window, click the Bill of Materials tab. Note that the safety bracket part is automatically added.

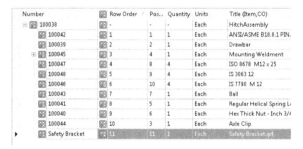

| Number | Row Order | Pos... | Quantity | Units | Title (Item,CO) |
|---|---|---|---|---|---|
| ⊟ 100038 | - | - | - | Each | HitchAssembly |
| 100042 | 1 | 1 | 1 | Each | ANSI/ASME B18.8.1 PIN. |
| 100039 | 2 | 2 | 1 | Each | Drawbar |
| ⊞ 100045 | 3 | 4 | 1 | Each | Mounting Weldment |
| 100047 | 4 | 8 | 4 | Each | ISO 8678 M12 x 25 |
| 100048 | 5 | 9 | 4 | Each | IS 3063 12 |
| 100046 | 6 | 10 | 4 | Each | IS 7790 M 12 |
| 100043 | 7 | 7 | 1 | Each | Ball |
| 100041 | 8 | 5 | 1 | Each | Regular Helical Spring L |
| 100040 | 9 | 6 | 1 | Each | Hex Thick Nut - Inch 3/4 |
| 100044 | 10 | 3 | 1 | Each | Axle Clip |
| Safety Bracket | 11 | 11 | 1 | Each | Safety Bracket.ipt |

**Note:** The item numbers do not match the item numbers in the previous illustration.

# Chapter Summary

In this chapter, you learned how to use to Autodesk Vault Professional to work with other applications, such as Autodesk Inventor.

Having completed this chapter, you can:

- Manage bills of materials (BOMs).
- Describe the integration of Inventor and Vault Professional and the relationship between an Inventor bill of materials (BOM) and the associated Vault Professional item BOM.

# Administering Autodesk Vault Professional

This chapter describes how to manage Autodesk® Vault Professional software. You learn about configuring Items, configuring and mapping Item properties, and configuring Change Orders.

Autodesk Vault Professional is an extension to Autodesk® Vault. Therefore, to effectively manage a Vault Professional installation, you should also be familiar with the following Autodesk Vault management topics.

- Backing up and restoring vaults.
- Moving file stores.
- Detaching vaults.
- Creating and deleting vaults.
- Re-indexing properties.
- Defragmenting databases.
- Using the content indexing service.
- Configure users, groups and folder level permissions.

## Objectives

After completing this chapter, you will be able to:

- Create unit and categories, create new Item numbering schemes, and create custom objects.
- Set up Change Orders including routing lists, user-defined properties, and Change Order numbering.

# Lesson: Configuring Items

## Overview

This lesson describes how to configure Items. You learn how to create unit and categories, create new Item numbering schemes, and change lifecycle rules.

All of the workflows described in the chapter are accessed from the Vault Settings dialog shown above. This dialog displays by selecting the Tools menu then selecting Administration>Vault Settings. You will need to be logged in as an Administrator to complete these workflows.

### Objectives

After completing this lesson, you will be able to:

- Describe Units of Measure.
- Describe Item categories.
- Create Item numbering schemes.
- Configure watermarking.
- Create units of measure and categories.
- Create Item numbering schemes.

# Units of Measure

Every Item is assigned a unit type. You can create new unit types if the supplied units do not meet your company's requirements. The following illustration shows the complete set of units that ship with Vault Professional.

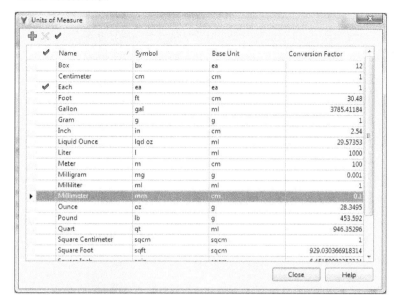

## About Units of Measure

Unit types define the units of measure for Items. You use unit types to specify the quantity of an Item in a bill of materials. Many Items use a special unit type, such as each, when the number of required Items is countable. Other Items are assigned specific unit types, such as meters or grams, when a measurable quantity is required, rather than an Item count. Several predefined unit types are supplied, but if those types do not meet your requirements, you can define new ones.

Each unit type is derived from a base unit and a conversion factor. For example, centimeters are the base unit for length and all length units are defined with respect to centimeters. You can create new base units if you cannot define the new unit from the existing base units.

The following illustration shows the length units that are defined using the centimeter base unit. The conversion factor relates the unit to the base unit. For example, one inch is 2.54 centimeters and one foot is 30.48 centimeters.

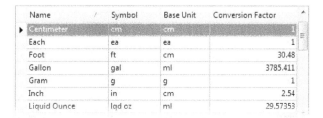

## Procedure: Create a New Unit of Measure

One of the Items in your product's bill of materials is measured in kilograms. You define a new unit type to support this unit of measure. The new unit uses grams as the base unit.

1. In the Vault Settings dialog box, select the Items tab.

2. Select Configure in the Units group to display the Units of Measure dialog box.

3. In the Units of Measure dialog box, click Plus sign to display the Add Unit dialog box.

4. Enter the Name, Symbol, Base Unit, and Conversion factor information.

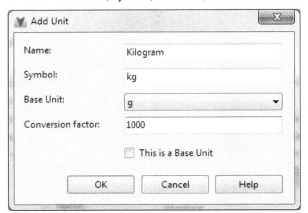

5. Click OK to dismiss the Add Unit dialog box.

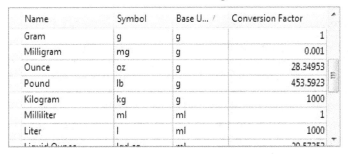

6. The Units of Measure dialog box shows the new unit.

7. Click OK to dismiss the Unit of Measure dialog box.

# Item Categories

Every Item has a category, such as part, assembly, or product, which helps to identify the Item. Some categories, such as part, assembly, and purchased, are assigned automatically based either on the type of file or the CAD file's bill of materials (BOM). You assign other categories manually when you create Items.

There are several predefined categories, as shown in the following illustration. If these do not match the categories you use, you can create new types to meet your requirements.

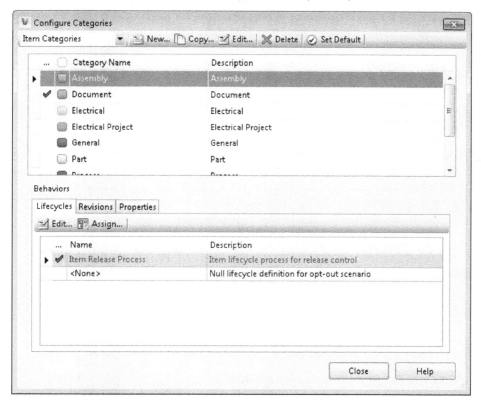

## Procedure: Create a New Item Category

Your company manufactures industrial machinery. Frames are often built by one division of the company then brought to a central area for assembly. In your current ERP system, you identify the frame as a weldment.

1.  In the Vault Settings dialog box, select the Behaviors tab and click Categories in the Categories group to display the Configure Categories dialog box.

2.  Select Item Categories from the drop-down list. The Item Categories display.

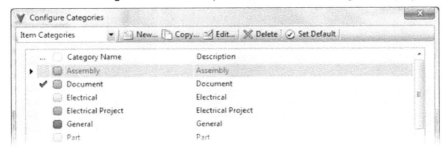

3.  Select New from the toolbar to display the Category Edit dialog box. Enter the new Item Category Name, pick a Category Glyph color, and optionally enter a Description. Ensure that Available is selected.

4.  Click OK to dismiss the Category Edit dialog box.

5.  The new Item Category is added to the list.

6.  Optionally assign a different Lifecycle definition, a different Revision scheme, and set of default properties to add to the Item when it is created.

7.  Click Close to dismiss the Configure Categories.

# Item Numbering Schemes

Item numbers uniquely identify Items. When you set up Vault Professional, create Item-numbering schemes to match your company standards.

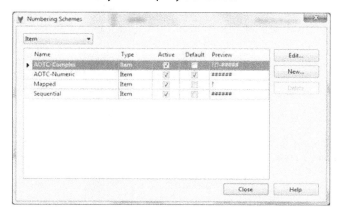

## Item Number Components

Item numbering schemes can consist of one or more of the following components. For a simple numbering scheme, use a single automatically generated sequential number. For a complex scheme, combine several components together.

| Field type | Description | Examples |
|---|---|---|
| Automatically generated sequence | Sequential number | 100058 |
| Delimiter | Single character | - |
| Fixed text | Fixed text string | ABC |
| Free text | User-entered text string | ANYTHING |
| Predefined list | List of choices | FAST, STRU, ELEC, OTHR<br>100, 200, 300, 400, 500 |
| Workgroup label | Workgroup ID | WG1 |

Autodesk Vault Professional is shipped with predefined Item numbering schemes named Sequential and Mapped. Neither scheme can be modified. The default Sequential Item numbering scheme uses a single, automatically generated number that numbers Items from 00000000 to 99999999. The Mapped Item-numbering scheme accepts a text string. It is automatically used when you assign an Item to a file and the file contains a property that is mapped to the Item's Number property. It is recommended that you define your own numbering scheme rather than using one of the supplied schemes.

### Procedure: Defining an Item Numbering Scheme

1.  In Vault Settings, select the Behaviors tab and select Define from the Numbering group.

2.  The Numbering Schemes dialog box opens. Select Item from the drop-down list to display the Item Numbering Schemes.

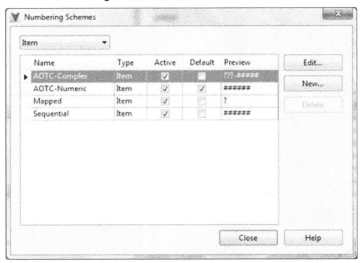

3. Click New to display the New Numbering Scheme dialog box. Enter a Name for the new numbering scheme and then select New.

4. The Add Field dialog box opens. Create the first part of the numbering scheme. In this case, a predefined list with list values 100, 200, and 300 representing Parts, Assemblies, and Purchased Items.

5.  Click OK to dismiss the Add Field dialog box. The first part of the sequence is shown in the New Numbering Scheme dialog box. Note the preview of how the number will look. Add two more parts to the sequence repeating step 4.

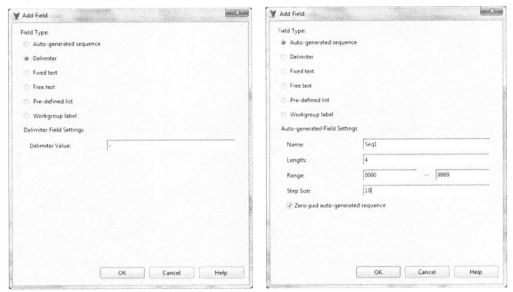

6.  Return to the New Numbering Scheme dialog box to see the final sequence.

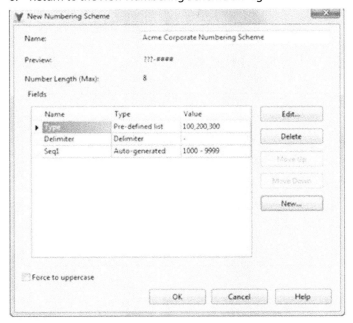

7. Click OK to dismiss the New Numbering Scheme dialog box and return to the Numbering Scheme dialog box.

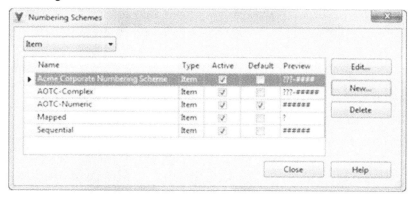

8. Select the checkbox Default if you want this to be the default numbering scheme.

 Note that numbering schemes that require user input are not good choices for default since in automated processes like Assign Item there is no chance to prompt for the input. In this case the number generated will always use the default value. You will be required to go back and edit the Item if you want to use a different value.

## Guidelines

- Do not use one of the default numbering schemes

  You should define your own numbering scheme rather than using the default, even if you want to use a simple sequential number. If you want to use a single sequential numbering scheme, start the first Item number with a 1 rather than 0 (for example, use 1000001 rather than 0000001) because leading zeros might be suppressed when you share data with other applications.

- Create as many numbering schemes as required

  You can create and use more than one Item numbering scheme if required. For example, you might use a simple sequential numbering scheme for users who assign Items. After the Items are created, the ERP Manager can renumber Items, using a more complex scheme to make Item numbers compatible with other company systems.

- Consider adding user-defined Item properties to enhance searching

  Although complex numbering schemes can be used to identify categories using fields in the Item number, you can also use Item properties to group and sort Items. Properties are more flexible and are more easily searched than complex Item numbers. For example, if you use a complex Item numbering scheme such as 100-ELEC-10345-545, consider using a simple scheme. Add user-defined properties to Items to include the information that is inherent in the numbering scheme. You can search on the properties to find Items and new or casual users will be able to better identify and locate Items.

# Edit Lifecycle State Security for Files Associated with Items

By default, no security is enabled on files associated with items. You can apply an item's security to its associated files, customize the security for files associated with items, or clear security overrides on associated files.

1. In the Vault Settings dialog box, select the Behaviors tab. Click Lifecycles to display the Lifecycle Definitions dialog box.

2. Select the state from the Lifecycle States list.

3. Select the Security tab.

4. Select the Security for associated files of items checkbox to enable security on associated files.

5. Click Configure.

6. On the Security for Associated Files of Items dialog, select one of the following actions from the drop-down list:

- **Apply item security to associated files**

   When selected, the Access Control List settings for the item for this state are also applied to the associated file.

- **Apply custom security to associated files**

   When selected, administrators can set an Access Control List that is different from the one applied to the item for that state.

- **Clear security override from associated files**

   When selected, if there is a current override Access Control List on the associated file, the security override is removed when the item enters this state.

7. If you selected Apply custom security to associated files, add or remove members and roles, and then configure permissions.

8. Click OK to save your changes and return to editing state security.

# Item Revision Schemes

Autodesk Vault Professional includes several predefined revision numbering sequences. You can use one of the predefined sequences or create your own.

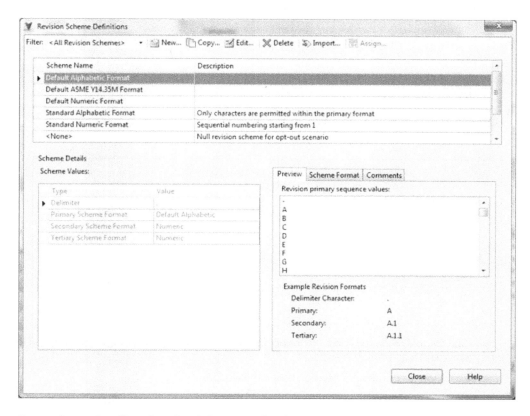

## Procedure: Configuring Revision Numbering Sequences

The following steps show how to create a revision number sequence for Items.

1.  Before creating a new revision sequence you must first create a text file that contains all of the revision numbers. When you specify a new revision, you must either enable the system to choose the next character in the sequence or manually specify a character that is the imported sequence. An example is shown in the illustration.

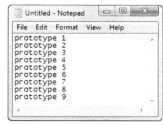

2.  In the Vault Settings dialog box, select the Behaviors tab then click Revisions for the Lifecycle and Revisions tab. Click Import to create a new Revision Scheme Definitions.

3.  In the Import dialog box, specify the Name by browsing to the file. Then enter a Description and enter which of the Item Categories to associate the revision scheme with.

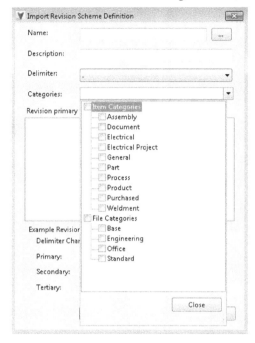

4.  Click OK to dismiss the Import Revision Scheme Definition dialog box and return to the Revision Schemes Definitions dialog box.

5.  Click Close to dismiss the Revision Scheme dialog box.

6.  Close the Vault Settings dialog box.

# Item Watermarking Configuration

Item watermarks can automatically be generated based on:

-   an item's lifecycle state,
-   a specified item property, or
-   customized text.

The default watermarks are based on the system life cycle names. Administrators can configure the watermark style and position.

**Note:** If you customize the display name for a life cycle state, then you should also change the default watermark.

## Configure an Item Lifecycle State Watermark

1.  Click Tools>Administration>Vault Settings.

2.  In the Vault Settings dialog box, select the Items tab.

3.  In the Watermarking section, select Lifecycle-based from the drop-down list and then click Configure.

4.  In the Lifecycle Watermarks dialog, select the lifecycle that you want to use for the state-based watermarks.

    **Note:** A lifecycle called Item Release Process is provided by the Autodesk Vault software.

5.  Select the lifecycle state for which you want to edit the watermark.

6.  Click the ellipses (...) in the Watermark Text column to open the Watermark Text Entry dialog box and edit the text of the watermark.

7.  Perform one of the following steps:

    ▪ Select the Input text for display in the watermark option to enter text of your choice for the watermark.

    ▪ Select a property to display as the watermark from the Insert a property from below drop-down list.

    ▪ Create a multi-line watermark by performing one of the two steps above and clicking Plus (+) to add it to the Watermark Text Display field. Use Plus (+) to add additional watermarks and Minus (-) to remove existing watermarks. You can also use the up or down arrows to arrange the order in which the watermarks display.

8.  Click OK to close the Watermark Text Entry dialog.

9.  On the Customize Watermarks dialog, select a location for the watermark from the Location drop-down list. The watermark can be placed:

    ▪ Diagonally

    ▪ Horizontally

    ▪ In the Border

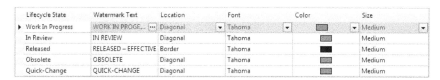

| Lifecycle State | Watermark Text | Location | Font | Color | Size |
|---|---|---|---|---|---|
| ▶ Work In Progress | WORK IN PROGR... [...] | Diagonal ▾ | Tahoma ▾ | ▾ | Medium ▾ |
| In Review | IN REVIEW | Diagonal | Tahoma | | Medium |
| Released | RELEASED – EFFECTIVE | Border | Tahoma | | Medium |
| Obsolete | OBSOLETE | Diagonal | Tahoma | | Medium |
| Quick-Change | QUICK-CHANGE | Diagonal | Tahoma | | Medium |

10. Select a font for the watermark from the Font drop-down list.

11. Select a color for the watermark from the Color drop-down list.

12. Select a size for the watermark from the Size drop-down list.

13. Click OK.

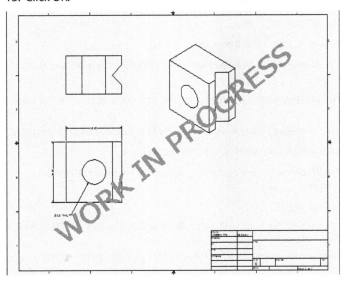

## Configure a Property-Based Watermark

The Watermark value is based on a specific item property that you set using the Property-based Watermark Settings dialog box.

**Note:** You are automatically prompted to identify an item property the first time you select this option.

1. Click Tools>Administration>Vault Settings.

2. In the Vault Settings dialog box, select the Items tab.

3. In the Watermarking section, select Property-based from the drop-down list and click Configure.

4. On the Property-based dialog, select a property from which to draw the text for the watermark from the Property-based watermark drop-down list.

5. Select a location for the watermark from the Location drop-down list. The watermark can be placed:
- Diagonally
- Horizontally
- In the border

6. Select a font for the watermark from the Font drop-down list.

7. Select a color for the watermark from the Color drop-down list.

8. Select a size for the watermark from the Size drop-down list.

9. Click OK.

## Configure a Custom Watermark

The Watermark value comes from a value you enter in the Custom Watermark Settings dialog box.

**Note:** You are automatically prompted to identify a text value for the watermark the first time you select this option.

1. Click Tools>Administration>Vault Settings.

2. In the Vault Settings dialog box, select the Items tab.

3. In the Watermarking section, select Custom from the drop-down list and click Configure.

4. On the Custom Watermark Settings dialog, enter the text for the watermark in the Text field.

5. Select a location for the watermark from the Location drop-down list. The watermark can be placed:
- Diagonally
- Horizontally
- In the border

6. Select a font for the watermark from the Font drop-down list.

7. Select a color for the watermark from the Color drop-down list.

8. Select a size for the watermark from the Size drop-down list.

9. Click OK.

# Assign Item Configuration

You can configure whether BOM rows are automatically displayed or hidden during item assignment.

1. Click Tools>Administration>Vault Settings.

2. In the Vault Settings dialog box, select the Items tab.

3. In the Assign Item section, click Configure to access the Configure Assign Item dialog.

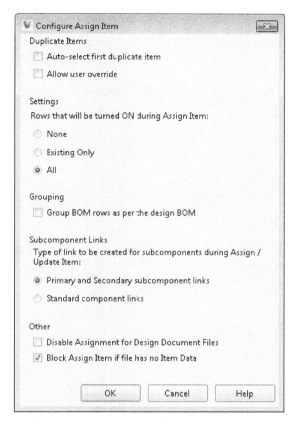

4. Select whether you want Vault to automatically select the first duplicate item in a list and assign it to the selected file. If you do not select this option, a new item is created instead.
   If this option is selected, child BOM Components will attempt to link to an existing item using the Equivalence Value property.

   **Note:** Standard components will always attempt to link to an existing item.

5. Select the Allow user override checkbox if you want the user to be able to choose a duplicate item other than the one automatically selected by Vault.

6. If you want to configure how BOM Rows are turned on during Item Assignment, select one of the following options:
   - **None** – Components that link to existing items are not turned on. All new item rows are turned off.

     **Note:** This is the default setting for new vaults.
   - **Existing Only** – Components that link to existing items are turned on. Components not linked to items remain as BOM components
   - **All** – Components that do not link to existing items have new items created for them. All new rows are turned on.

     **Note:** This is the default setting for Vaults migrated from Vault 2014 or earlier releases.

   **Note:** These rules apply until a row is linked to an item. Once a row has an item identified, rows are not turned on or off during subsequent updates.

7. Select Group BOM rows as per the design BOM if you want BOM rows merged or unmerged based on how the CAD application has them. If the checkbox is not selected, BOM rows are automatically merged, regardless of how the CAD application has them. For example, if Inventor has BOM rows unmerged and the checkbox is not selected, the rows are automatically merged in Vault regardless of how Inventor has them.

8. Select Disable assignment for Design Document files if you want to disable the ability to assign item to design files such as .IDW files. If this option is checked, design files will only be linked to the Items for which they represent.

9. Select Block Assign Item if file has no Item Data to prevent items from being assigned to CAD files that can have item data but do not yet have any. This option is selected by default.

10. Click OK to save your changes.

# Property Write-Back Configuration

By default, item properties are written back to the associated file from Vault add-ins, Vault Explorer, and the Job Processor. Item properties take precedence over file properties and mappings. If the file's properties are edited and properties are synchronized, the item properties will overwrite the file properties.

**Note:** Editing and saving a property can result in an item property being written back to a File.

You can manually synchronize properties on files associated with items.

Important: The Write Item properties back to the file checkbox on the Items tab must be selected for item properties to be written back to a file.

### Synchronize Associated File Properties

1. In the Item Master, select the item for which you want to synchronize file properties.

2. Select the General tab in the preview if it is not already selected.

3. Right-click on the Associated Files section and select Synchronize Properties.

4. Item properties are written back to the associated file.

# Other Configuration

- Determine whether or not a user is able to assign a category to an item when the item is created. By default, this option is selected. Clear the Allow user to assign category when creating a new item option checkbox to disable this option.

- When the Break file links from items based on Equivalence Value during item update option is selected, Vault automatically breaks the link between an item and a file if the equivalence values do not match during an Update of the item. This setting is off by default.

# Exercise: Configure Items

In this exercise, you create a new unit and new category, and configure an item lifecycle state name.

1. Start Autodesk Vault Professional and login with the following information.
   - User Name: Administrator
   - No password
   - Vault: AOTCAdminVault

2. Select the Tools menu then Administration>Vault Settings to display the Vault Settings dialog box.

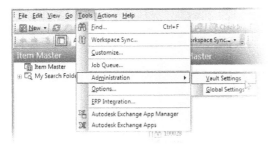

3. Select the Items tab.

## Unit of Measure

1. Select Configure in the Units section to display the Units of Measure dialog box.

2. Click the Plus-sign to display the Add Unit dialog box. This is where you will define the new unit – microns.

3. Do the following:
   - For Name, enter **Micron**.
   - For Symbol, enter **um**.
   - For Base Unit, select centimeters (cm).
   - For the conversion factor, enter **.0001**.
   - Ensure that This is a Base Unit is unchecked.
   - Click OK to create the new unit.

| Name | Symbol | Base Unit | Conversion Fa... |
|------|--------|-----------|------------------|
| Centimeter | cm | cm | 1 |
| Millimeter | mm | cm | 0.1 |
| Meter | m | cm | 100 |
| Inch | in | cm | 2.54 |
| Foot | ft | cm | 30.48 |
| Yard | yd | cm | 91.44003 |
| Micron | um | cm | 0.0001 |
| Each | | | 1 |

4. Confirm the new unit is added. Select Close to dismiss the Units of Measure dialog box and return to the Vault Settings dialog box.

## Item Category

1. In the Vault Settings dialog box, select the Behaviors tab.

2. Select Categories in the Categories section to display the Configure Categories dialog box.

3. Select Item Categories from the drop-down list.

4. In the Configure Categories toolbar, select New to display the Category Edit dialog box.

5. In the Category Edit dialog box, enter the following information:

   - For Name, enter **Weldment**.
   - For the Color, select a color of your choice.
   - Select the Available checkbox if not already enabled.
   - For Description, enter **Frame Weldments**.

6. Click OK to dismiss the Category Edit dialog box and return to the Configure Categories dialog box.

7. Click Close to dismiss the Configure Categories dialog box and return to the Vault Settings dialog box.

## Check Lifecycle State Transition Action

1. Select the Behaviors tab and select Lifecycles to display the Lifecycle Definitions dialog box.

2. Select Item Release Process and click Edit.

3. For the Lifecycle State of Work In Progress, select the Transitions tab.

**4.** Select the row that has a From State of Released and To State of Work In Progress.

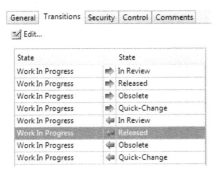

**5.** Click Edit and then the Actions tab to see the Bump primary revision action for this lifecycle State change.

**6.** Click OK.

## Configure Item Lifecycle State Name

**1.** Select the In Review lifecycle state and click the General tab.

**2.** Replace In Review with the string For Review.

**3.** Select OK. The Lifecycle State name is updated in the list.

Lifecycle States:

| ✔ | Name | Description |
|---|------|-------------|
| ✔ | Work In Progress | Item is available for editing |
|   | For Review | Item is awaiting further acti... |
|   | Released | Item is ready for production |
|   | Obsolete | Item is no longer used in ac... |
|   | Quick-Change | State for controlling Item ac... |

**4.** Click Close.

## Watermarking

1.     Select the Items tab, and then in the Watermarking section select Configure to display the Lifecycle Watermarks dialog box.

2.     Select the row for the Lifecycle State of For Review.

3.     Change the text to be consistent with the change. Click the button next to the Watermark Text IN REVIEW to display the Watermark Text Entry – For Review dialog box.

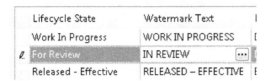

| Lifecycle State | Watermark Text | |
|---|---|---|
| Work In Progress | WORK IN PROGRESS | [ |
| For Review | IN REVIEW ... | |
| Released - Effective | RELEASED – EFFECTIVE | [ |

4.     In the Watermark Text Display list, select the current text and then click the '-' button to remove it.

5.     Select the Input text for display in the watermark radio button and enter the text **For Review**.

6.     Click the '+' button to add this text to the list.

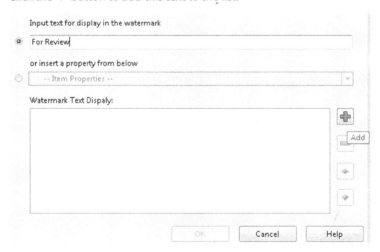

7.     Click OK to dismiss the Watermark text Entry – For Review dialog box and return to the Lifecycle Watermarks dialog box.

**8.** Note the change in the Watermark Text for the For Review State.

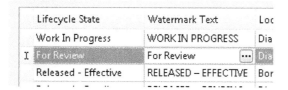

| Lifecycle State | Watermark Text | Loc |
|---|---|---|
| Work In Progress | WORK IN PROGRESS | Dia |
| I For Review | For Review [···] | Dia |
| Released - Effective | RELEASED – EFFECTIVE | Bor |

**9.** Click OK to dismiss the Lifecycle Watermarks dialog box and return to the Vault Settings dialog box.

**10.** Click Close to dismiss the Vault Settings dialog box.

# Exercise: Create Item Numbering Schemes

In this exercise, you create two Item numbering schemes. One scheme consists of a simple sequential number. The other is a more complex numbering scheme, with a list, delimiter, and sequential number.

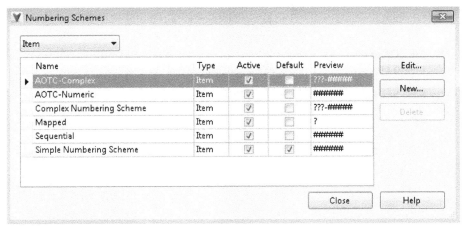

The completed exercise

## Create Simple Item Numbering Scheme

1. Select the Behaviors tab in the Vault Settings dialog box.

2. In the Numbering section, select Define to display the Numbering Schemes dialog box.

3. In the Numbering Schemes dialog box, in the drop-down list, select Item to display the Item Numbering Schemes.

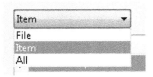

4. Click New to create a new Item Numbering Scheme.

5. The New Numbering Scheme dialog box displays.

6. In the Name field, enter **Simple Numbering Scheme**.

7. Click New to display the Add Field dialog box.

8. In the Add Field dialog box do the following:
   - For Field Type, select Auto-generated sequence.
   - For Name, enter **Number**.
   - For Length, enter **6**.
   - For Range, enter **100001** for the starting number and do not change the ending number.
   - Leave Step Size at the default (1).

9. Click OK to return to the Numbering Schemes dialog box.

## Create Complex Numbering Scheme

1. Click New to create a new Item Numbering Scheme.

2. The New Numbering Scheme dialog box displays. In the Name field, enter **Complex Numbering Scheme**.

3. Click New to display the Add Field dialog box.

4. In the Add Field dialog box do the following:
   - For Field Type, select Auto-generated sequence.
   - For Name, enter **Number**.
   - For Length, enter **5**.
   - For Range, enter **10001** for the starting number and do not change the ending number.
   - Leave Step Size at the default (1).

5. Click OK to dismiss the Add Field dialog box and return to the New Numbering Scheme dialog box.

6. Click New to display the Add Field dialog box.

7. In the Add Field dialog box do the following:
   - For Field Type, select Delimiter.
   - For Delimiter Value, enter '-' (hyphen).

8. Click OK to dismiss the Add Field dialog box and return to the New Numbering Scheme dialog box.

9. Click New to display the Add Field dialog box.

**10.** In the Add Field dialog box do the following:

- For Field Type, select Pre-defined list.
- In the Predefined List Field Settings section, for the name, enter **Type**.
- In the first row of the Enter code list: section, enter **100**.
- Select the Description field right next to it and enter **Part**.
- A second row is added to the list. In the Code field, for this new row, enter **200**.
- Select the Description field right next to it and enter **Assembly**.
- A third row is added to the list. In the Code field, for this new row, enter **300**.
- Select the Description field right next to it and enter **Purchased**.
- Select the first row and click Set as Default.

Your entries should look like the following illustration.

**11.** Click OK to return to the New Numbering Scheme dialog box.

**12.** Select the Type row then select Move Up twice to move it to the top of the list.

**13.** Now select the Delimiter row and click Move Up once to move it between the Type and the Number. Your Fields list should display like the following illustration.

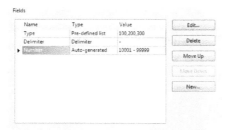

**14.** Click OK to dismiss the New Numbering Scheme dialog box and return to the Numbering Schemes dialog box.

**15.** In the Numbering Schemes dialog box select the default checkbox in the Simple Numbering Scheme row. This numbering scheme will now be applied to new Items. Click Close to dismiss the Numbering Schemes dialog box.

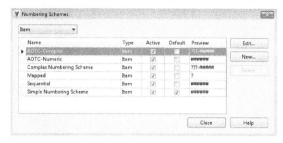

# Lesson: Configuring Change Orders

## Overview

This lesson describes how to set up and configure Change Orders to better match your company's requirements.

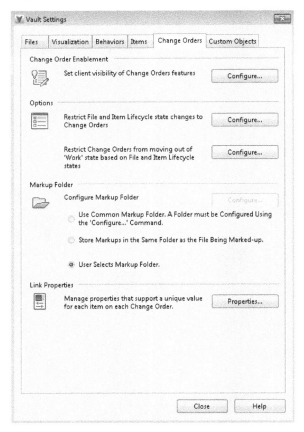

### Objectives

After completing this lesson, you will be able to:

- Set Change Order options.
- Configure a Change Order markup folder.
- Add user-defined properties to Change Orders.
- Define Change Order routing lists.
- Define Change Order numbering schemes.
- Configure email notification.

# Change Order Options

As an administrator, you can set several options for Change Orders that determine Change Order workflows. The Change Orders option settings are shown in the following illustration.

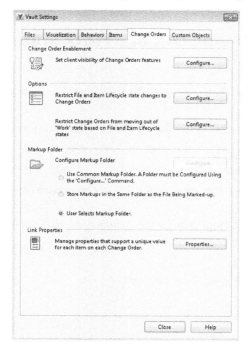

# Configure Restrictions for Lifecycle State Changes Using Change Orders

Specify whether item or file lifecycle state changes are controlled only by change orders.

When the Restrict File and Item Lifecycle state changes to Change Orders setting is enabled, a File or Item lifecycle state cannot be changed outside of a change order unless the user is an Administrator. Users must change file and items record states using the Change State command inside the Change Order.

You can select whether users with administrative permissions can override these restrictions.

## Configure Restrictions

1. In the Vault Client, click Tools>Administration >Vault Settings.

2. In the Vault Settings dialog box, select the Change Orders tab.

3. Click Configure next to Restrict File and Item Lifecycle state changes to Change Orders.

4. Select whether you want to restrict File and Item lifecycle changes to Change orders.

5. To enable users with administrative permissions to override the restriction for that entity, select Allow Administrator Override.

6. Click Close to save your changes.

# Prevent a Change Order from Moving Out of a Work State Based on Item and File States

Prevent a change order from leaving its work state unless its item and file records are in selected lifecycle states.

These files and items must be listed in the Records tab of the change order, and not the Files tab.

1. In the Vault Client, click Tools>Administration >Vault Settings.

2. In the Vault Settings dialog box, select the Change Orders tab.

3. Click Configure next to Restrict Change Orders from moving out of 'Work' state based on File and Item Lifecycle states.

4. Select the lifecycle states that an item or file cannot be in for the change order to move out of a work state.

5. Click Close.

6. Select whether you want these settings to apply to Items, Files, or both.

7. Click OK to save your changes.

# Configuring a Markup Folder

During the Change Order process, markups are often used to discuss changes. By default, the markup files are placed in the same folder as the associated file. As an administrator, you can enable the user to select a markup folder or you can configure a markup folder in the vault where all of the markup files are stored.

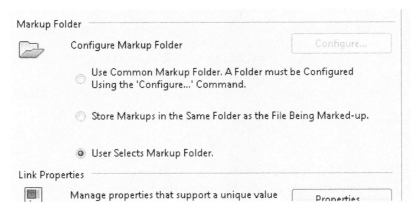

The following illustration shows a markup folder named Markups that was added under the root of the vault.

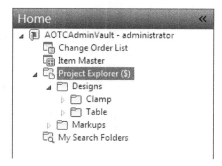

## Procedure: Configuring a Markup Folder

The following steps describe how to configure a markup folder.

1. In the Vault Settings dialog box, select the Change Orders tab.

2. In the Markup Folders sections click Use Common Markup Folder. Configure, in the same group, is now enabled.

3. Click Configure to display the Select a Vault Location dialog box.

4. If the folder already exists, select it otherwise use the New Folder command to create a new folder.

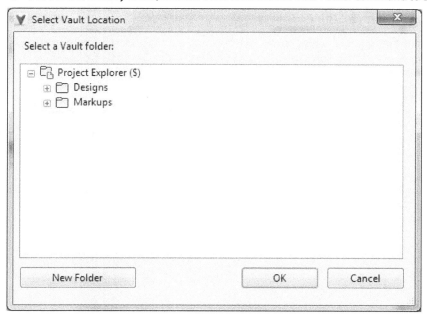

5. Dismiss the Select Vault Location dialog box by clicking OK and return to the Vault Settings dialog box.

# Link Properties

## Introduction to Link Properties

Link properties are unique to Change Orders and enable you to support a unique value for each Item on the Change Order. Link properties are Item properties, but only in the context of the Change Order that they are associated with. If the Item is not on a Change Order, it does not have this property.

Link Properties are unique in the sense that they are administered in a dialog box different in File, Item, and Change Order properties. However, they do support Property Compliance. The following Change Order shows the two ICU Valve Buttons on a Change Order to remove the paint. The cost of the change for each button is $400 to change the tooling and update the process documentation.

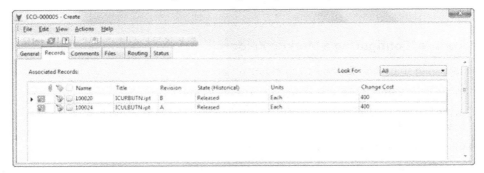

## Procedure: Adding a Link Property

1.  In the Vault Settings dialog box, select the Change Order tab. In the Link Properties section click Properties to display the User Defined Linked Properties (Change Orders) dialog box. There are no default properties shipped with the product.

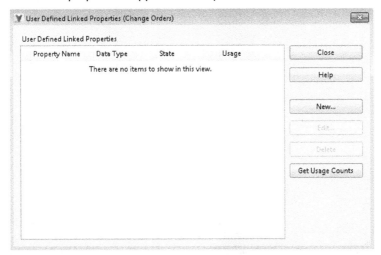

2. Click New to display the New Change Order Link Property dialog box. Enter the Name, select the type from the drop-down list then specify the Settings for the property. Enter Initial Value and List Values if required. Click OK to dismiss the dialog box and return to the User Defined Linked Properties (Change Orders) dialog box.

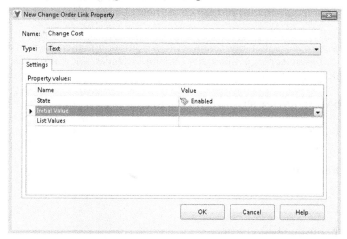

3. The new link properties display in the list. Click Close to return to the Vault Settings dialog box.

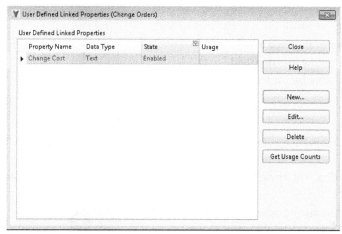

# Change Order Numbering

The default Change Order numbering scheme uses a three-letter prefix, ECO, and an auto-generated six-digit number. If the supplied Change Order numbering scheme does not match your company standards or does not meet your requirements, you can create new Change Order numbering schemes.

If your company standards require more than one Change Order numbering scheme, you can create multiple numbering schemes. The person originating the Change Order can select the appropriate scheme when they create the Change Order.

### Procedure: Define a Change Order Numbering Scheme

1. In the Vault Settings dialog box, select the Behaviors tab.
2. In the Numbering section, click Define.
3. In the Numbering Schemes dialog box, select Change Order.
4. Click New.
5. Enter the scheme name.
6. Click New to add fields for the numbering scheme.
7. In the Add Field dialog box, select one of the following field types:
   - Auto-generated
   - Delimiter
   - Fixed text - Enter a name for the fixed text field.
   - Free text - Enter a name for the free text field.
   - Predefined list - Enter a name for the free predefined list field.
   - Workgroup label
8. Click OK.
9. The New Numbering Scheme dialog box displays a preview of the settings defined in the Add/Edit dialog box.
10. To change the settings, click Edit. To delete, click Delete. To add another numbering scheme, click Add.
11. To display text in all capital letters, select the Force to upper-case checkbox.
12. Click OK to save the scheme.
13. When a new change Order is created, the user selects the button next to the Change Order Number field to change the scheme used.

---

# Routing Definition - Workflow Selection

There are two possible workflows possible with Vault Professional:

1. **Standard:** In the workflow definition a Change Order moves from the Work State to the Review State. The Responsible Engineer or Change Administrator moves the Change Order out of the Work State and the Approvers can either reject the Change Order to the Rejected State or Approve it to the Approved State. This is the default workflow.

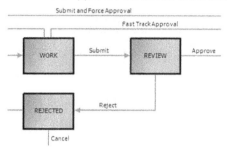

2. **Check State:** In this workflow definition a new State Check and Routing Participant Checker is added to the standard workflow. This is a common workflow where someone checks the work of the Responsible Engineer to ensure adherence to company standards, etc. before it is submitted to final review. In this workflow the Responsible Engineer or Change Administrator submits the Change Order to the Check State. There the Checker can either Approve it to the Review State or Reject it back to the Work State.

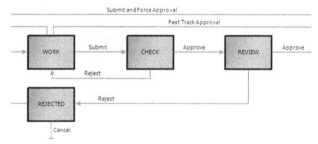

3. The workflow can be changed by selecting the Tools menu then selecting Administration and Global Settings dialog box.

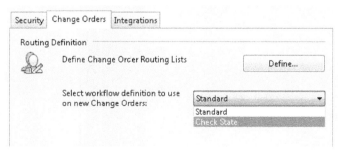

# Routing Definition - Change Order Routing Lists

As an administrator, you define one or more routing lists to define Change Order participants and their roles in the Change Order process. When users create a Change Order, they select which routing list to use. Small companies might require only one routing list and large companies might require many. Because routing lists are shared across all vaults, only one set of routing lists is required regardless of the number of vaults you use.

The following illustration shows the creation of a Change Order routing list.

When a change order is created, you must specify a routing. A routing is a list of participants with predefined roles. Each of the different routing roles has specific permissions and responsibilities.

The Change Administrator, Responsible Engineer, and Approver roles control the progression of the change order. The Reviewer role can add markups, view, add, and reply to comments.

The person creating the change order automatically becomes the Change Requestor.

The task a routing participant can perform depends on the routing participant role.

**Note:** Only users with Administrator or Change Order Editor privileges can be assigned routing roles.

## Change Order Roles

Change order participants are assigned one or more of the following roles.

| Role | Task Availability |
|------|-------------------|
| Change Requestor | Initiated the change order. |
| Change Administrator | Can add or remove Approvers, Change Administrators, and Responsible Engineers. This participant can edit the title of the change order, add or remove files or items, and modify user-defined properties. Can submit the new Change Order to the Open State.<br><br>The Change Administrator is also responsible for:<br><br>■ Canceling the change order or reopen a closed change order.<br>■ Evaluating change orders in the Open State to determine whether they should be processed or canceled, and so is responsible for submitting the Open change order to Work or canceling it.<br>■ Rejecting change orders to determine whether they should be canceled or can be re-worked. When a change order is Approved, the Change Administrator is responsible for closing the change order and releasing the associated items and files. |
| Responsible Engineer | Can edit the change order when in the Work State, make required revisions, and submit the change order for review. |
| Checker | Participates only in the Check State (when enabled). Can add comments in the Check State. Can approve to the Review State or reject back to the Work State. |
| Reviewer | Can only view, add, and reply to comments. |
| Approver | Can review, approve, and reject a change order. |
| Notification User | Receives notification when the change order is closed. |

## Example

A small company wants to track change. They install Autodesk Vault Professional and need to set up a single Change Order routing list. Two engineers are responsible for all aspects of the Change Order process and the production manager wants to be notified of change.

A Change Order routing list is created with three participants. Each of the two engineers is assigned as Change Administrator, Responsible Engineer, and Approver. The production manager is assigned as a Notification User.

## Procedure: Creating a Change Order Routing List

The following steps outline the creation of a routing list.

1. Open the Global Settings dialog box (Tools menu>Administration>Global Settings) and select the Change Orders tab. In the Routing definition section click Define to display the Routing dialog box.

2. A number of Routings have been defined, but only one, Default, is currently active and set as the default. Click New to display the Edit Routing dialog box.

3. Enter a Routing Name then select one of the users from the Change Order participants list and click Add to display the Edit Roles dialog box.

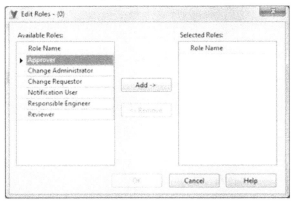

4. Select a role from the list of Available Roles and click Add to add it to the list of Selected Roles.

5. Repeat the previous step to add any additional roles.

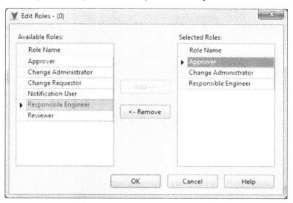

6. Click OK to return to the Edit Routing dialog box. Note the Routing Roles assigned to the first selected user.

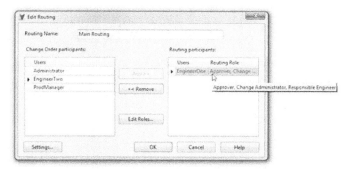

7. Repeat Steps 3 to 5 to add the rest of the Change Order participants and define their Routing Roles.

 Note that you must add users in the Change Administrator, Responsible Engineer, and Approver role. If you are using the optional Check state a Checker must also be added.

8. If you have more than one approver, use Settings to display and select the approval type required.

9. Click OK to dismiss the Edit Routing dialog box and return to the Routing dialog box.

10. In the Routing dialog box, select the new Routing and drag it from the All routings list to the Active routings list.

11. In the Routing dialog box select the new Routing. If this is to be the new default Routing, click Set as Default.

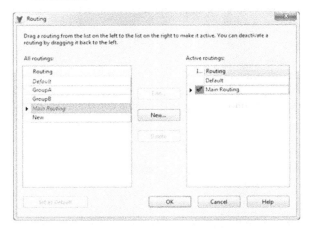

12. Click OK to dismiss the Routing dialog box and return to the Global Settings dialog box.

# Configure Email Notification

As an administrator, you must configure email settings if you want notifications emailed to participants on the routing list when a Change Order enters a State that requires attention. For example, the Responsible Engineer is notified when the Change Order enters the Work State, Approvers are notified when the Change Order enters the Review State, and Notification Users are notified when the Change Order enters the Closed State.

The following illustration displays the Email dialog box in which you enable email notification and enter the email server information.

## Procedure: Configuring Email Notification

The following steps describe how to configure email notification.

1. Ensure that all users that will be participating in Change Orders have email addresses.

2. Log in to the Autodesk Data Management Server console as Administrator.

3.  In the Tools menu, select Administration.

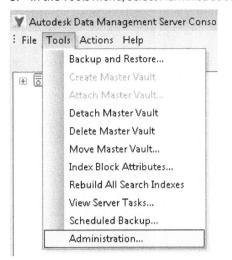

4.  Select the Advanced Settings tab. In the Email section, click Email to display the Email dialog box.

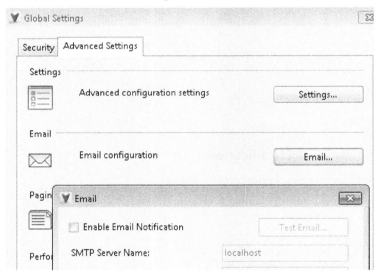

5.  Select Enable Email Notification, then enter the appropriate SMTP Server Name and address that will show up ir the From address in the email and the SMTP Server Port Number. If your company requires authentication, check the box to enable SMTP Authentication and provide the user credentials.

6.  Use Test Email to verify that the configuration is correct.

7.  Click OK to dismiss the Email dialog box and return to the Global Settings dialog box.

8.  Click Close to cismiss the Global Settings dialog box and log out of the Autodesk Data Management Server console.

# Exercise: Set Up Change Orders

In this exercise, you set up a markup folder, add a user-defined Change Order property, create a new Change Order numbering scheme, and add a new Change Order routing list.

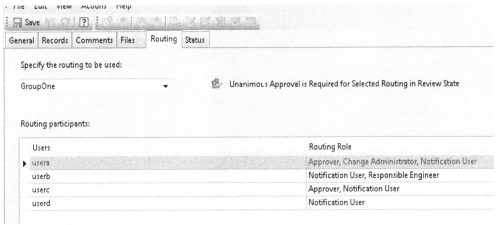

The completed exercise

## Configure Change Orders

1.  Start Autodesk Vault Professional logging in with this information:
    - User Name: Administrator
    - No password
    - Vault: AOTCAdminVault

2.  Open the Vault Settings dialog box by selecting Tools from the menu then Administration>Vault Settings.

3.  Select the Change Orders tab and review the default options.

## Markup Folders

1.  In the Markup Folder section select Use Common Markup. Configure, in the same section, is now enabled.

2.  Click Configure to display the Select Vault Location dialog box.

3.  Select New Folder to create a new folder named Markups in the Project Explorer ($) root folder.

**4.**     Enter **Markups** in the New Folder dialog box and then OK to dismiss the dialog box.

**5.**     Click OK to dismiss the Select Vault Location dialog box and return to the Vault Settings dialog box.

## Add Link Properties

**1.**     In the Vault Settings dialog box, select Properties in the Link Properties section to display the Link Properties dialog box.

Note that unlike other properties, there is no default Link Properties.

**2.** Click New to display the New Change Order Link Property dialog.

**3.** Enter the following information for a new Link Property Disposition.

- For the Name, enter **Disposition**.
- Keep the default Type as Text.

**4.** In the List Values dialog box do the following:

- In the Click here to add a new row section, enter **Revise** followed by the ENTER key.
- Enter **Substitute** followed by the ENTER key.
- Enter **Obsolete** followed by the ENTER Key.

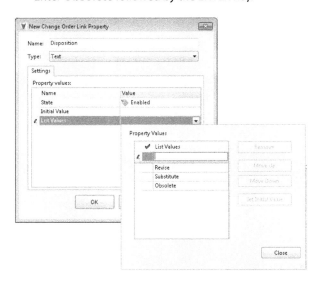

5. Select the entry for Revise then select Set Initial Value to make this the default value.

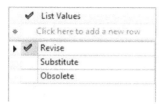

6. Click Close to close this dialog box and return to the New Change Order Link Property dialog box.

7. Review the entries. They should look like the following list:

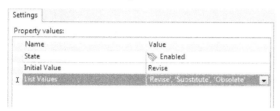

8. Click OK to return to the User Defined Linked Properties (Change Orders) dialog box and then Close to return to the Vault Settings dialog box.

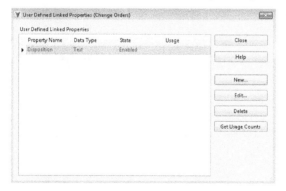

## Change Order Numbering

1. In the Vault Settings dialog box, in the Behaviors tab, in the Numbering section, select Define to display the Numbering Schemes dialog box.

2. Select Change Order from the drop-down list.

3. Click New to create a new Change Order Numbering Scheme.

4. Enter the following:

- For Name, enter **AOTC ECO**.
- Select the Auto-generated number Value field and pick Edit.
- For Starting Number, enter **1**.
- Keep the default number of digits (3).

5. Click OK to return to the Numbering Schemes dialog box.

6. Select the new numbering scheme and then click the Default checkbox to set it as the default.

7. Click Close to dismiss this dialog box and return to the Vault Settings dialog box.

## Create Routing List

1. Click Close to dismiss the Vault Settings tab.

2. In the Tools menu under Administration, select Global Settings to display the Global Settings dialog box.

3. In the Global Settings dialog box select the Change Orders tab.

4. Click Define to display the Routing dialog box.

5.      Click New to display the Edit Routing dialog box.

6.      Do the following:

- For Name, enter **GroupOne**.
- Press <Shift> and select usera, userb, userc and userd from the Change Order Participants list and click Add to add them to the Routing Participants.
- In the Edit Roles dialog box that opens, select Notification User from the Available roles list then Add to add that to the Selected Roles list.
- Click OK to dismiss the dialog box and return to the Edit Routing dialog box.

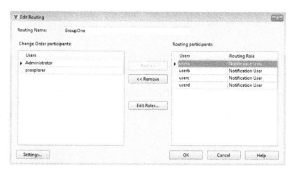

7.      In the Routing participants list select usera then click Edit Roles to display the Edit Roles dialog box.

8.      Hold <Ctrl> and select Change Administrator and Approver from the list.

9.      Click Add to add these roles to the Select Roles list.

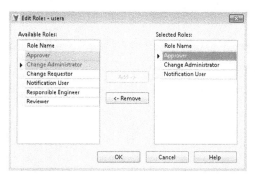

10. Click OK to dismiss this dialog box and return to the Edit Routing dialog box.

11. Do the following:
    - Select userb in the Routing participants list.
    - Click Edit Roles.
    - In the Edit Roles dialog box, select Responsible Engineer from the Available Roles list.
    - Click Add to add this role in the Selected Roles list.
    - Click OK to dismiss the dialog box and return to the Edit Routing dialog box.

12. Do the following:
    - Select userc in the Routing participants list.
    - Click Edit Roles.
    - In the Edit Roles dialog box, select Approver from the Available Roles list.
    - Click Add to add this role in the Selected Roles list.
    Click OK to dismiss the dialog box and return to the Edit Routing dialog box.

13. Examine the Edit Routing dialog box to see the Routing participants and their roles you setup.

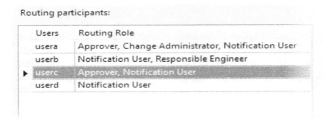

14. Click Settings from the lower left part of the dialog box.

15. Select Unanimous approval for Review state required.

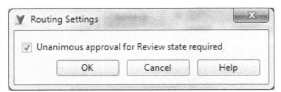

16. Click OK to dismiss this dialog box and return to the Edit Routing dialog box.

17. Click OK to dismiss the Edit Routing dialog box.

18. In the Routing dialog box, select the new routing GroupOne and drag it to the Active routings list.

**19.** In the lower left corner of the dialog box, click Set as Default.

**20.** Click OK to dismiss this dialog box and return to the Global Settings dialog box.

**21.** Click Close to close this dialog box.

**22.** Exit Vault Professional.

# Lesson: Custom Objects Definition Administration

## Overview

This lesson describes how to create and configure Custom Objects to suit your company's requirements. Custom Objects enable Vault administrators to use an extensible system to create new Vault entities to meet the requirements of their team, organization, or company. Right out-of-the-box, the administrator can create a Custom Object definition and assign it categories, lifecycles, and properties. Once the Custom Object definition is created, users can create instances of that custom object directly through the user interface. As with files and folders, users can perform many common Vault tasks with custom objects.

Custom Object Definitions are created, edited, and deleted in the Configure Custom Objects dialog box. You can access the Configure Custom Objects dialog box through the Custom Objects tab in the Vault Settings dialog box. You must be an administrator to create and modify custom object definitions.

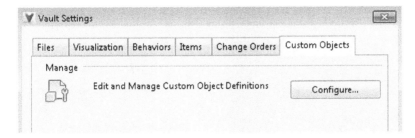

### Objectives

After completing this lesson, you will be able to:

- Create a Custom Object definition.
- Edit a Custom Object definition.
- Delete a Custom Object definition.

# Create a Custom Object Definition

The Custom Object definition is the type of entity that is being created. For example, an administrator can create a custom object definition called Contacts or Tasks.

When the user creates a new custom object based on a definition, it is considered an instance. For example, an administrator creates a custom object definition called Contact. A user could then create an instance of that custom object called Bob Smith.

Users can attach files, folders, and other Vault entities to a custom object with a link. For example, if a custom object definition has been created called Tasks and a user has created a task called Review John's Design, the task (Review John's Design) can be linked to John's design in the vault.

Custom Object instances can be checked in, checked out, undergoes a change state, and managed with many common Vault commands. Similarly, linked objects are also affected, depending on the user's settings for the Vault function.

For example, if a user wants to check out a custom object and the custom object has links to files, folders, items, or change orders; the files associated with that linked data are gathered and checked out as well.

## Procedure: Create a New Custom Object Definition

Follow these steps to create a new custom object definition:

1. In Autodesk Vault Professional, click Tools>Administration>Vault Settings.
2. In the Vault Settings dialog box, select the Custom Objects tab and click Configure.
3. On the Configure Custom Objects dialog box, click New.

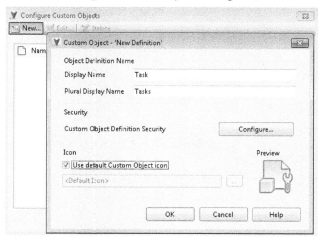

4. Enter a new Display name for a Custom Object. This name is used in the Vault User Interface when the new Custom Object displays.

 A display name and plural display name are required because vault uses both contexts throughout the interface. Since there is no universal way to make a name plural, the administrator requirements to insert the value upon creation.

5. By default, new custom objects use object-based security. This can be customized by configuring different permissions for individual users and groups.

6. New Custom Objects can use any icon file (*.ICO). Defining four different sizes of the icon, provide the best looking icons throughout the Vault interface (16x16, 32x32, 64x64, or 128x128). If only one size is defined, it is stretched or compressed to fit each size. If no icon is available, the Use default Custom Object icon should be selected.

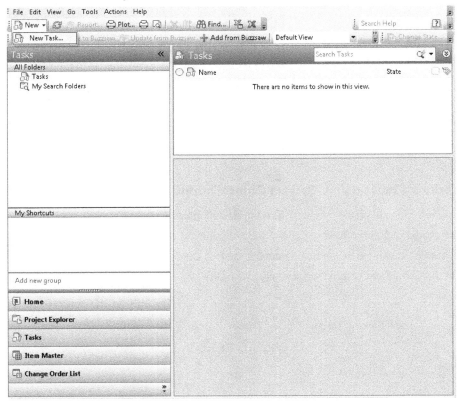

 New Custom objects do not display in the user interface until the user logs out and logs back in after the Custom Object is created.

# Edit a Custom Object Definition

Once a custom object definition is created, the administrator can navigate back to the Configure Custom Objects dialog box and modify the existing settings.

### Procedure: Edit Name

1. In Autodesk Vault Professional, click Tools>Administration>Vault Settings.
2. In the Vault Settings dialog box, select the Custom Objects tab and click Configure.
3. Select a custom object definition and click Edit.

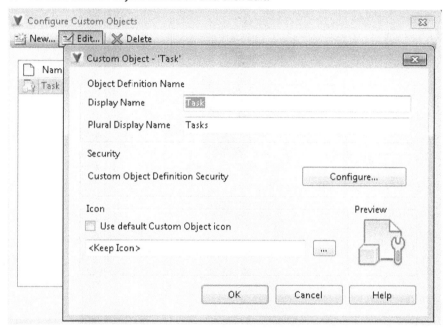

4. Modify the value in the Display Name and Plural Display Name fields.
5. Click OK.

 The changes made to the custom object name are seen after logging out and logging back into the Vault client.

## Procedure: Edit Security

1.  In Autodesk Vault Professional, click Tools>Administration>Vault Settings.

2.  In the Vault Settings dialog box, select the Custom Objects tab and click Configure.

3.  Select a custom object definition and click Edit.

4.  Click Configure under the Security section.

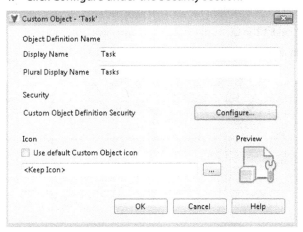

5.  Make edits to the existing access control list.

6.  Select OK.

▪ Edits to the security are made immediately to all instances of the custom object definition.

---

## Procedure: Edit Icon

The icon associated with a custom object definition can be changed after the definition is created.

1. In Autodesk Vault Professional, click Tools>Administration>Vault Settings.
2. In the Vault Settings dialog box, select the Custom Objects tab and click Configure.
3. Select a custom object definition and click Edit.
4. Change the icon by either choosing to use the default custom object icon or browsing to a new .ICO file.

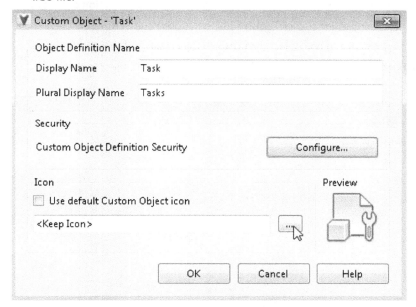

5. Click OK.

 The changes made to the custom object icon are seen after logging out and logging back into the Vault client.

# Delete a Custom Object Definition

A user can delete an existing Custom Object at any time using the Configure Custom Objects dialog box. As long as the custom object is not in use, the definition can be deleted from the Vault.

 All instances of a custom object definition have to be removed from the vault before the definition can be deleted.

Once an instance of a custom object definition has been created, the definition cannot be deleted.

1. In Autodesk Vault Professional, click Tools>Administration>Vault Settings.
2. In the Vault Settings dialog box, select the Custom Objects tab and click Configure.
3. On the Configure Custom Objects dialog box, select the Custom Object to delete.
4. Click Delete.

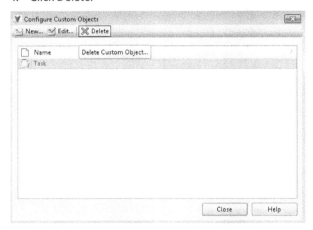

5. Perform one of these tasks:

   If no instances of the custom object were created in the Vault, click Yes in the Confirm Deletion dialog box.

   If there are instances of the custom object in the Vault:

   - Click OK in the dialog box that confirms the definition is in use.
   - Search the Vault for the custom object instances.
   - Delete the instances.
   - Navigate back to the Custom Object Configuration dialog box and select the definition.
   - Click Delete.
   - Click Yes on the Confirm Deletion dialog box.
   - The custom object definition is deleted. A new definition can be created using the same name, if required.

 If there are properties associated with the custom object definition, the administrator is restricted from deleting it.

# Chapter Summary

As a Vault Professional administrator, you need to configure Vault Professional to meet your company's requirements.

Having completed this chapter, you can:

- Create unit and categories, and create new Item numbering schemes.
- Create, edit, and map item and change order properties
- Set up Change Orders including routing lists, user-defined properties, and Change Order numbering.
- Create, edit, and delete Custom Object Definitions.

# Reporting

Autodesk® Vault Professional provides the ability to generate formatted reports representing data contained in a vault. You can generate reports for files, items, and change orders, and organize the report based on specific properties. For example, a report can display files grouped by a category, summarize currently open change orders, or show the distribution of lifecycle states across a model. Reports can display the data in a variety of ways, including charts, tables, and data sheets. You can also format data using dozens of predefined operators.

In this chapter, you learn how to use report templates so that you can customize Vault reports that contain information relevant to your business, in a format that suits your needs.

## Objectives

After completing this chapter, you will be able to:

- Create reports from an advanced search and configure how the data displays.
- Identify the different out-of-the box report templates and the information they are formatted to display.
- Create project reports, also known as folder reports or folder dashboards.

# Lesson: Creating Reports

## Overview

In this lesson you learn how to create a report from an advanced search and configure how the report data displays.

Use search reports to illustrate details about files, items, and change orders stored in the vault by using charts, tables, and data sheets.

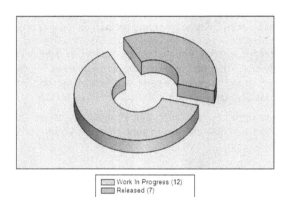

## Objectives

After completing this lesson, you will be able to:

- Create reports from an advanced search.
- Understand how to use each of the out-of-the box templates included with Autodesk Vault Professional.

# About Reports

Working with reports is a way of illustrating file details for those who do not have direct access to the vault. Reports can be organized to suit the needs of your business and to illustrate certain file, folder, item, or change order details.

The properties displayed in the report, as well as the report layout, are specified in a report template file that is selected during the report generation. After selecting a template during report generation, the information displays for viewing. Through the report template, you can control the report content, layout, and format.

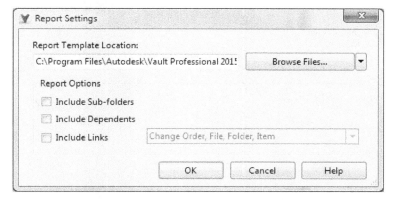

You can also generate and view reports by creating an advanced search with specified parameters then clicking Report. Search options specified in the Advanced Find dialog determine which vault objects display in a report.

Finally, you can also generate and view reports from the Reports tab, built into the preview pane of a folder. These reports are known as folder reports or vault project reports and are based on data contained in the selected folder. You can also include data from subfolders, dependents, and links in these reports.

An example of a folder report using the Project Dashboard template is shown below.

Folder reports can also be generated by clicking Report on the Standard toolbar after a folder has been selected.

## Example of Creating a Report

A report must be generated to show the current state of the change orders in a particular project. You create an advanced search with the condition that the search returns all of the change orders for a specific project folder. Once the search is complete, you generate a report and choose the template that shows the state of each change order. Once the report is generated, you save a copy to the vault and email a copy to the project manager for review.

# Report Templates

Report descriptions for Vault reports are contained in RDLC files stored on the Vault client machine. These report description files are referred to as report templates. Vault report templates are fully RDLC compliant, but Vault requires certain naming conventions in the <DataSet> section of the template for integrating Vault data into the report.

A report template authoring utility is installed with the vault client to help you create simple client report definition files (.RDLC) for storing search data. This utility provides only a raw template structure for categorization purposes. A more sophisticated template authoring tool is required for custom visual layouts.

## Pre-existing Report Templates

When the Vault Client is installed, several pre-existing report templates are provided. The following table describes each template.

| Template Name | Description |
|---|---|
| BOM – First-Level | Displays the BOM First Level details. |
| BOM – Multi-Level | Displays the BOM Multi-Level details. |
| BOM – Parts-Only | Displays the BOM Parts-Only details |
| ECO Average Close Rate | Displays the average number of days it takes to close an ECO. |
| ECO By State | Displays the ECOs in groups based on ECO state. |
| ECO Detail | Displays the ECO Number, Change Order Properties, Sate, Due Date, and submission information without table formatting. |
| ECO Status Created on Month | Displays the number of ECOs per State. |
| ECO Table | Displays the ECO Number, Change Order Properties, State, Due Date, and submission information in table format. |
| File by Category | Displays the filename, revision, state, comments, and check-in information in a pie-chart organized by category. |
| File by Lifecycle State | Displays the filename, revision, state, comments, and check-in information in a graph by lifecycle state. |
| File Checked Out By | Displays checked out by information in a graph. |
| File Detail | Displays the filename, revision, state, check-in information, and comments without table formatting. |
| File Table | Displays the filename, revision, state, check-in information, and comments in a table format. |
| File Transmittal | Displays the filename, revision, state, vault folder location, and date the version was created for each file. |
| Item By State | Displays the item information in groups based on state. |
| Item Detail | Displays the item name, revision, state, type, units, modification information, compliance status, and description without table formatting. |

| Item Table | Displays the item name, revision, state, type, units, modification information, compliance status, and description in table format. |
|---|---|
| Project Dashboard | Displays the filename, revision, state, comments, and check-in information as well as pie-charts organized by lifecycle state and category distribution. |
| Vault Professional In-CAD | Displays check out information, lifecycle state, category, designer, and other In-CAD data displayed in pie-charts. |

## Microsoft Report Viewer

Vault uses the Microsoft Report Viewer to generate and display reports. Microsoft Report Viewer contains a full-featured, highly customizable reporting engine to display reports for SQL Server Reporting Services. However, the report viewer can also be run in "local mode" - enabling applications like Vault to provide data for report rendering without requiring the overhead of SQL Server Reporting Services. Vault runs the report viewer in local mode. Report descriptions for Vault reports are contained in RDLC files stored on the Vault client machine.

Change Orders By State Report

Folder Name      : $/Projects
Generated By     : Administrator
Date             : 8/15/2014 11:15:00 AM
Search Root      :
Search Conditions :

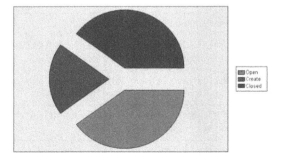

## Creating Search Reports

To create a search report, you must be familiar with how to generate searches with conditions. Familiarize yourself with the template you intend to use before creating the search. Once you understand which file, item, or change order properties will be displayed, you can specify search conditions to return the required vault objects for the report.

Report templates can be stored in a local folder or in a vault. During installation, the pre-existing report templates are placed in a local folder at *C:\Program Files\Autodesk\Vault <edition><version>\ Explorer\Report Templates*.

### Procedure: Creating a New Search Report

The following steps describe how to create a new search report.

1. Click Find. The Find dialog box displays.
2. Click the Basic tab or the Advanced tab depending on the type of criteria for which you want to search.
3. Specify the search criteria for this report.
4. Click Report. The Select Report Template dialog box displays.
5. Enter the path of a template that you would like to use or click Browse to navigate to the required template. The last selected report template displays by default.
6. Click OK to generate a report. If none of the search criteria is set to "ask me later", the report is created and displayed automatically.
7. If any of the criteria has a value set to "ask me later", the Specify Search Values dialog box displays. Specify the search values for the listed properties and then click OK. The Select Report Template displays.
8. Click OK to generate and view the report. The report automatically displays in Microsoft Report Viewer.
9. In Microsoft Report Viewer, click Page Setup to configure printing preferences. Click Print to print the report.
10. To export the report, click Export and select whether to export the report as an Excel file, PDF file or a Word file.

# Creating Autodesk Vault Project Reports

To create a vault project report, also known as a folder report, ensure that all objects (files, subfolders, items, or change orders) or links to the objects that are being reported on are in one project folder.

### Procedure: Creating a Vault Project Report

The following steps describe how to create a vault project report.

1. Select a project folder in the main pane.
2. Select the Reports tab in the preview pane and select Configure.
3. In the Report Settings dialog box, select Browse Files to navigate to the required template. The last selected report template displays by default.
4. Select the required report template and click Open.
5. Select one or more report options if required.
6. Click OK to generate and view the report. The report automatically displays in the preview pane.

# Exercise: Create Reports

In this exercise, you create a search report using a pre-existing template and save the report to the vault. You also create a vault project report.

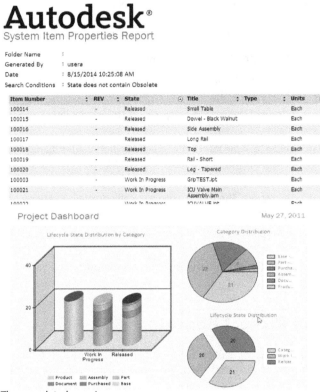

The completed exercise

## Create a Search Report

1. Start Autodesk Vault Professional. Log in using the following information:
   - User Name: **usera**
   - Password: **vault**
   - Database: AOTCVault

2. In the navigation pane, click Home.

3. Select the Item Master list. Alternatively you can click Item Master.

4. Click Find on the toolbar.

**5.**     In the Find dialog box, click the Advanced tab.

**6.**     On the Advanced tab, do the following:

- Select State from the Property drop-down list.
- Select does not contain from the Condition drop-down list.
- Enter **Obsolete** in the Value field.
- Click Add.

> Find items that match these criteria:
>
> State does not contain Obsolete

**7.**     Click Find Now. All of the items that are not in an Obsolete state are listed in the Report.

**8.**     Click Report.

**9.**     On the Select Report Template dialog box, do the following:

- Click the ellipses (…) button.
- Select Item Table.rdlc on the Select Report Template dialog.
- Click Open.

**10.**    Click OK on the Select Report template dialog box. The report is generated and immediately launched in Microsoft Report Viewer. The generated report might vary slightly depending on the files in your database.

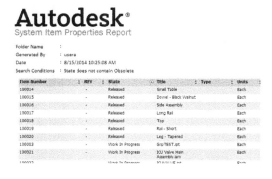

**11.** Click Export on the View Report toolbar.

**12.** Select PDF as the format in which you will save the report.

**13.** On the Save As dialog box, navigate to the desktop.

**14.** Name the report and click Save to store it on your desktop.

**15.** Close the View Report and Find dialog boxes.

## Create a Vault Project Report

**1.** Click Project Explorer.

**2.** Right-click Project Explorer ($) and select New Folder.

**3.** Create a new folder called Projects.

**4.** Right-click Projects and select New Folder to create a new folder called 10-A-555. Click OK.

**5.** Click *Designs\TrailerHitch*.

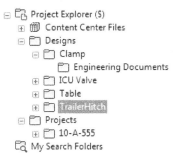

**6.** Select all of the folder's files using <Ctrl>+<A>.

**7.** In the Edit menu, select Copy.

**8.** Navigate to the 10-A-555 project folder.

**9.** In the Edit menu, select Paste as link.

**10.** Select Item Master.

**11.** Select all of the items using <Ctrl>+<A>.

**12.** In the Edit menu, select Copy.

**13.** Navigate to the 10-A-555 project folder.

**14.** In the Edit menu, select Paste as link.

**15.** In the main pane, select the 10-A-555 project folder.

**16.** In the Reports tab of the Preview pane, click Configure.

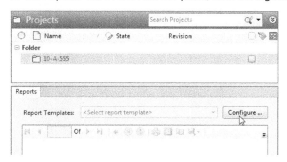

**17.** In the Report Settings dialog box, ensure all Report Options are selected and click Browse Files.

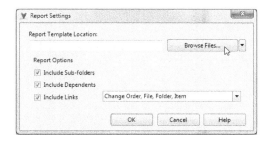

**18.** Select the Project Dashboard.rdlc template and click Open.

**19.** Click OK. The report is automatically displayed in the Preview pane. The generated report might vary slightly depending on the files in your database.

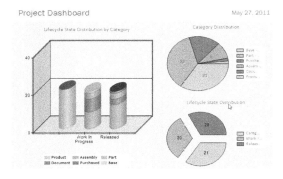

# Chapter Summary

All Autodesk Vault Professional users can create reports to illustrate file, item, and change order details. These reports are useful in understanding design statuses by visually organizing vault data based on specified properties.

You can use existing report templates to display your data in the form of charts, graphs, and tables.

Having completed this chapter, you can:

- Create reports from an advanced search and configure how the data displays.
- Identify the different out-of-the box report templates and the information they are formatted to display.
- Create project (folder dashboard) reports.

# Working with AutoCAD Civil 3D

This chapter gives an overview of using the Autodesk® Vault Professional software with the AutoCAD® Civil 3D® software.

## Objectives

After completing this chapter, you will be able to:

- Describe the workflow of working with the Autodesk Vault Professional software and the AutoCAD Civil 3D software.
- Share AutoCAD Civil 3D software objects using the Autodesk Vault interface.
- Manage Drawing Ownership.
- Understand how Sheet Set Manager is integrated.
- Work with Sheet Set Manager integration.

# Lesson: AutoCAD Civil 3D Data Management

## Overview

The Autodesk Vault Professional software provides AutoCAD Civil 3D software users with additional project management functionality. When the Autodesk Vault Professional software is installed with the AutoCAD Civil 3D software, the Prospector tab in the Toolspace displays a Projects tree. Using this tree, AutoCAD Civil 3D software users can safely share their drawing files and individual AEC objects with other team members. The Vault shortcuts enable users to share design data, such as surfaces, alignments, profiles, pipe networks, and view frames.

### Objectives

After completing this lesson, you will be able to:

- Access the Vault from the AutoCAD Civil 3D software.
- Use a typical workflow for the AutoCAD Civil 3D software and the Autodesk Vault Professional software.
- Manage drawing ownership.

# AutoCAD Civil 3D Data Sharing

The integration between Autodesk Vault and the AutoCAD Civil 3D software provides a consistent user interface between the Prospector tab and Vault Explorer. When AutoCAD Civil 3D software objects are shared they act like files in Autodesk Vault, enabling you to easily see the relationship between source drawings, objects, and consumer drawings. This also enables you to search for specific objects or drawing files using the Vault search capabilities. AutoCAD Civil 3D software projects can be searched based on folder properties. Also, when working in a Connected Workgroups environment, it is possible to manage drawing and object ownership right from the AutoCAD Civil 3D software.

You can access the data management tools provided by the Autodesk Vault add-in from a number of locations, including the Prospector tab in the Toolspace, the X-ref manager, and the Vault tab on the ribbon.

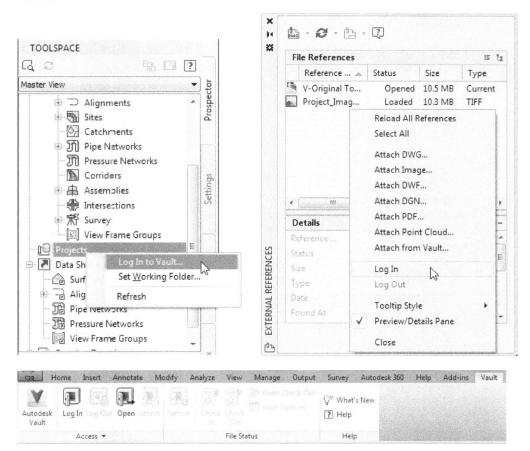

## Workflow: Using AutoCAD Civil 3D and Autodesk Vault Professional

Your workflow varies depending on where you are in the design cycle. The following steps describe a basic workflow for the Autodesk Vault Professional software and the AutoCAD Civil 3D software.

1. Using the Autodesk Data Management Console, configure the Autodesk Vault to work with the AutoCAD Civil 3D software. You can do this when you create the vault or after the vault has been created.

   When the vault is being created, you can choose one of the following configuration templates for your vault instead of accepting the Default Vault configuration:

   - **Building**: Creates a vault with inherent properties for Architectural, Engineering, and Construction (AEC) design workflows.
   - **Infrastructure**: Creates a vault with inherent properties for Engineering, Natural Resources, and Infrastructure (ENI) design workflows.
   - **Manufacturing**: Creates a vault with inherent properties for Manufacturing (MFG) design workflows.

   **Note:** The Civil 3D template is included with all three industry templates.

   If the vault has already been created, open the Autodesk Data Management Console and right-click on the Vault name. Select Import Configuration, and select one of the three industry templates as noted above.

2. Launch the AutoCAD Civil 3D software and log in to the Vault.

3. Enable the Master View in the Toolspace. On the Prospector tab in the Toolspace, set the Working Folder by right-clicking on Projects and selecting Set Working Folder. In the Browse For Folder dialog box, browse to and select the working folder.

4. On the Prospector tab in the Toolspace, right-click on Projects and select New to create a new project. In the New Project dialog box, define the project. Consider using a project template to set a default project directory structure that you can modify to suit your company's standard.

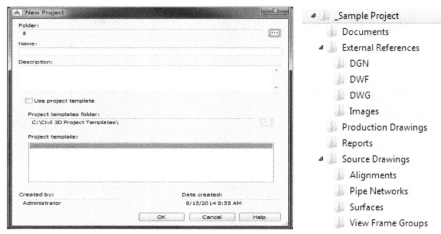

5. In the AutoCAD Civil 3D software, open a file that you want to add to the vault or start a new drawing.

6. Attach any required external reference files (xrefs) to the open AutoCAD Civil 3D software file, using either the Attach command or the Attach from Vault command.

7. Create any AutoCAD Civil 3D software objects that you need to share, such as surfaces, alignments, profiles, etc.

8. Save the drawing in the current working folder under the project that you created.

9. On the Prospector tab, right-click on the drawing name and select Check in. Alternatively, you can select Check In on the Vault tab or use the Xref Manager.

10. Navigate to the required folder in the Project folder. Select the AutoCAD Civil 3D objects that you want to share (surfaces, alignments, pipe networks, etc.) and click OK.

11. Create a new file or open an existing file into which you want to reference Autodesk Vault data. To create reference, right click on the shared object and select Create Reference.

12. On the Prospector tab, expand the project tree, and then open and check out other files from the vault using the Open from Vault command.

13. Check the edited files back into the Vault.

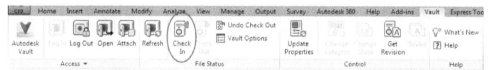

# Manage Drawing Ownership

In many multidisciplinary firms, multiple groups are responsible for editing civil project drawings at different times throughout the course of the project. A project typically starts with the surveying department, and then gets turned over to the engineering department, then over to the drafters/designers, and back to the surveyors for staking out the project. Lastly, it goes to the construction managers to ensure that it is built correcly.

To open the Manage Ownership dialog box in Autodesk Vault, right-click on the file (or group of files) that you want to share and select Manage Ownership. Files that are available for the current workgroup (either owned by them or have an expired lease for another workgroup) display in bold. This indicates that you can change ownership of the file(s). You can also include related documentation when changing file ownership. Select the checkbox to have direct documentation parent to the file that is included when ownership is requested. Files can be paired together so that when the ownership of one changes, the other also changes. You can do this by selecting the checkbox to have ownership transferred to items related to the files in the list.

**Note:** Manage Ownership is only available in a replicated Autodesk Vault environment.

### Workflow: Assign Ownership to a Different Workgroup

1. In the Autodesk Data Management Server Console, go to Tools>Administration.

2. On the Advanced Settings tab, click Settings… in the Ownership Lease area.

3. Set the required lease duration.

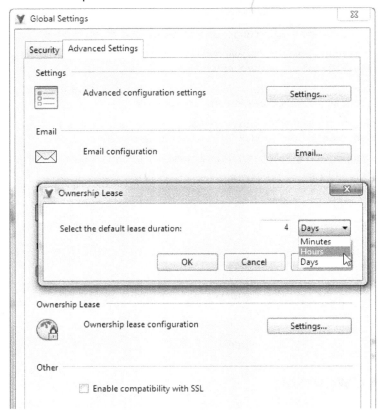

4. Open a drawing or start a new file. Make the required design changes.

5. Check in the file.

6. In the Autodesk Vault Professional software, right-click on the file and select Manage Ownership.

7. Select the next group that needs to work on the file so that they have ownership.

## Icons and Font Colors in AutoCAD Civil 3D

Icons and the font color used for the filename indicate the status of files in the vault. The icons indicate whether you have a local copy, if your copy is up-to-date, if you have a current version, etc. The font color indicates whether the file is not checked out, is checked out to you, or is checked out to another user.

## Status Fonts

| Font Color / Weight | Description |
|---|---|
| Black/Normal | The file is not checked out. |
| Blue/Bold | The file is checked out to you. |
| | **Note:** Files that are checked out to you and have changes in memory that have not been saved have an asterisk appended to their filenames (e.g., Fork-Damper.dwg*). |
| Gray/Italic/Strikethrough | The file is checked out to another user. |

## Status Icons

| Option | Description |
|---|---|
| | If an icon is not displayed, the file is in the vault but you do not have a local copy of the file on your computer. You can quickly identify any files that are new to the vault. Use Get/Checkout to retrieve a copy of the file. |
| ○ | The file is in the vault and available for check out. This is the leading version of the leading revision of the file. Use Get/Checkout to retrieve a copy of the file. |
| ✓ | The file is checked out to you and the local version is the same as the one in the vault. This is also referred to as the latest version of the leading revision. Use Check In to check the file back into the vault or select Undo Checkout to cancel any changes and check the file back into the vault. |
| ● | The local file is newer than the file in the vault. |
| ✓ | The file is checked out by you and the local copy is newer than the latest version in the vault. This typically means that you have made changes to the file since it was checked out but have not checked it back in. |
| ◑ | The local copy of the file is the released version of the latest revision, but is not the latest version of the latest revision. This typically happens when you have a local copy of the released version and a quick change has been made by another user. |
| ✛ | The file is not in the vault. You can add the file using the Check In feature. |
| △ | The local copy is a historical revision of the leading revision in the vault. |
| ⟳ | The local copy of the file does not match the latest version in the vault. Use the Refresh from Vault feature to obtain the latest version of the file. |
| 🔒 | The file is locked and the local copy is up-to-date. |
| 🔒 | The file is locked and the local copy is not up-to-date. |
| ⓘ | There has been an unexpected result with the file (e.g., the local file has been changed without being checked out). See the tooltip for more information. |

# Exercise: Working with AutoCAD Civil 3D Files

In this exercise you will create a new project, add files to it, and share AutoCAD Civil 3D software objects between drawings. You will also practice changing the drawing ownership from one group to another. Note that the AOTCVaultCivil3D Vault that is used in this exercise had the Building configuration file (*AECVault.cfg*) imported into it when it was created. As *AECVault.cfg* includes the Civil 3D template, the vault has already been configured to use with the Civil 3D software.

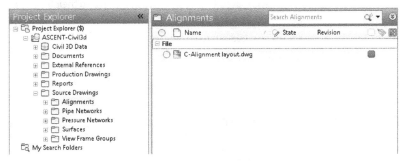

The completed exercise

## User Setup

1. Start the Autodesk Vault Professional software.

   - User Name: **Administrator**
   - Password: leave blank
   - Vault: AOTCVaultCivil3D

2. In the Tools menu, select Administration.

3. Select Global Settings.

4. Select Groups.

**5.** Click New Group.

- For Group Name, enter **Surveyors**.
- For Vaults, select AOTCVaultCivil3D.
- For Roles, select Document Editor (Level 2) and Document Manager (Level 2).

Add usera as a group member and click OK.

**6.** Repeat Step 5 for the following groups (including roles):

- For Group Name, enter **Engineers**.
  Add userb as a group member in the Engineers group.
- For Group Name, enter **Drafters**.
  Add userc as a group member in the Drafters group.
- For Group Name, enter **Construction Managers**. Add userd as a group member in the Construction Managers group.

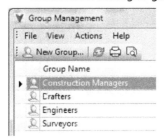

**7.** Close the Group Management and Global Settings dialog boxes.

## Create Categories

**1.** In the Tools menu and select Administration>Vault Settings.

**2.** On the Behaviors tab, click Categories.

**3.** In the top left of the window, select File Categories. A default list is provided based on the configuration used during Vault set up.

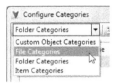

**4.** Click New...

- For Name, enter **Survey**.
- For color, select Green.

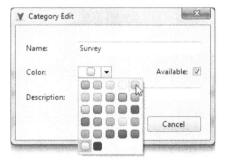

- In the Description field, enter **Survey Drawings**.
- Click OK.

**5.** Repeat Step 4 for the following:

- For Name, enter **Civil**.
- For color, select Blue.
- In the Description field, enter **Civil Drawings**.

**6.** Repeat Step 4 for the following:

- For Name, enter **Architectural**.
- For color, select purple.
- In the Description field, enter **Architectural Drawings.**

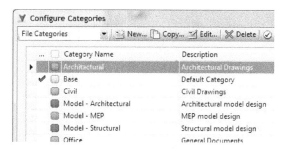

**7.** Close the Configure Categories dialog box.

## Create Rules for Categories

**1.** On the Behaviors tab of the Vault Settings dialog box, click Rules.

**2.** In the top left window, select File Rules, if not already selected. Default rules are provided based on the configuration used during vault set up.

**3.** Click New. Create the following three rules (Survey, Architectural, and Civil) and associate each with their correct Category Assignment.

**4.** In The Rule Condition Builder for the Survey Rule, set the following criteria using the File Name property:

- For the Property, select File Name.
- For the Condition, select starts with.
- For the Vault, enter **V-**.
- Click Add.

**5.** Ensure the Apply rules on object creation option is selected.

**6.** Repeat step 12 for the Architectural and Civil rules, as follows:

- For Architectural, set the Property to File Name, set the Condition to starts with, and for the Value, enter **A-**.
- For Civil, set the Property to File Name, set the Condition to starts with, and for the Value, enter **C-**.

**7.** Click Apply and OK.

**8.** Close all dialog boxes.

## Start a new project

**1.** Launch the AutoCAD Civil 3D software.

**2.** Open *C:\AOTG VAULT Professional\Civil 3D Files\V-Original Topo.dwg*.

**3.** On the ribbon, select the Vault tab>Access panel and select Log In.

**4.** Log in to the vault using the following information:

- For User Name, enter **usera**.
- For Password, enter **vault**.
- For Vault, select AOTCVaultCivil3D.

**5.** In the AutoCAD Civil 3D software's Status Bar tray, hover the cursor over the Vault icon. The vault user name and vault name display.

Next you will set the working folder and create an AutoCAD Civil 3D software project. This will set the location in which you will store the Autodesk Vault projects. The default working folder for AutoCAD Civil 3D software projects is: *C:\Civil 3D Projects*.

**6.** On the Prospector tab, set the View to the Master View, if not already set.

**7.** In the Prospector tab, right-click on Projects>Set Working Folder.

**8.** Browse to and select *C:\AOTG VAULT Professional\Civil 3D Files*.

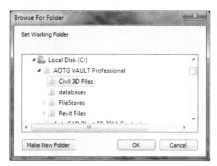

**9.** Click OK.

**10.** Save the drawing.

**11.** Right-click on Projects again and select New.

**12.** For the Name, enter **ASCENT-Civil3d**. Checkmark the Use project template option and click OK.

**13.** On the Vault tab, click Check In. Select the ASCENT-Civil3d project and click Next.

**14.** Select Surfaces under the Drawings>Source Drawings folder. Click Next.

**15.** Under the DWF publishing options, select Do not create, if not already selected. Ensure that everything has a checkmark and click Next.

**16.** Checkmark the Existing Ground surface. Click Finish.

**Note:** The drawing should close.

**17.** On the Vault tab, click Autodesk Vault. If the option is not available, launch the Vault Professional software.

**18.** Log in to the vault using the following information:

- For User Name, enter **usera**.
- For Password, enter **vault**.
- For Vault, select AOTCVaultCivil3D.

**19.** Expand the Project Explorer>ASCENT-Civil3D project>Source Drawings>Surfaces folders.

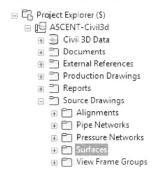

**20.** Note that the category assigned to the newly checked in file should be Survey since the File Name started with V- as the rule stated.

## Reference Vault Data

**1.** In AutoCAD Civil 3D, start a new drawing from the _AutoCAD Civil 3D (Metric) NCS template. Save it as *C-Alignment layout.dwg* under *C:\AOTG VAULT Professional\Civil 3D Files\ASCENT-Civil3d\ Source Drawings\Alignments*.

**2.** Log out of Vault from the AutoCAD Civil 3D software.

3. Log in to the vault using the following information:
   - For User Name, enter **userb**.
   - For Password, enter **vault**.
   - For Vault, select AOTCVaultCivil3D.

4. On the Vault ribbon, on the Access panel, select Attach.

5. In the Select File dialog box, open *ASCENT-Civil3d\Source Drawings\Surfaces\V-Original Topo.dwg*.

6. When prompted that the files are not checked out, click Yes to check them out.

7. Use the default settings in the Attach External Reference dialog box and click OK.

8. Zoom to the extents of the drawing by entering **ZE**.

9. Under Projects in the Prospector tab, expand Surfaces, right-click on Existing Ground, and select Create Reference...

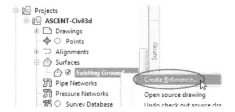

10. Accept the default settings in the Create Surface Reference dialog box, and click OK.

11. Create an alignment from Objects.

12. For the XREF, enter **X**. Select the green line running along the canal as shown in the following illustration.

13.    Press Enter twice to open the Create Alignment from Objects dialog box.

- For the alignment name, enter **Michelle Way**.
- Change the Alignment label set to Major and Minor only.
- Leave all other defaults and click OK.

14.    Create an existing ground profile without creating the profile view.

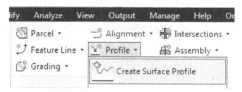

15.    In the Create Profile from Surface dialog box, click Add. Click OK.

16.    Save the drawing.

17.    On the Vault tab, click Check In and Select the *Drawings\Source Drawings\Alignments* folder as the path to check in to. Click Next.

18.    Ensure that the Keep files checked out option is not selected. For the DWF publishing options, select Do not create. Also ensure that all folders/files are selected. Click Next.

19.    Checkmark the Alignments. Click Finish.

20.    Now go to Vault by clicking Autodesk Vault on the Vault tab or opening the Vault software.

21.    Go to the Alignments folder. Note that the category assigned to the newly checked in file should be Civil since the File Name started with C- as the rule stated.

# Lesson: Sheet Set Manager Integration

## Overview

Sheet Set Manager is the AutoCAD® software tool that is used for managing layouts from drawing files and that makes printing entire projects much easier. Autodesk Vault Workgroup and Autodesk Vault Professional integrate with the AutoCAD software Sheet Set Manager for supported AutoCAD software products.

### Objectives

After completing this lesson, you will be able to:

- Generate sheet sets from vaulted data.
- Add sheet sets to Autodesk Vault software.
- Access and edit vaulted sheet set data.

# About Sheet Set Manager Integration

The Autodesk Vault family of products integrates with the AutoCAD software's Sheet Set Manager. With the integration, sheet set functionality can be done in Vault, such as searching for sheets and sheet sets based on properties in the Sheet Set Manager. Property management, plotting, and publishing tasks can also be done through the Vault integration. In the Vault, sheets are represented as files to maintain the relationship between sheets and their associated drawings.

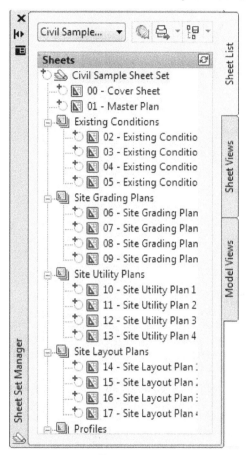

The plan production tools in the AutoCAD Civil 3D software automate the creation of plan and profile sheets for a project. Two separate wizards quickly break the design alignment into multiple sheets. The first wizard creates view frames along the alignment, defining how many sheets are required according to the alignment length and selected sheet size. The second wizard creates the sheets and a sheet set in which they are to be placed.

# Working with Sheet Set Manager Integration

When working with Sheet Set Manager, the first thing you need to do is to set up the title block with fields that the AutoCAD Civil 3D software can automatically fill in for you. Vault can use the fields to help you search your drawings. Using one of the default drawing templates that are supplied with the AutoCAD Civil 3D software enables the software to fill in the project name, address, creation date, and sheet number.

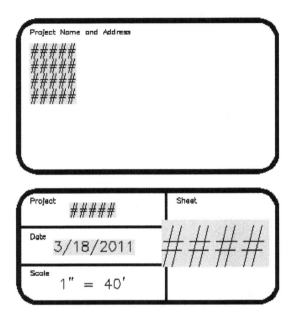

You can manage ownership of an individual sheet or an entire sheet set through the Manage Ownership command. If the Manage Ownership command is accessed from the sheet node, only the ownership of a single sheet is changed. If the same command is accessed from the Sheet Set node, ownership for all sheet drawings in that sheet set is changed.

**Note:** Copy Design is not supported with sheet set files such as .DSS, .DSU and .DSH. It is also recommended to perform all edit operations (such as Rename, Remove, Move, etc.) inside the Sheet Set Manager. The Autodesk Vault software will update the related data files (DSS, DSU and DSH), if required. It is not recommended to perform the above edit operations on the data files by accessing them directly in the Autodesk Vault software. Any changes (such as Rename or Move) that are made in the Vault Client are ignored when you open the edited sheet set in the Sheet Set Manager.

# Exercise: Sheet Set Manager Integration with AutoCAD Civil 3D Files

In this exercise you will create view frames that will divide the alignment into multiple views. You will then create sheets and a sheet set for the view frames and place them in the Vault.

The completed exercise

## Create a Sheet Set

1. Log out of Vault from the AutoCAD Civil 3D software.

2. In the AutoCAD Civil 3D software, log in to the vault using the following information:
   - For User Name, enter **userc**.
   - For Password, enter **vault**.
   - For Vault, select AOTCVaultCivil3D.

3. Check out the C-Alignment Layout.dwg by expanding the *Alignments\Centerline Alignments* under the Project, right-click on Michelle Way, and select Check out source drawing.

4. Accept the defaults in the Check Out Drawing dialog box and click OK.

5. On the Output tab, click Create View Frames.

6. On the Create View Frames – Alignment page, select Michelle Way as the Alignment and click Next.

**7.** On the Create View Frames – Sheets page, ensure that the template is set to ISO A0 Plan and Profile 1 to 500. Click OK.

**8.** Accept all other default settings and click Create View Frames. Three View Frames should have been created, as indicated by the three blue view frame rectangles on the drawing.

**9.** On the Output tab, click Create Sheets.

**10.** For the Layout Creation options, select Number of layouts per new drawing. Enter **1**. Click Next.

**11.** For the Sheet Set name, enter **Civil Plans**.

**12.** For the Sheet set storage location click the Vault icon to the right and select Production Drawings. Click OK.

**13.** Click Next.

**14.** Accept all other defaults and click Create Sheets. Click OK to save the drawing.

**15.** Pick a point to the right of the plan view to place the profile view. A sheet set with three sheets is created.

**16.** In the Check In 'Civil Plans' dialog box, click OK to check in the three new sheet drawings.

**17.** Click OK in the Vault Add-In dialog box.

**18.** Return to Vault and click Find on the toolbar. Select the Basic tab and enter **\*.dsu** to search the database for Sheet Sets. Run the search. This enables you to search for sheet sets created and added to the Vault.

**19.** Right-click on the located file and select Go To Folder. In the main pane, you will see that the .DSU file along with the .DSH files are in the VFG-Michelle Way – (1) folder.

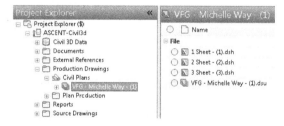

**20.** Navigate up one level to the Civil Plans folder and note that the .DSS file is located there.

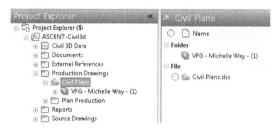

# Chapter Summary

Autodesk Vault Professional software provides product lifecycle management for your designs. A common interface provides access to files, folders, revisions, and AEC Objects.

Having completed this chapter, you can:

- Describe the workflow of working with the Autodesk Vault Professional software and AutoCAD Civil 3D software.
- Share AutoCAD Civil 3D software objects using the Autodesk Vault interface.
- Manage Drawing Ownership.
- Understand how Sheet Set Manager is integrated.
- Work with the Sheet Set Manager integration.

# Working with Autodesk Revit

This chapter gives an overview of using the Autodesk® Professional software with Autodesk® Revit® products.

## Objectives

After completing this chapter, you will be able to:

- Describe the workflow of working with Autodesk Vault and Autodesk Revit software for shared and non-shared projects.
- Use the Autodesk Revit Vault Add-in commands.
- Configure Autodesk Revit and Autodesk Vault Add-In Options.

# Lesson: Autodesk Revit Vault Add-in

## Overview

The Autodesk® Vault Professional software with Revit Vault Add-in offers Autodesk Revit users with file security, version control, and multi-user support. Autodesk Vault integrates with Autodesk® Revit® Architecture, Autodesk® Revit® MEP, and Autodesk® Revit® Structure.

### Objectives

After completing this lesson, you will be able to:

- Access the Autodesk Vault from the Autodesk Revit software.
- Describe the workflows of working with Autodesk Vault and Autodesk Revit for shared and non-shared projects.
- Use the Autodesk Revit Vault Add-in Commands.
- Configure Autodesk Revit and Autodesk Vault Acd-In Options.

# Autodesk Revit Vault Add-in Concepts

There are two essential concepts to understand when working with the Autodesk Revit Vault add-in.

- Using Autodesk Revit Server or work shared central files: The Autodesk Revit add-in does not require a check out. This behavior is unique and is unlike all other Autodesk Vault add-ins where you must check a file out of the vault before you can modify it. Copies of the project file are added to Autodesk Vault at specified milestones or automatically after a Revit Synchronization with Central.

- Using Autodesk Vault with non-shared project files: The project file can be downloaded using the Open from Vault command. This will automatically check out the file for editing. Once you are done editing the file, check the file back into the vault by using the Save to Vault command.

# General Workflow for Shared Project Files

Follow these steps to work with a shared project file:

1. In Autodesk Revit, log into Autodesk Vault using the Log In command in the Autodesk Vault ribbon tab.

2. Open or create a local copy of the project file.

3. Perform one of the following steps:

- Synchronize with Central. A copy of the synchronized file is automatically added to your vault.

- Select Save to Autodesk Vault in the Vault ribbon. A new file version is added to the vault without synchronizing with the Autodesk Revit Server.

 You might be prompted to select a folder location in Autodesk Vault. This prompt can be hidden by configuring the Share Path property in Vault.

# General Workflow for Non-shared Project Files

Follow these steps to work with a non-shared project file.

1. In Autodesk Revit, log into Autodesk Vault using the Log In command on the Vault ribbon tab.

2. Open a project file with Autodesk Revit or click Open from Vault on the Vault ribbon.

Open from Vault automatically checks the file out of the vault.

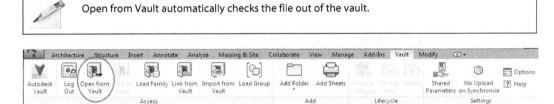

3. Make your changes to the file.
4. Select Save to Vault on the Vault ribbon.

If this is the first time the file is being saved to Autodesk Vault, it is added to the Vault as a new file and checked in. If the file already exists in the Vault, the file is checked back into Autodesk Vault as a new version.

# Autodesk Revit Vault Add-in Commands

The Autodesk Revit Vault Add-in commands can be found on the Vault ribbon tab.

## Open from Vault

Opening a Autodesk Revit file from the Autodesk Vault opens an existing file previously added to Vault. When selecting the latest version of a file, Autodesk Revit Server files and Central work shared files are opened from their respective locations just as they would be if opened from Autodesk Revit.

Opening a historical version of a file or a Read Only version of the file downloads a copy of the file from Vault and opens it for viewing.

Opening a non-work shared file for editing automatically checks out the file unless the Read-Only option is selected.

Each of the following conditions must be met to open a file from Autodesk Vault for editing:

- You must be logged into the vault that contains the file that you want to edit.
- The file must be in a checked-in state. It cannot be checked out to another user.
- You must have permissions to check out the file for editing.

To open Autodesk Revit File from Autodesk Vault:

1. Click Open from Vault on the Vault ribbon in Autodesk Revit.
2. Navigate to the file that you want to open and click OK.

 You might be prompted to select a folder location in Autodesk Vault. This prompt can be hidden by configuring the Share Path property in Vault.

## Save to Autodesk Vault

 Save to Vault can only be used on Non-work shared files and Autodesk Revit Family files.

Non-work shared files are added to Vault using the Save to Vault command. When a file is saved to Vault, it is automatically checked into the Vault.

Ensure that your folder mappings are in place before adding files to the Vault with the Revit Vault Add-in. This folder mapping is used to determine where to add or update the file in Vault.

After saving a file to Vault, if you continue to edit the file, the file is automatically checked back out.

## Load a Family from Autodesk Vault

In Autodesk Revit, you can search or browse Autodesk Vault for Revit family files and load, or load and place them into the current project. Load Family supports files of type .RFA with or without type catalogs.

 Files of type .ADSK must first be opened from Vault and converted into the .RFA format before they can be loaded into a project.

1.  Open your project with Autodesk Revit and log into the Vault.
2.  Select Load Family from the Autodesk Vault ribbon.

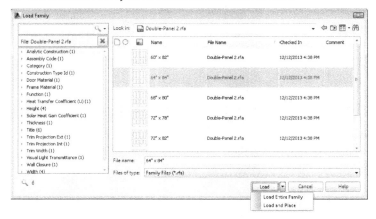

3.  From the Load Family dialog box, you can perform the following tasks:
    a.  **Search family types:** You can search for family types based on categories, a family file, or by

        entering a text string in the Search field  .

 The Autodesk Revit Indexing Service must be enabled by an administrator in the ADMS Console before you can search family types.

    b.  **Browse family types based on the family file:** You can browse for the family types in vault by clicking on a family file and drilling down to the family type that you want to load.

    c.  **Search the Vault**: You can locate a specific file by clicking Find 🔎 and entering your search criteria in the Vault Search dialog box.

4.  Do one of the following three tasks:

-   Select one or more family types and click Load.
-   Select a single family type in the family that you want to load and select Load Entire Family from the Load drop-down. All family types in the family are loaded. Depending on the number of family types in the family, the Load Entire Family option can take some time to complete.

- Select a single family type in the family that you want to load and place into the active by selecting Load and Place from the Load drop-down. Click on the appropriate element in the active model to place the family type.

The Load Family dialog box enables you to locate family types quickly across multiple family files. Understanding how the search interface works enables you to use this functionality effectively. The table below describes the interface components.

| | |
|---|---|
| **Content Search Box**<br><br>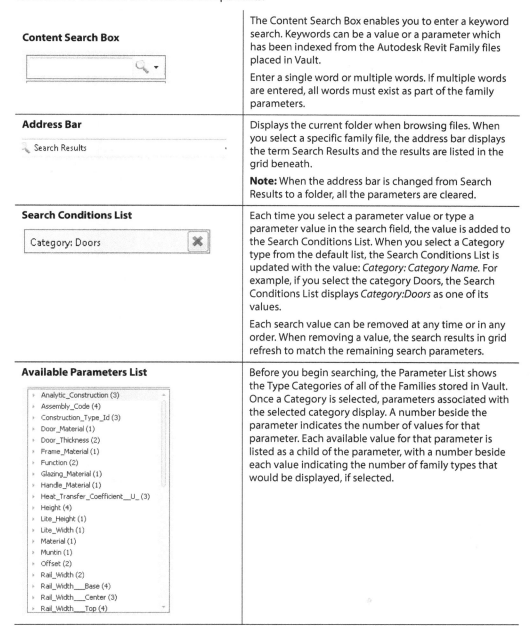 | The Content Search Box enables you to enter a keyword search. Keywords can be a value or a parameter which has been indexed from the Autodesk Revit Family files placed in Vault.<br><br>Enter a single word or multiple words. If multiple words are entered, all words must exist as part of the family parameters. |
| **Address Bar**<br><br>Search Results | Displays the current folder when browsing files. When you select a specific family file, the address bar displays the term Search Results and the results are listed in the grid beneath.<br><br>**Note:** When the address bar is changed from Search Results to a folder, all the parameters are cleared. |
| **Search Conditions List**<br><br>Category: Doors | Each time you select a parameter value or type a parameter value in the search field, the value is added to the Search Conditions List. When you select a Category type from the default list, the Search Conditions List is updated with the value: *Category: Category Name.* For example, if you select the category Doors, the Search Conditions List displays *Category:Doors* as one of its values.<br><br>Each search value can be removed at any time or in any order. When removing a value, the search results in grid refresh to match the remaining search parameters. |
| **Available Parameters List**<br><br>Analytic_Construction (3)<br>Assembly_Code (4)<br>Construction_Type_Id (3)<br>Door_Material (1)<br>Door_Thickness (2)<br>Frame_Material (1)<br>Function (2)<br>Glazing_Material (1)<br>Handle_Material (1)<br>Heat_Transfer_Coefficient__U_ (3)<br>Height (4)<br>Lite_Height (1)<br>Lite_Width (1)<br>Material (1)<br>Muntin (1)<br>Offset (2)<br>Rail_Width (2)<br>Rail_Width___Base (4)<br>Rail_Width___Center (3)<br>Rail_Width___Top (4) | Before you begin searching, the Parameter List shows the Type Categories of all of the Families stored in Vault. Once a Category is selected, parameters associated with the selected category display. A number beside the parameter indicates the number of values for that parameter. Each available value for that parameter is listed as a child of the parameter, with a number beside each value indicating the number of family types that would be displayed, if selected. |

| | |
|---|---|
| **Grid** 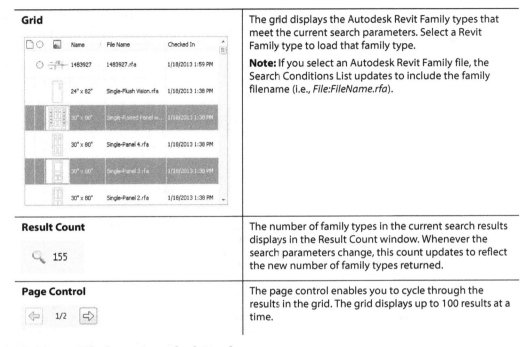 | The grid displays the Autodesk Revit Family types that meet the current search parameters. Select a Revit Family type to load that family type.

**Note:** If you select an Autodesk Revit Family file, the Search Conditions List updates to include the family filename (i.e., *File:FileName.rfa*). |
| **Result Count**

🔍  155 | The number of family types in the current search results displays in the Result Count window. Whenever the search parameters change, this count updates to reflect the new number of family types returned. |
| **Page Control**

⬅  1/2  ➡ | The page control enables you to cycle through the results in the grid. The grid displays up to 100 results at a time. |

## Linking a File from Autodesk Vault

Link from Vault enables the user to select a file in Autodesk Vault to be linked into the current Autodesk Revit Project. The advantage of using the Link from Vault is that there is no need to know where the latest version of the file is. If the latest version is located on the Autodesk Revit Server then the server version is linked too. If the file is a non-work shared file, it is downloaded from Autodesk Vault and linked to the current project and will continue to be managed by Autodesk Vault. To link a file:

1. Click Link from Vault from the Autodesk Revit Vault ribbon.

2. Select the file to be linked from Autodesk Vault.

3. Select Specify in the Layers/Levels field and select a list of Levels to link. Click OK to return to the Link a File from Vault dialog.

4. Select your positioning preference from the Positioning drop-down.

5. Click Link. The file is imported and linked based on your positioning selection.

The following file formats can be linked: .RVT, .DWG, .DXF, .DGN, .SAT, .SKP, .IFC, .DWF, and .DWFX.

## Importing a File from Autodesk Vault

Import from Vault enables you to import CAD files or images stored in a vault into the current Revit project. You can also specify position options for the imported file on the Import from Vault dialog. However, unlike Link from Vault, when the project is saved to Vault, only the project is updated. Any uses/used-by relationship between the project and the imported file are not saved. This means if a link is modified, the file must be re-imported to see the changes. To import a file:

1. Launch the Import from Vault.
2. Select the file to be imported from Autodesk Vault.
3. Select Specify in the Layers/Levels field and select a list of Levels to link. Click OK to return to the Link a File from Vault dialog.
4. Select your positioning preference from the Positioning drop-down.
5. Click Import. The file is imported based on your positioning selection.

The following file formats can be imported: .DWG, .DXF, .DGN, .SAT, .SKP, .BMP, JPG, JPEG, and .TIF.

## Load Group from Autodesk Vault

Vault supports loading Model groups, Detail groups, and Attached groups from a Revit project in the Vault into the current project. To load a group:

1. Open the Revit project file and ensure that you are logged into the Vault.
2. Select Load Groups from the Autodesk Revit Vault ribbon. The Select Project with Groups dialog box opens.

 If a sheet is in the active view, the Load Groups command is disabled.

3. Select a .RVT file and click Select to see which groups are available. Unlike in Revit, you can select which groups are loaded from Vault.
- If a parent group is selected, all children groups are automatically selected for loading.
- If a child group is cleared off, the parent group is automatically also cleared and will not be loaded either.
- If a file has an attached detail group type and that group is chosen, all children files are loaded as well as its model group.
- Groups can have the same name in one file only if they are different group types.

4. Select one or more groups to load and click OK. This loads an instance of the selected groups into the current Revit project.

## Add Autodesk Revit Files to Autodesk Vault

Use the Add Files command to add a selection of files to the Autodesk Vault. Relationships between Autodesk Revit files and associated files are created as new versions of the files are added to vault.

 You must be logged into the vault to add files

1. On the Vault ribbon tab, select Add Files.
2. In the Open dialog box, select the files to add.

 When adding linked files using Add Files, all children files should be added before adding parent files. Consider keeping the number of files under 1000 to reduce processing time.

3. Specify any selection changes. If a file is unchecked the file will not be added to vault. The list view supports sorting by type and multi select for efficient selection.
4. Under Settings... you might enable or disable the visualization attachment for this session.
5. The Target Location in Autodesk Vault specifies the vault folder to which the selected file is added. If the Share Path property has been configured, the vault path should be automatically set.
6. Click OK. The selected content is added to the vault.

## Add Autodesk Revit Folders to Autodesk Vault

Use the Add Folder command to add multiple files contained in a Windows folder to Autodesk Vault. Relationships between Autodesk Revit files and associated files are created as new versions of the files are added to Vault.

1. On the Vault ribbon tab, select Add Folder from the Add File drop-down list.
2. In the Browse For Folder dialog box, select the folder to add.

 When adding linked files using the Add Folder option, all children files should be added before adding the parent files.

3. Click OK.
4. Under Settings... you might enable or disable the visualization attachment for this session.
5. The Target Location in Vault specifies the vault folder to which the selected folder is added. If the Share Path property has been configured the vault path should be automatically set.
6. Click OK. The folder and the selected content are added to the vault.

## Add Sheets to Autodesk Vault

The Add Sheets feature enables users to print all sheets in the active Autodesk Revit file and place them directly in the vault. To add sheets:

1. Click the Add Sheets icon on the Vault ribbon.

2. Select which of the sheets to include in the sheet set.

3. Create a sheet set or choose an existing sheet set to use as a name for the plot set file. Any sheets that are excluded from the plot job are struck through in the list. These sheets are still included in the set.

   **Note:** Sheets can only be excluded in the Plot Manager in the Vault Client. If you create a new sheet set, you must identify the location of the sheet set for Vault, the Sheet Set Name, and a Sheet Name Prefix.

4. Select the DWF Properties tab to modify properties associated with the DWFs, if required.

5. Click OK to add the selected sheets to the Vault.

## Lifecycle Options (Change Category, State, and Revise)

The Autodesk Revit Vault Add-in supports changing categories, states, and revise file workflows enabling you to manage your design files directly in Revit.

The Change Category command enables users to modify the lifecycle category for a file or group of files. To change categories:

1. Open the file for which you want to change the category and click Change Category on the Revit Vault ribbon.

 Change Category is disabled if the open file has not already been added/saved to the vault.

2. In the Change Category dialog box, select the new category from the list of available categories. The Next Category field updates adjacent to the filename with the new category.

3. Enter any comments regarding the category change in the Comment field.

4. Click OK to save the changes and close the Change Category dialog.

The Change State command enables you to modify the lifecycle state of a file. Examples of states include, Work in Progress, Quick Change, and Obsolete. To change states:

1. Open the file for which you want to change the state and click Change State on the Revit Vault ribbon.

2. In the Change State dialog box, the current lifecycle of the file and lifecycle definition name display.

3. Select the new lifecycle state from the list of those available for selection.

4. Enter any comments regarding the lifecycle state change in the Enter Comments field, or select a comment from the drop-down list.

5. Click OK to save the changes and close the Change State dialog.

With revisions, you can label a significant milestone or set of changes to a document and its related files. The label itself is the revision, and the collection of files affected in that revision are considered a revision level. A revision level can be retrieved later so that a document and the version of the related files associated with that particular revision are preserved. To set a new revision:

1. Open the file to be revised and click Revise on the Revit Vault ribbon.

2. In the Revise dialog box, select whether you want to perform a Primary, Secondary, or Tertiary revision in the Select next revision drop-down list.

3. Enter any comments regarding the new revision in the Enter Comments field, or select a comment from the drop-down list.

4. Click OK on the Revise dialog box to save the changes and close it.

## Shared Parameters

Shared parameters are definitions of parameters that you can add to families or projects. Shared parameter definitions are stored in a .TXT file independent of any family file or Revit project, which enables you to access the file from different families or projects. This file is referred to as the Shared Parameters file. The Shared Parameters file can be stored in the Vault and activated from the Shared Parameters button on the Revit Vault ribbon.

 Autodesk recommends creating a single folder to store shared parameters in the vault. As there might be multiple .TXT files inside a vault, a shared parameters folder helps users to immediately and easily identify the parameter files.

To use a shared parameters file:

1. Open a project file and select Shared Parameters on the Autodesk Revit Vault ribbon.

2. In the Select Shared Parameter File dialog box, the currently active Shared Parameters file is shown at the bottom left of the File dialog.

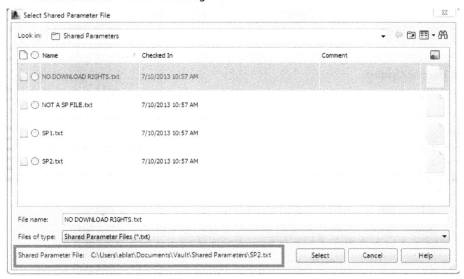

3. Select the Shared Parameters .TXT file that you want to activate and click Select. The latest version of the file is downloaded and set as the active Shared Parameters file.

 Vault does not confirm the legitimacy of the shared parameters file. If you select an invalid .TXT file, it is activated as the Shared Parameters file despite being an improper file.

## Sync on Demand

When working with Work share-enabled files, you can add or update a file in the Vault through the Upload on Synchronize command on the Vault add-in tab in Revit. This button toggles between Upload on Synchronize and No Upload on Synchronize.

Upload
on Synchronize    **TO**    No Upload
on Synchronize

Additional options for uploading are found in the Vault Options dialog box on the Sharing tab.

# Configure Autodesk Revit and Autodesk Vault Add-In Options

To optimize collaboration, you can configure sharing and mapping options in Autodesk Revit. To access these options, select Options on the Revit Vault ribbon. The Vault Options dialog box has three tabs that can be used to configure the system: Sharing, Mapping, and Searching.

## Sharing Options

All sharing options are available on the Sharing tab. Each of these options are user specific.

### Vault Upload Options

Vault Upload options enable you to configure when a synchronized file is added to the vault.

- Always Upload on Synchronize with Central: Every time a Synchronize with Central command is performed, a new version of the file is added to the vault.
- Upload Every # Hours on Synchronization: When a Synchronize with Central command is performed, if the version is older than the set number of hours a new version is added to the vault.
- No automatic upload on Synchronization: When a Synchronize with Central command is performed, no upload occurs.
- Upload on Close: A new file version is added to the vault whenever a file is closed.

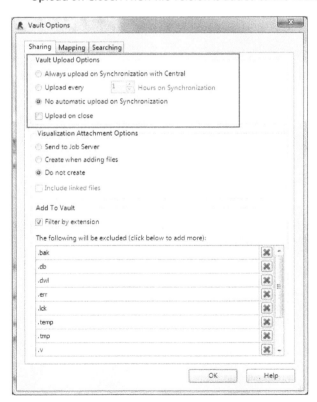

### Visualization Attachment Options

Visualization Attachment Options control how Visualization files are created when files are added through the Vault add-in for Autodesk Revit.

- Send to Job Server: When a file is added to vault, a job is queued to an active job server.
- Create when adding files: Each file generates a visualization file during the add process.

 This option adds processing time to the add operation.

- Do not create: No visualization files are generated when a file is added to the vault.
- Include linked files: Ensures that any selected options list above also apply to linked files.

### Add to Vault

Use the Add to Vault section to define which file extensions are to be excluded from the database when files are added. If a file extension is listed, that file format cannot be added to the vault with Add File or Add Folder commands. Clear the Filter by extension checkbox if you do not want to filter out files with the listed extensions. This enables you to keep the list, and toggle the filter on and off as required.

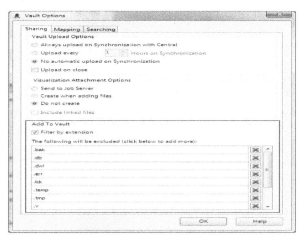

## Mapping Options

The Mapping tab enables you to map any local, network, or Autodesk Revit server folder to any Vault folder. This can only be done as Administrator.

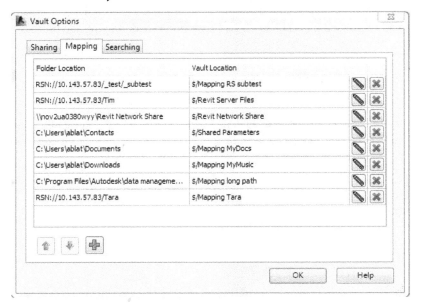

To add Mapping settings:

1. Click Options on the Vault add-in ribbon and select the Mapping tab.

2. Click '+' (Plus) at the bottom of the Mapping tab to define mappings.

3. Select the File system folder option to select a local folder, or select the Revit Server folder to define a Revit server folder.

4. Enter the path for the folder or click the ellipses (...) button to browse to and select the folder location. Click OK.

 If you want to map to a network shared folder (\\), enter the beginning of the network path in the browse field (e.g., \\network879). By doing this, you do not have to manually navigate to the network directory, which can be time-consuming depending on the size of the network and speed of your connection.

5. Click Next. The Mapping Wizard will validate the specified local or server path.

6. On the Select the Vault folder screen you define the Vault folder to map to. Enter the path or click the ellipses (...) button to browse to and select the Vault folder.

7. Click Next. The Mapping Wizard will validate the specified Vault path. If the mapping is valid, a confirmation displays showing the new mapping configuration.

 If the mapping is not valid, an error message displays and the wizard displays the attempted settings. An error can occur if one or both of the folders being mapped are already part of an existing mapping configuration. Modify your mapping settings and click Next to validate the changes.

---

8. Click Finish to close the wizard.

9. Click OK on the Vault Options dialog to save the mapping settings.

 If you do not click OK on the Vault Options dialog, your mapping changes are not saved.

Mappings are listed in order or priority. Select a mapping entry and use Up and Down to arrange the mappings in the preferred order. Mappings can also be edited or deleted. To edit an existing mapping, select the pencil button adjacent to the mapping to be changed and use the mapping wizard to make the required changes. To edit a mapping, select it and select X. Click OK at the bottom of the Vault Options dialog box to confirm any changes, otherwise they will not be saved.

## Configure the Share Path

Share Path is a vault property that can be added to a vault folder. This property provides vault with the location of the Autodesk Revit central project files on your network. The advantage of using the Share Path is that the Revit add-in will duplicate the folder structure of the network share inside vault. Having the Share Path configured also removes the need for users to select the vault folder while adding files.

By configuring Share Path, the folder structure on the network share is duplicated automatically in the vault as files are added.

**Note:** Share path is only required for the Add Files and Add Folder commands. All other Revit commands use the mapped folders defined in the Mapping options.

To configure the Share Path:

1. Log in to the Autodesk Vault Professional software.

2. Select or create a vault folder that contains the project folders.

3. Go to the Edit menu and select Edit Properties.

4. On the Property Edit dialog box, click Select Properties.

5. On the Customize Fields dialog box, set the Select available fields to Folders.

6. Select Share Path on the left side of the dialog box, click Add -> to move Share Path to the right side.

7. Click OK to close the dialog box.

8. On the Property Edit dialog box, enter the path to the network share location of the Revit project folders in the Share Path field.

9. Click OK to close the Property Edit dialog box.

10. Review the Property Edit Results and click OK if everything is accurate.

11. Open a local copy of a Revit project that has its central file in the network share path that you just added to the vault.

12. Log into Autodesk Vault from Autodesk Revit.

13. When the next Revit Synchronize with Central is performed, a new version of the file is added to the vault.

 When using Autodesk Revit Server, the Sharepath value should match the value in the RSN.ini file for the Autodesk Revit server being mapped. For example if the server's IP address is 10.1.1.10 then the value for the Share path should be RSN://10.1.1.10.

## Searching Options

You can control which categories and parameters display in searches in the left pane of the Load Family dialog box by configuring the settings on the Searching tab of the Vault Options dialog box. For example, you can determine the types of parameters that show up for the category Doors, and whether you want Balusters and Callout Heads displayed as categories.

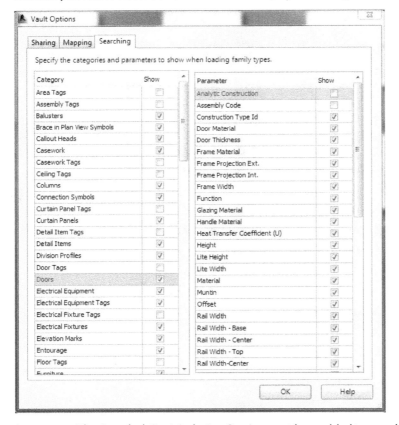

**Important:** The Autodesk Revit Indexing Service must be enabled to search family types.

 **Configure Searching Options**
You must be an administrator to modify the settings on the Searching tab.

1.  Click Options on the Vault add-in ribbon.
2.  Select the Searching tab on the Vault Options dialog box. A list of all indexed Categories in the Vault displays.
3.  Select the checkbox for any categories you want to show up in the Family Search. By default, all categories are selected.
4.  Select a Category to modify its parameters.
5.  Select the checkbox for each parameter that you want displayed in the Parameters list when searching this category. As an alternative you can use the shortcut menu to perform any of the following to more efficiently select parameters:

Select all
Clear all

Show parameter
Hide parameter

Show in all categories
Hide in all categories

Restore all to default

- Right-click anywhere in the list of parameters and choose Select all to select all parameters for that category.
- Right-click anywhere in the list of parameters and select Clear all to clear all parameters for that category.
- Select a particular parameter, right-click, and select Show parameter to select that parameter.
- Select a particular parameter, right-click, and select Hide parameter to clear that parameter.
- Select a particular parameter, right-click, and select Show in all categories to select that parameter across all categories.
- Select a particular parameter, right-click, and select Hide in all categories to clear that parameter across all categories.
- Right-click anywhere in the Searching tab and select Restore all to default to reset all the parameters to their original settings.

6.  Click OK to save the changes.

# Exercise: Working with Autodesk Revit Files

In this exercise, you will first save an Autodesk Revit family to the Autodesk Vault. You will also use the Add Files and Add Folder commands to add Autodesk Revit projects to Autodesk Vault from the Autodesk Revit Architecture and Autodesk Revit Structure software interfaces, respectively. Finally you will modify a vaulted project and save the changes to Autodesk Vault.

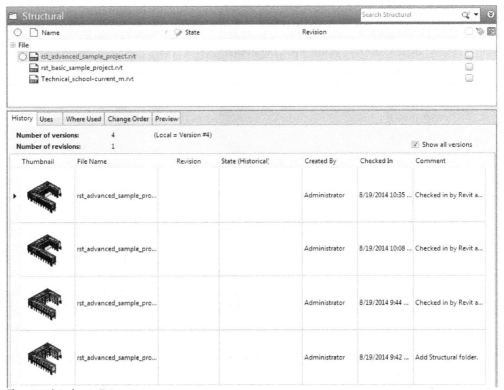

The completed exercise

## Folder Setup and Set Working Folder

1.    Start the Autodesk Vault Professional software. Login using the following information:
   - For User Name, enter **Administrator**.
   - No Password
   - For Vault, select AOTCVault.

2.    In the Navigation Pane, select Project Explorer ($).

**3.**     Click New>New Folder.

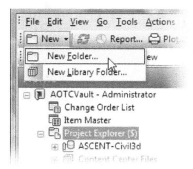

**4.**     Name the new folder Architectural and click OK.

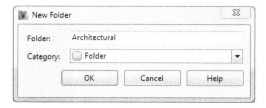

**5.**     Select File>Set Working Folder.

**6.**     Browse to *C:\AOTG VAULT Professional*. Click Make New Folder to create a folder called Working Folder. Click OK.

## Save a Family to Vault

**1.**     Launch the Autodesk Revit Architecture software.

**2.**     Open the following family, *C:\AOTG VAULT Professional\Revit Files\Double-Glass 1.rfa*.

**3.**     On the ribbon, select the Vault tab and select Log In.

**4.**     Log in to the vault using the following information:

- For User Name, enter **Administrator**.
- No Password
- For Vault, select AOTCVault.

**5.**     On the Vault tab select Save to Vault.

**6.** Select the Architectural folder and click OK.

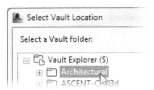

## View Files in Autodesk Vault

**1.** On the ribbon, select the Vault tab and select Autodesk Vault to open Autodesk Vault. Login if required.

**2.** In the Navigation Pane, select Project Explorer ($) and click the Architectural folder to view its file.

## Add Files

**1.** Return to the Autodesk Revit Architecture window.

**2.** On the ribbon, select the Vault tab and select Add Files.

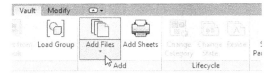

**3.** Navigate to the *C:\AOTG Vault Professional\Revit Files* folder.

**4.** Use <Ctrl> to select rac_advanced_sample_project.rvt and rac_basic_sample_project.rvt. Click Open.

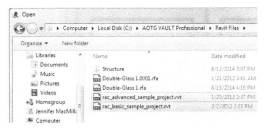

**5.** In the Add Files to Vault dialog box, click Settings.

**6.** In the Add To Vault Settings dialog box, select Create when adding files and click OK.

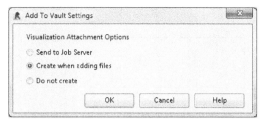

**7.** Click the ellipses (…) button for Target Location in Vault and in the Select Vault Location dialog box, select Architectural. Click OK.

**8.** Enter comments in the Enter Comments field and click OK.

**9.** On the ribbon, select the Vault tab and select Autodesk Vault to open Autodesk Vault.

**10.** Click Refresh icon to refresh the Architectural folder files. Note that the two new projects have been added.

**11.** Select rac_basic_sample_project.rvt. Select the Preview tab to view the Version 1 visualization file of the project.

## Add Folder

**1.** Return to the Autodesk Revit software.

**2.** On the ribbon, click Add Folder from the Add Files drop-down list.

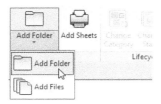

**3.** Navigate to the *C:\AOTG Vault Professional\Revit Files\Structure* folder and click OK.

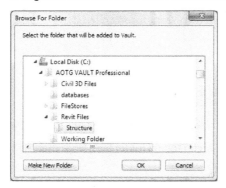

**4.** In the Add Files to Vault dialog box, click Settings.

**5.** In the Add To Vault Settings dialog box, accept the default settings and verify that Do not create is selected. Click OK.

**6.** Click the ellipses (…) button for Target Location in Vault.

**7.** In the Select Vault Location dialog box, select New Folder and enter **Structural** as the new folder name. Click OK twice to return to the Add Files to Vault dialog box.

**8.** Enter comments in the Enter Comments field and click OK.

**9.** On the ribbon, select the Vault tab and select Autodesk Vault to open Autodesk Vault.

**10.** Click Refresh icon and select the Structural folder. Note the new files that you added using the Add Folder command.

**11.** Select rst_advanced_sample_project.rvt. Select the Preview tab, select the thumbnail, and note that the visualization file does not display as the visualization setting was set to Do not create.

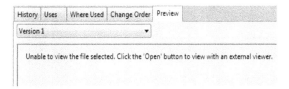

## Open from Autodesk Vault and Modify

**1.**      Return to Autodesk Revit.

**2.**      On the ribbon, select the Vault tab and click Open from Vault.

**3.**      Navigate to the Structural folder and select rst_advanced_sample_project.rvt to open it in Autodesk Revit.

**4.**      Delete the wall as highlighted below and save the file.

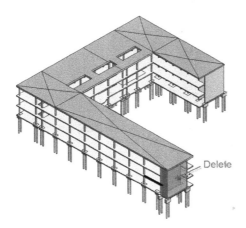

**5.**      On the ribbon, select the Vault tab and select Save to Vault.

## Link from Autodesk Vault

**1.**      On the ribbon, select the Vault tab and click Link from Vault.

**2.**      Navigate to the Architectural folder, select rac_advanced_sample_project.rvt and click Link.

**3.** Note that rac_advanced_sample_project.rvt is now linked to rst_advanced_sample_project.rvt.

    ⊟ ⊶ Revit Links

        ⬇ rac_advanced_sample_project.rvt

**4.** On the ribbon, select the Vault tab and click Save to Vault.

**5.** Click Yes to save and continue.

**6.** Click Autodesk Vault to return to the Autodesk Vault.

**7.** Select rst_advanced_sample_project.rvt and click the Preview tab. Note that the number of versions indicates the number of times the project is saved (checked in). There is no preview available based on how the file was initially checked in.

# Chapter Summary

The Revit Vault Add-in offers Autodesk Revit users with file security and version control for shared and non-shared projects. It also provides options to configure the software to suit specific workflows.

Having completed this chapter, you can:

- Describe the workflow of working with Autodesk Vault and Autodesk Revit for shared and non-shared projects.
- Use the Revit Vault Add-in commands.
- Configure Autodesk Revit and Autodesk Vault Add-In Options.

# Thin Client

With Autodesk® Vault Thin Client you are able to access Files and Items in a Vault via the web. Employees or groups can view, search, and print details of items and files. This chapter covers the default installation, along with how to access and view files and items in the vault.

## Objectives

After completing this chapter, you will be able to:

- Explain Requirements for Vault Thin Client.
- Configure the Browser settings.
- Sign In and Out of Thin Client.
- Navigate the folders and files in the Thin Client.
- Search Files and Items using the Thin Client.
- Configure view display settings.
- Print using the Thin Client.
- Access and identify the panes in the File Details page for a selected file.
- Navigate between the History, Uses, and Where Used pages for a selected file.
- Preview a selected file.
- Access the Actions menu to download files from the vault.
- Access the Item Master list in the Thin Client.
- Access and identify the panes in the Item Details page for a selected item.
- Navigate between the Bill of Materials, History, Where Used, and Attachments pages for a selected item.
- Preview a selected item.

# Lesson: Getting started with the Thin Client

## Overview

In this Lesson you will review the requirements for Vault Thin Client on various browsers and learn how to sign in and out of the vault using the web-browser interface. Once in the Thin Client, you will navigate the vault, locate files using search tools, configure view displays, and preview and print files.

### Objectives

After completing this lesson, you will be able to:

- Explain Requirements for Vault Thin Client.
- Configure the Browser settings.
- Sign In and Out of Thin Client.
- Navigate the folders and files in the Thin Client.
- Search Files and Items using the Thin Client.
- Configure view display settings.
- Print using the Thin Client.

### Requirements

 Vault Workgroup requires a Vault Office license to use the Thin Client. Vault Professional provides read-only access through the Thin Client by default. A Vault Office license is required for read/write access.

The Autodesk Vault Thin Client is supported by the following web browsers.

- Internet Explorer
- Google Chrome

In addition, the Vault Thin Client supports DWF viewing across all browsers with the Autodesk Design Review (ADR) plug-in. If the browser does not have the ADR plug-in installed, the DWF is downloaded instead.

# Configure the Browser settings

There are four Web browser settings that affect the Thin Client.

- Cookies
- Scripts
- ActiveX controls (for Internet Explorer only)
- Pop-up windows

# Internet Explorer

### Allow cookies

1. In Internet Explorer, click Tools>Internet Options.
2. In the Internet Options dialog box click the Privacy tab.
3. Move the slider to select the setting that allows cookies. The Medium setting is acceptable because it restricts first-party cookies, without completely blocking them.

### Enable ActiveX controls

1. In Internet Explorer, click Tools>Internet Options.
2. On the Internet Options dialog box, click the Security tab.
3. On the ActiveX control settings, select Enable.
4. If Autodesk Design Review has been installed but you still cannot view DWF files, ensure that Run ActiveX control and plug-ins is enabled by selecting Enable on the Run ActiveX control and plug-ins setting.

### Allow any Web site to run scripts and ActiveX controls on your computer

1. In Internet Explorer, click the Tools>Internet Options.
2. Click the Advanced tab and then in the Settings list, scroll to the Security section.
3. Select the Allow active content to run in files on My Computer checkbox, and then click OK.

### Allow pop-up windows

Pop-up windows must be enabled for the Thin Client to work correctly.

1. In Internet Explorer, click Tools>Internet Options.
2. On the Internet Options dialog box click the Privacy tab.
3. Clear the option that allows Pop-up Blockers.

# Google Chrome

### Allow cookies

1.  In Chrome, click Customize and Control Google Chrome>Settings.
2.  In the Google Chrome Settings dialog box, click Show advanced settings.
3.  In the Privacy section, click  Content settings.
4.  In the Cookies section, select Allow sites to save and read cookie data (recommended).

### Allow pop-up windows

Pop-up windows must be enabled for the Thin Client to work correctly.

1.  In Chrome, click Customize and control Google Chrome>Settings.
2.  In the Google Chrome Settings dialog box, click Show advanced settings.
3.  In the Privacy and security section, click Content settings.
4.  In the Popups section, enable Allowed to show pop-ups. Customize permissions for specific websites in the Block and Allow sections.

# Log In and Log Out

### Log In

You must log in using a unique user name and password assigned by the administrator. If an account has not been set up for you, contact your administrator. To login:

1.  In the browser address field, enter the URL for the Thin Client application. For example, **http://[servername]/AutodeskTC**, where server name is either the IP address or the name of the computer hosting the Autodesk Data Management Server (For this class it is '**localhost**').

2.  On the Sign in page, specify the type of account with which to sign in. From the Authentication drop-down, select:
-   Vault Account to log in with an Autodesk Data Management Server account.
-   Windows Account if your server is configured to use Active Directory.

3.  On the Sign In page, enter the user name and password for the Autodesk Data Management Server account assigned to you by your system administrator (For this class use Administrator as user name and password is empty).

4.  In the Server box, enter the name of the server (**localhost**) to which to connect.

5.  In the Vault box, enter the name of the database that you want to connect to, or click Browse and then select the vault from the Vaults dialog box, and then click OK.

6.  By default, you are restricted to read-only access to files in the vault. Clear the Read Only Access checkbox to check in non-CAD files using the Vault Office license.

 A Vault Office license is required for read/write access through the Thin Client.

7.  Click Sign In.

8.  The Welcome page displays at the top of the browser to review information about the Thin Client. Click Close at the top right-hand side of the Thin Client to close the Welcome page banner. This can be opened again by selecting Help at the top of the window.

### Log Out

1.  To Sign Out of the session with the current server, click Sign Out, in the Account menu. You are logged out of the current vault server and returned to the Log In page.

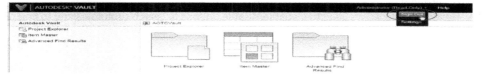

# File Navigation

Once logged into the Thin Client there are two main panes displayed in the browser. The left-hand side of the Browser is a Menu of three options that enable you to activate the Project Explorer, Item Master, and the results from a previously-executed advanced find. The pane on the right-hand side is the Files List page, which displays the vault data based on the option chosen on the left.

To navigate and display files in the Vault, select Project Explorer. The Files List page updates to display all the data at the top most level of the vault. Files in this folder or subfolder display in the file list. If no files are contained in a selected folder, a message indicating that there are no files to show displays in the file list. Consider the following to further navigate and select files:

-   Select folders on the Files List page to navigate through the vault database.

-   Select files on the Files List page to access the Files Details page. More information on this is covered in the next lesson.

-   Use the breadcrumb trail above the files list to show the path or select previous folders in the trail to navigate backwards in the vault.

### Paging

The Thin Client displays objects using paging. A certain number of objects are initially displayed. If you scroll to the bottom of the page and there are more objects to display, additional objects are automatically loaded. Each time you reach the bottom of a page, the next batch of objects are loaded until everything displays. By default, the number of objects loaded each time is 200. You can change paging options in the Administration dialog in the Autodesk Data Management Server console.

# Searching

You can search for files and items in Autodesk Vault Professional using the Thin Client.

### Basic Search

Basic search only finds objects in the current context. If you are in Project Explorer, a basic search locates only files in the current folder and, optionally, subfolders. If you are in Item Master, a basic search locates only items. To conduct a Basic Search:

1. Enter search criteria in the Search text box. The search string can contain letters, numbers, or a combination of both.

2. Press Enter or click Search. The items or files matching the search criteria display on the Search Results page.

- Hover the cursor over Search to enable/disable options to search subfolders and to find the latest version. Clear either of these options before searching, if required.

### Advanced Search

Use Advanced Find to create more complicated searches with multiple criteria.

1. Expand the Search option and click Advanced Find.

2. At the top of the Advanced Find dialog box, select the search context type in the Look In area. The default context is the one in which you are currently working. Select from the following options:

- Vault: look for files and items (if available)
- Project Explorer: look for files only
- Item Master: look for items only (if available)

3. The search criteria consists of a property, a condition, and a value. Specify the search criteria by selecting or typing in each of these fields.

4.  Click the green '+' (Plus) button to add the criteria. Once added, a new entry line is added to further refine the criteria. To remove a defined criteria hover the cursor over the entry and select the red X button to delete it.

5.  Click Search.

6.  The objects matching the search criteria display on the Search Results page. You can also perform a basic search on the results on this page.

The last search results that were reported using an Advanced Find always remain listed in the Advanced Find page until another Advanced Find is conducted. To return to this page, select Advanced Find in the Autodesk Vault menu on the left-hand side of the Thin Client interface.

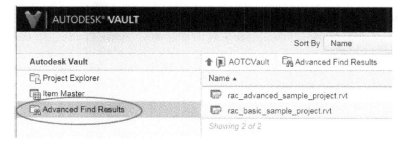

## Search File Content

The content of files can be searched by changing the search settings on the Thin Client Options page.

 Autodesk Data Management Server (ADMS) Content Indexing Service must be enabled in the ADMS Console. See the ADMS Console help for more information.

The Active Content Search feature is disabled by default. This is strictly an administrator controlled setting. Non-administrators cannot access this setting. If an administrator enables content searches (and the server is indexing content), then all user searches include content when searching. To enable:

1.  Go to the account menu>Settings.

2.  In the Search Settings section, toggle on Search file content.

3.  Click Done.

# Customizing the Thin Client View

Users can customize how data is viewed in the Thin Client. This can be done by changing the layout, specifying the sort order, and/or configuring which properties display.

## View Layout

There are three different views for displaying content in the Thin Client. The options are located at the top of the Thin Client interface as shown below. The options include:

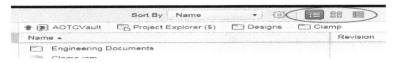

- **Grid:** Displays the content in a table layout with column headers.
- **Tile:** Displays the content as large thumbnails.
- **Planks:** Displays the content as large thumbnails with properties alongside.

Once a layout is selected it remains active until it is changed, regardless of being signed out or not.

## Sort

You can sort the contents of any view in ascending or descending order, based on any property configured for that view. Use any of the following to sort content in a view:

- Click a column heading to sort by that property. As an alternative, in the Sort by drop-down list, select the property by which to sort.
- Click the column heading to switch between ascending and descending sort order. Using the Sort drop-down list, select the same property a second time to switch between ascending and descending order.

 When in the Tile and Plank view the configured properties and their headers are not displayed so you must use the Sort By drop-down list to sort.

## Filter BOM View

You can filter whether ON rows or OFF rows only show in the BOM view. In addition, you can specify whether the BOM view displays non-released items.

 Your administrator must grant you permission to see both ON and OFF rows and non-released items for the filter to permit these controls.

1. Select an item and click any BOM view.
2. Click Filter to restrict which types of items display in the BOM.
3. Toggle the settings on or off for each filter option.
4. Click Apply to save your changes.

## Toggle Item History View

If the administrator has enabled you to see all versions of an item, you can toggle between all versions and only the latest version of an item by clicking Toggle All Versions in the History view.

## Configure Properties

A user can configure which properties to display in a view in the Thin Client. This is done using the Configure Properties dialog box.

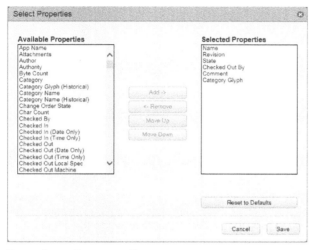

To configure the properties:

1. Click Configure Properties in the view you want to configure.

2. In the Available Properties list, select the properties you want to display and then click Add to move them to the list on the right side. In the Selected Properties list, select the properties you want removed and then click Remove.

3. Select a property and then click Move Up or Move Down to adjust its display order.

 Press <Ctrl> or <Shift> to select multiple properties.

4. Click Save.

Each view can have a unique property configuration. To return to the default set of properties originally chosen by the administrator, click Reset to Defaults and click Save.

# Thin Client Administrator Settings

The Administrator can customize the look-and-feel of the Thin Client, as well as some of the behaviors. The Settings are available once the Administrator has signed in via the Account menu.

The Settings window enables you to customize the following:

- Page Layout
- Search Settings
- File and Item Display Settings
- File Download
- Default Properties

## Page Layout

The banner displayed at the top of the Thin Client can be customized to show your company logo. Click Upload to use the Open dialog box to locate and assign an image to use as a banner. The banner area is 250x30 pixels. Images are resized as required. Click Reset to return to the original Autodesk banner.

## Search Settings

By default, only file properties are examined when searching files. You can perform a more thorough search by also including file contents in the search. To enable this type of search, select Search file content.

### Search Settings

Specify options for performing searches

☐ Search file content

## File and Item Display Settings

You can modify which files and items display on the page.

- Select the Released items checkbox to display only the items that are released. Clear the checkbox to show all items.
- Select Latest Version to display only the latest versions of items. If this checkbox is unselected, all versions of items and item data display.
- Select Released file versions to show only released files. Clear to show all files.

> Since the Uses and Where Used tabs show entire assemblies, any files that are unreleased display as non-linked text.

## File Download

The File Download area enables you to toggle if files with visualization attachments can be downloaded or not. If this option is enabled only the visualization file can be downloaded from the vault, an associated CAD model cannot be. If cleared, the visualization file and the CAD model can both be downloaded.

**File Download**

Customize the download behaviors

☑ Restrict download of file with visualization attachment

## Default Properties

The administrator can enforce the default properties and prevent users from configuring views. To ensure enforcement of the property display settings once set, select Enforce default properties at the top of the Default Properties area. Once set, Configure Properties at the top of each view in the Thin Client will not be visible to users.

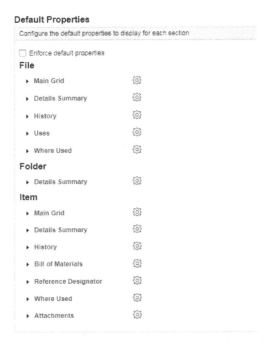

To review the default properties that are assigned for each view (File, Folder or Item), expand a view to see which properties display. If required, this list can be modified similar to how users configure views in the Thin Client. To configure the default properties for each view:

1.  Click Configure Properties for the view (File, Folder or Item), you want to configure.

2.  In the Available Properties list, select the properties you want to display and then click Add to move them to the list on the right side. In the Selected Properties list, select the properties you want removed and then click Remove.

3.  Select a property and then click Move Up or Move Down to adjust display order.

4.  Click Save Defaults.

To return to the default set of properties originally chosen by the administrator, click Reset to Defaults and click Save.

# Printing

## Print Pages

Use the browser print feature to print pages from the Thin Client.

## Print Tabs

A Print button is available on the History, Uses, Where Used, and Bill of Materials tabs in the Thin Client. Click Print to create a printer-friendly preview of the tab. You can toggle Row Numbers to include or omit row numbers in the printout. If printing items, select BOM Levels to include the BOM levels in the printout. Click Print on the preview page to print.

# Exercise: Get started with the Thin Client

In this exercise you will ensure the browser settings for the Thin Client are correctly set, Sign into the Vault using the Thin Client, navigate the vault, change the layout and configuration of the properties displayed in a view, and search the vault.

1. Open a browser to access the Autodesk Vault Thin Client.

2. Ensure the specific browser configurations for cookies, scripts, ActiveX controls, and pop-up windows are set as explained at the beginning of Lesson 1.

3. Type in the URL to access the Thin Client Login page (**http://localhost/AutodeskTC**) for this class)

4. Set the Authentication to Vault Account, enter your user name (**Administrator**), password (empty) and enter the correct server (**localhost**) and database (**AOTCVault**).

5. Click Sign In.

6. Select the Project Explorer on the left-hand side on the Thin Client page.

7. In the Project Explorer's File list page, navigate to the Designs>TrailerHitch folder. Note that there are no files displayed in the folder. This is because the Setting for the Thin Client is by default set to only show Released Items and Files. Currently there are no Released Items or Files in this folder.

**8.** Expand the Login drop-down list and select Settings.

**9.** In the Thin Client Options window, scroll to the File and Item Display Settings area and clear the checkbox adjacent to the Released items and Released file versions options.

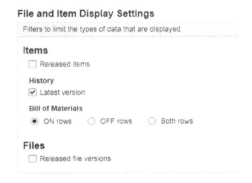

**10.** Click Done to close the window. Note how all the files are now displayed in the view in the Thin Client.

**11.** In the header above the list of files, Grid is the default view option. Select the other view options to change the display to Tile and Planks. Return the view to Grid.

**12.** In the Sort By drop-down list, select one of the Properties to sort by. Return the sort by Name.

**13.** Select the arrow beside the Name property header to change the sort order for the names.

**14.** Select Configure Properties.

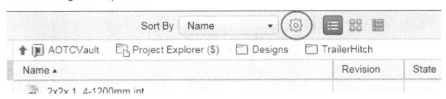

**15.** Select the Category Glyph in the Selected Properties pane and select Move Up till it is listed after the name property.

---

**16.** Select Created By in the Available Properties pane and then select Add to move it to the Selected Properties pane. Move it before the Comment property.

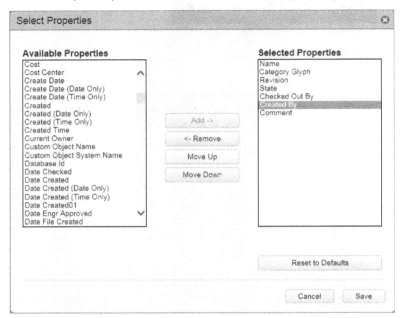

**17.** Select Save. Note that the display for the current folder has changed. Switch to other folders and note that the properties displayed are consistent.

 Using the Settings option, default properties can be set for each view in the Thin Client. For example the Main Grid, Details Summary, History views for files and items. These settings can also be enforced so users can't change them.

**18.** Select Configure Properties. Select Reset to Defaults to return to the default property display. Click Save.

**19.** Navigate up to the Project Explorer.

**20.** In the Basic Find field enter **ICU\*** and press Enter. The results of the search are returned in the Grid display.

**21.** Expand the Search option and click Advanced Find.

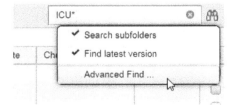

**22.** At the top of the Advanced Find dialog box, ensure that the Project Explorer is the context type that is selected for searching.

**23.** In the search criteria field expand the property list and select Created By, select Equals as the condition, and enter **usera** as the value.

**24.** Click the green '+' Plus button to add another criteria.

**25.** In the search criteria field expand the property list and select Checked Out By, select Contains as the condition, and enter **Administrator** as the value.

**26.** Click Search. The files matching the search criteria display on the Search Results page. Modify the search if this doesn't return any files that are checked out.

**27.** Return to the Project Explorer to clear the Search Results from display.

**28.** In the left-hand pane in the Thin Client select Advanced Find Results to return to the previously executed search results. Note that the search results are still visible.

# Lesson:  Working with Files

## Overview

This lesson covers how to view details of the files in the Vault using Thin Client. You will learn how to access the File Details page and how the panes on this page can be used to get information on the active file. This includes viewing its system and user-defined properties, file History, Uses, and Where Used information. Additionally you will learn to preview the file and access the options on the Action menu.

### Objectives

After completing this lesson, you will be able to:

- Access and identify the panes in the File Details page for a selected file.
- Navigate between the History, Uses, and Where Used pages for a selected file.
- Preview a selected file.
- Access the Actions menu to download files from the vault.

# Viewing File Details

From the Files list page, click the filename to view detailed information about the selected file on the File Details page.

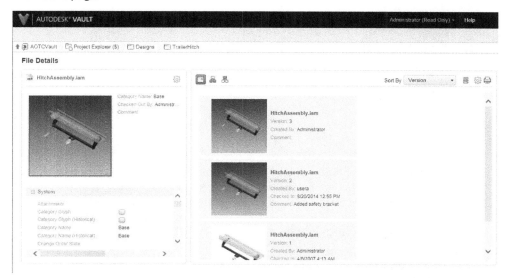

The File Details page displays a summary of the file, the full set of system and user-defined properties, as well as the history, uses, and where used data for the selected file. The properties displayed in file summary, the History tab, the Uses tab, and the Where Used tab can be configured independently of each other using Configure Properties in each of their respective panes.

## The Details Pane

The Details pane on the left side of the File Details page displays a thumbnail of the current file (if available) as well as selected properties.

- Hover the cursor over the thumbnail image and click Preview (bottom left corner) to view a large preview image of the file.
- If the file is a CAD file with an associated DWF, the file opens in a new browser window and provides access to Autodesk Design Review functionality in the browser.
- When there is no attachment, a File Download dialog box displays and prompts you to open or save the file. If you choose Open, it is opened with the associated application.

Below the summary is the complete list of system and user-defined properties.

- Scroll down or across to review all the properties in the summary pane.
- Click the +/- icons in the System and User-Defined property headers lists to expand or collapse the respective properties.

 On the History, Uses, and Where Used tabs, clicking a file or version to view updates the Details pane with the selected files details.

Further details on the file are available using the History, Uses, and Where Used tabs that display in the right-hand pane on the File Details page.

### History Tab

The History tab displays the file version history list. The following can be done in the History tab:

- Select a property from the Sort By drop-down to change the sort order of the file versions. You can sort by any of the properties displayed in the History tab.
- Click Configure Properties to select which properties display in the History tab.
- By default, only the latest version of the file displays. Click Show All Versions to display a complete list of all revisions and versions for the file.
- Select Print to print the tab.

### Uses Tab

The Uses tab enables you to view files that the current file uses. The following can be done in the Uses tab:

- Select a property from the Sort By drop-down to change the sort order of the files. You can sort by any of the properties displayed in the Uses tab
- Click Configure Properties to select which properties display in the Uses tab.
- Select Print to print the tab.

### Where Used Tab

The Where Used tab enables you to view a list of files that use the current file. If the file is not used in any other file the "There are no items to show in this view" message displays. The following can be done in the Where Used tab:

- Select a property from the Sort By drop-down to change the sort order of the files. You can sort by any of the properties displayed in the Where Used tab
- Click Configure Properties to select which properties display in the Where Used tab.
- Select Print to print the tab.

# File Actions

In the File Details page you can interact with the file by hovering the cursor over the thumbnail image and using either the Preview or Action options that display at the bottom of the image.

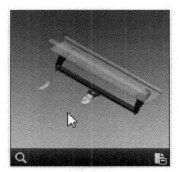

## Action Menu

Depending on the type of file that is active in the File Details page and whether you are signed in with read/write access (Vault Office license), the Action menu options vary. With Read-only access the Thin Client enables you to download files (visualization files or the CAD model). Select the download option and use the Opening dialog box to decide whether to open the file in the source CAD file or download locally.

 A Vault Office license is required for read/write access through the Thin Client. With this type of license the additional Action command are available for checking in or out, adding files to the vault, and updating visualization files.

## Preview

Selecting Preview enables you to preview a larger image of the file if a DWF visualization file exists. Use the tools on the toolbar and ViewCube to navigate and review the file. Additional tools are available in the tabs along the top of the window (Home, Markup & Measure, Tools, and Resources) that provide Design Review functionality to the Browser to markup the file.

> If no DWF file exists for the selected file the thumbnail image opens in a new window. Close the window to return to the Thin Client.

# Exercise: Working with Files

In this exercise you will navigate through the file structure to locate a file. Once located you will access the File Details page and view the details of the file using the History, Uses, and Where Used views. You will also open the DWF preview of the file.

**1.** In the Project Explorer navigate to the Designs>TrailerHitch folder or conduct a search for Hitch.

**2.** In the Files List, click the *HitchAssembly.iam* filename to view the detailed information about the file on the File Details page.

**3.** The Thumbnail for the selected file displays in the left-hand pane of the File Details page.

**4.** Below the thumbnail is the detailed summary of the System and User-Defined properties. Scroll through the list to review the details.

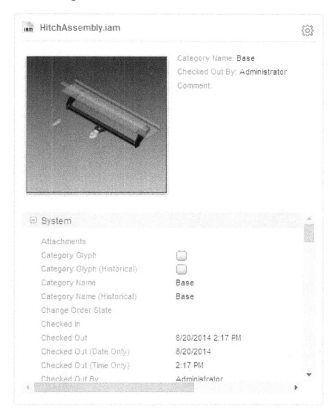

**5.** In the right-hand pane the History tab displays by default.

**6.** In the header of the History tab, select Toggle all versions to show all three versions of the file.

**7.** Select the Uses tab to display all the files that are used in the HitchAssembly.iam file. Scroll through the list.

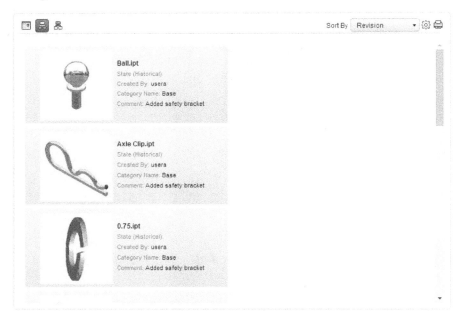

**8.** Select Axle Clip.ipt thumbnail in the Uses tab. The thumbnail and summary details update to show the new part. This is now the active file listed on the File Details page.

**9.**   Select the Where Used tab to display where the Axle Clip is used. This part is only used in the HitchAssembly.

**10.**   Select the HitchAssembly thumbnail in the Where Used tab to make it the active file. Note that the Where Used tab now displays a message that "There are no items to show in this view". This is because the top-level assembly is not used in any other files.

**11.**   In the Details pane, hover the cursor over the HitchAssembly thumbnail to activate the Actions that can be done on the file. Two buttons displays at the bottom of the thumbnail.

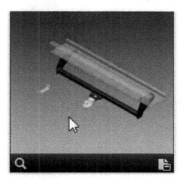

**12.**   Select Actions on the bottom right. The available commands enable you to download the file or the visualization. The options available in this menu depend on if a DWF file exists. Clear this selection. No files will be downloaded.

 A Vault Office license is required for read/write access through the Thin Client. The options in the Action menu will enable write access if a Vault Office license is available.

**13.** Hover over the thumbnail again and select Preview on the bottom left of the thumbnail. This opens a DWF of the file into the Browser viewer.

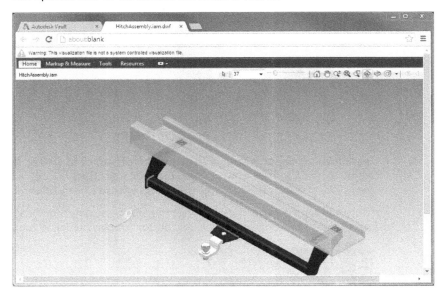

**14.** Using the toolbar and the ViewCube navigate the assembly to review it.

**15.** Select the Home option to return the model to its default orientation.

**16.** Select the Markup & Measure tab in the Browser. If this tab is not available review the browser settings discussed in Lesson 1 or try using another browser.

**17.** In the Callouts panel, select Rectangle Callout. In the model, select the component that is located away from the main assembly. Drag the callout box away from the component and select again to place it.

**18.** Enter **Please Review** in the text box to add this markup to the file.

**19.** Select the text and using the font options in the Markup & Measure tab, change the size of the font and bold setting. Press Enter.

**20.** On the Markup & Measure tab, select Length to add a measurement. Select the overall length by selecting two vertices on parallel edges at the extent of the model. Select to place the dimension. Change the font for the measurement, if required.

**21.** Add a second Rectangular Markup that indicates that the FrameRail component needs to be enlarged to 1700mm.

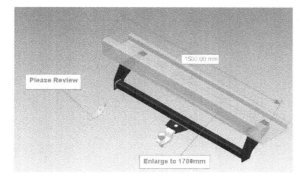

**22.** Select the Home tab.

**23.** Select Save As to save a local copy of the marked up DWF file to share in your design team.

 A Vault Office license is required for read/write access through the Thin Client. With this license the markup could be added back to Vault.

**24.** Close the DWF Preview and return to the Thin Client window.

# Lesson: Working with Items

## Overview

This lesson covers how to view the details of items in the Vault using the Thin Client. You will learn how to access the Item Master list and the Item Details page for a selected item. Similar to working with files, you will learn how the panes on the Item Details page can be used to get information on the active item. This includes viewing its system and user-defined properties, Bill of Materials, file History, Where Used, and Attachment information. Additionally you will learn to preview the item.

### Objectives

After completing this lesson, you will be able to:

- Access the Item Master list in the Thin Client.
- Access and identify the panes in the Item Details page for a selected item.
- Navigate between the Bill of Materials, History, Where Used, and Attachments pages for a selected item.
- Preview a selected item.

# Viewing Item Details

The Item Master displays the items that have been setup in the vault. Items refer to what a company manages, assembles, sells, and manufactures. An item is identified by its item number or part number. Items typically represent:

- Parts
- Assemblies
- Consumable goods such as fluids, lubricants, and artwork
- Bills of Materials

 The Items feature is available only in the Autodesk Vault Professional edition.

To display the list of items in the vault, select Item Master in the menu on the left-hand side of the browser. All items display in the Item List.

Similar to files, you can use the toolbar along the top of the browser to do any of the following:

- Change the view layout using the Grid, Tile, and Planks buttons.
- Sort the contents of Item Master view. You can sort in ascending or descending order based on any property configured by selecting the column headers or using the Sort By drop-down list
- Configure which properties to display in the Item Master view. This is done using the Configure Properties dialog box in the same way as done when configuring views for files.

## Item Details

Click an item to view detailed information about the item on the Item Details page.

The Item Details page displays a summary of the item, the full set of system and user-defined properties, as well as the Bill of Materials, history, where used data, and attachments for the item. The properties displayed in the views can be configured independently of each other.

## The Details Pane

The Details pane on the left side of the Item Details page displays a thumbnail of the current item (if available) as well as selected properties.

- Hover the cursor over the thumbnail image and click Preview (bottom left corner) to view a large preview image of the file.

Below the summary is the complete list of system and user-defined properties.

- Scroll down or across to review all the properties in the summary pane.
- Click the +/- icons in System and User-Defined property headers lists to expand or collapse the respective properties.

Further details on the file are available using the Bill of Materials, History, Where Used, and Attachment tabs that are displayed in the right-hand pane on the File Details page.

## Bill of Materials Tab

The Bill of Materials (BOM) tab enables you to view the Bill of Materials for the current item. There are three views available in the drop-down list:

- Multi-Level (default) expands or collapses the structure to show nested parts and assemblies.
- First-Level displays the first level of the BOM structure.
- Parts-Only displays the item total part count, but does not display intermediate subassemblies.
- Reference Designator individually displays only AutoCAD Electrical items and their reference designator properties.

The following can be done in the Bill of Materials tab:

- Select a property from the Sort By drop-down to change the sort order. You can sort by any of the properties displayed in the History tab.
- Click Configure Properties to select which properties display in the Bill of Materials tab.
- Select Print to print the tab.

### History Tab 🖳

The History tab displays the revision history of the item. The following can be done in the History tab:

- Select a property from the Sort By drop-down to change the sort order. You can sort by any of the properties displayed in the History tab.
- Click Configure Properties to select which properties display in the History tab.
- Select Print to print the tab.

### Where Used Tab 🖧

The Where Used tab enables you to view a list of items that use the current file. If the file is not used in any other file the "There are no items to show in this view" message displays. The following can be done in the Where Used tab:

- Select a property from the Sort By drop-down to change the sort order. You can sort by any of the properties displayed in the History tab.
- Click Configure Properties to select which properties display in the History tab.
- Select Print to print the tab.

### Attachments Tab 📎

The Attachments tab enables you to view the files attached to the current item. Select the attachment in this view to view further details. The following can be done in the Attachments tab:

- Select a property from the Sort By drop-down to change the sort order. You can sort by any of the properties displayed in the History tab.
- Click Configure Properties to select which properties display in the History tab.
- Select Print to print the tab.

## File Actions

### Preview 🔍

In the Item Details page you can interact with the file by hovering over the thumbnail image and using the Preview option that display at the bottom of the image. Selecting Preview enables you to preview the thumbnail image for the item in a new window. Close the window to return to the Thin Client.

# Exercise: Working with Items

In this exercise you will activate the Item Master view and review the information and tabs (Bill of Materials, file History, Where Used, and Attachment) available on the Item Details page for a selected item.

1. To display the list of items in the vault, select Item Master in the menu on the left-hand side of the Thin Client browser. All items that exist in the vault display in the Item List.

> If no items are listed in the Item Master check the Settings for the Thin Client and ensure that Released Items option in the File and Item Display Settings area is cleared.

2. In the header above the list of items, Grid is the default view option. Select the other view options to change the display to Tile and Planks. Return the view to Grid.

3. In the Sort By drop-down list select one of the Properties to sort by. Return the sort by Name.

4. Select the arrow beside the Name property header to change the sort order for the items.

5. Select Configure Properties and configure the properties that display in the default view.

6. Select Save. Note that the display for the Item Master view has changed.

7. Select Configure Properties. Select Reset to Defaults to return to the default property display. Click Save.

8. With the Item Master view still active use the Basic Find field to search on Work in Progress items. The results of the search are returned in the Grid display showing only those items identified in this view as Work in Progress. If no files have been assigned this State, search the Item List another way.

9. Select the X in the Basic Find field to clear the filtering of the list.

10. Select the 100038 item (HitchAssembly.iam) to open the Item Details page.

11. Hover the cursor over the Thumbnail in the left-hand pane. Note that only the Preview option is available for this option. Select it. It opens an independent window of the thumbnail. Close it.

12. Review the summary of the System and User-Defined properties in the left-hand pane.

13. By default the History tab is active. Note the history of this item.

14. Select the default option for the Bill of Materials tab (Multi-level) to display the Bill of Materials for this item.

15. Note how the Configure Properties, Sorting, and Printing buttons are the same as those available for options in the File Details page.

# Chapter Summary

With Autodesk Vault Thin Client users can access vault data using a convenient Web-browser interface. This enables users without a Vault Professional client installation to view and print data from all over the world, to review or present it in a professional way.

With Autodesk Vault Professional you are able to handle files and items.

Having completed this chapter, you can:

- Explain Requirements for Vault Thin Client.
- Configure the Browser settings.
- Sign In and Out of Thin Client.
- Navigating the folders and files in the Thin Client.
- Search Files and Items using the Thin Client.
- Configure view display settings.
- Print using the Thin Client.
- Access and identify the panes in the File Details page for a selected file.
- Navigate between the History, Uses, and Where Used pages for a selected file.
- Preview a selected file.
- Access the Actions menu to download files from the vault.
- Access the Item Master list in the Thin Client.
- Access and identify the panes in the Item Details page for a selected item.
- Navigate between the Bill of Materials, History, Where Used, and Attachments pages for a selected item.
- Preview a selected item.

# Working with Active Directory, Project Sync and Replication

There are several options to configure and manage your Autodesk® Vault for your needs. User and Group, and security options make Autodesk Vault highly flexible. The Project Sync feature provides file and folder synchronization between the Autodesk® Vault software and Autodesk® Buzzsaw® products. This capability enables Autodesk Vault users to automatically synchronize files from a folder in Autodesk Vault software with a folder in Autodesk Buzzsaw. The Autodesk Vault Professional software has multiple replication solutions available to suit your organization's needs, such as: the ADMS file store replication (multi-site, single workgroup configuration) for file store replication only, Full replication (connected workgroups configuration) for both file store and SQL database replication, and Autodesk Vault File Server (AVFS), an alternative file store replication solution. This chapter introduces these replication solutions and their associated components and configuration procedures.

## Objectives

After completing this chapter, you will be able to:

- Manage User accounts regarding the Active Directory.
- Manage Groups in Autodesk Vault.
- Administrate the Project Sync utility.
- Differentiate between an ADMS File Store Replication and a Full Replication.
- Enable and Disable Workgroup Replication.
- Add and Delete Workgroups.
- Enable and Disable a Vault for a Multi-Site Environment.
- Replicate a Vault, Files and Folders.
- Export, Import and Configure Replication Priorities.
- Schedule Replication for a Multi-Site Environment.
- Describe benefits of Autodesk Vault File Server (AVFS).

# Lesson: Active Directory

## Overview

An administrator can create a vault server account with credentials unique to the vault server or import a Windows Active Directory account. By using an Active Directory account, users can log into Autodesk data management clients using their Windows account credentials. Users and groups can then be managed using Windows permissions.

### Objectives

After completing this lesson, you will be able to:

- Understand the advantages of Active Directory
- Manage user accounts

# Managing Groups

Individual users have roles and permissions assigned to them that define what actions they can take and to which vaults they have access. You can create groups of users and assign roles and permissions to the group. As a member of a group, a user has all the permissions and roles assigned to the group. By default, every new user is added to a group called **Everyone**. The Everyone group is only available on an Access Control Lists. It does not display in the Groups dialog box. If the Everyone group is granted membership to a folder, all new users have access to that folder

Groups can be comprised of users or other groups. Groups can be disabled, toggling off all permissions assigned to the group. The permissions and roles assigned to a group are independent of individual user roles and permissions. Groups can also be restricted to specific folders in a vault, so you can keep projects and other data secure between groups.

By assigning users to groups and then granting folder membership to those groups, you can easily manage users and their access to vault folders. This is the best practice for creating a vault security model.

 Folder membership is only available with the vault server that is installed with Autodesk Vault.

## Manage Groups

You must be assigned the role of Administrator to perform this operation.

1. Select Tools>Administration>Global Settings.
2. In the Global Settings dialog, select the Security tab
3. Click Groups.
4. In the Group Management dialog box, you can list groups three different ways:
- Select View>List to view the groups in a flat list.
- Select View>By Vault to view the groups as a list grouped by the vaults to which they are assigned.
- Select View>By Role to view the groups as a list grouped by roles.

## Create a Group

1. Click New Group.
2. In the Group dialog box, specify the group settings, and then click OK.

## Edit an Existing Group

1. Select a group from the list.
2. Click Actions>Edit.
3. In the Group dialog box, specify the group settings, and then click OK.

# Import an Active Directory domain user account

 The Active Directory feature is only available with Autodesk Vault Professional and you must be assigned the role of Administrator to perform this operation.

Domain user accounts and domain user groups can be imported to the Autodesk vault server. This enables accounts to be created using Active Directory information and enables users to log into a data management client without requiring a new account. If a user account or group already exists on the server, it can be promoted to an Active Directory account or group. Likewise, an account or group created by importing an Active Directory account can be disconnected or demoted from the Active Directory domain, making the account or group unique to the server.

You cannot manage Active Directory accounts through the server console. You can only import Active Directory accounts, promote server accounts to the Active Directory accounts, or demote Active Directory accounts to standard server user accounts. To manage Active Directory user accounts and Active Directory group membership, you must use the User Accounts controls in the Windows Control Panel.

### Import User

1. Select Tools>Administration>Global Settings.
2. In the Global Settings dialog box, select the Security tab.
3. Click Users.

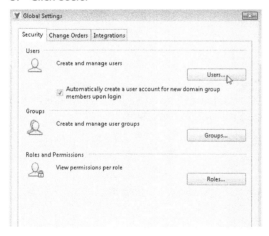

4. In the User Management dialog box, you can list user accounts three different ways:
- Select View>List to view the user profiles in a flat list.
- Select View>By Vault to view the user profiles as a list grouped by the vaults to which they are assigned.
- Select View>By Role to view the user profiles as a list grouped by roles.

5.  In the User Management dialog box, select Actions>Import Domain User.

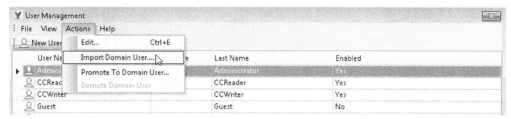

6.  In the Select User dialog box, click Locations to specify the domain containing the Active Directory accounts to import. In the Locations dialog, select the domain to use and then click OK.

7.  In the Select User dialog, enter the names of the users to add from the Active Directory domain or click Advanced to search for the users.

8.  Once the uses accounts have been specified click OK in the Select Users dialog box. The selected Active Directory domain user accounts are added to the User Management list.

Vault server user accounts imported from an Active Directory domain use the first name, last name, user name, e-mail address, and password associated with the Active directory account and cannot be edited. The domain name displays in front of the user name. Changes made to the Active Directory user account are updated in the vault server user account automatically.

 Imported users are not automatically assigned to a group, role, or vault unless they are members of a linked Active Directory group.

# Promote a vault server account to an Active Directory domain account

A vault server user account can be promoted to an Active Directory account. Promoting a vault server account to an Active Directory account maps the vault server account to an existing Windows account. Promoting an account replaces the vault server account information with the selected Active Directory account information.

1.  In the User Management dialog box, select a vault server user account and then select Actions>Promote to Domain User.

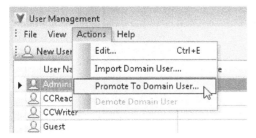

2.  In the Select Users dialog box, click Locations to specify the domain containing the Active Directory account to which the selected vault server account will be mapped. In the Locations dialog, select the domain to use and then click OK.

3. In the Select Users dialog box, enter the name of the Active Directory domain user to which the vault server account will be promoted or click Advanced to search for the user.

4. Once the user account has been specified, click OK in the Select Users dialog box. The vault server account information is replaced with the Active Directory account information and the properties in the vault database are updated with the new user name.

# Demote an Active Directory domain user account to a vault server user account

A vault server user account that was imported from an Active Directory account or promoted to an Active Directory account can be demoted, creating a vault server account. Once demoted, the account is unique to the vault server and no longer associated with the user's Active Directory account.

- In the User Management dialog box, select an Active Directory account and then select Actions>Demote Domain User. When the account is demoted, the domain name is removed from the user name. As a result, the demoted account might collide with an existing vault server account with the same name. If the vault server account name already exists, you are prompted to rename the demoted account.

The vault server account retains the vault server group membership and permissions but is no longer associated with the Active Directory account. The password for the demoted account is reset to be blank.

 Once an account has been demoted from the Active Directory, the associated user can no longer log into the vault server using Windows authentication.

# Import an Active Directory domain group

An administrator can create a group of users on the Autodesk vault server or Active Directory groups can be imported. Importing an Active Directory group imports all members of the group as well as sub-groups.

This enables accounts to be created using Active Directory information and enables users to log into a data management client without requiring a new account. If a user account or group already exists on the vault server, it can be promoted to an Active Directory account or group. Likewise, an account or group created by importing an Active Directory account can be disconnected or demoted from the Active Directory domain, making the account or group unique to the vault server.

### Import Group

1. In the Group Management dialog box, select Actions>Import Domain Group.

2. In the Select Groups dialog box, click Locations to specify the domain containing the Active Directory groups to import. In the Locations dialog, select the domain to use and then click OK.

 Only Security groups can be imported. Distribution groups cannot be imported.

3. In the Select Groups dialog box, enter the names of the groups to add from the Active Directory domain or click Advanced to search for the groups.

4. Once the groups have been specified, click OK in the Select Groups dialog box. The selected Active Directory domain groups are added to the Group Management list.

All members of the group as well as sub-groups are imported. Groups imported from an Active Directory domain retain the group name and e-mail address from Active Directory. The domain name displays in front of the group name.

 An imported domain group can be updated to reflect changes to the Active Directory group membership. For more information, see Update a Domain Group.

## Promote a vault server group to an Active Directory domain group

A vault server group can be promoted to a domain group. Promoting a vault server group to an Active Directory group maps the vault server group to an existing domain group. Promoting a group replaces the vault server group information with the selected domain information.

1. In the Group Management dialog box, select a vault server group and then select Actions>Promote to Domain Group.

2. In the Select Groups dialog box, click Locations to specify the domain containing the Active Directory group to which the selected vault server group will be mapped. In the Locations dialog, select the domain to use and then click OK.

3. In the Select Groups dialog box, enter the name of the Active Directory domain group to which the vault server group will be promoted or click Advanced to search for the group.

4. Once the group has been specified, click OK in the Select Groups dialog box. The vault server group information is replaced with the domain group information.

All members of the selected domain group will be imported.

## Demote an Active Directory domain group to a vault server group

A vault server group that was imported from an Active Directory group or promoted to an Active Directory group can be demoted, creating a vault server group. Once demoted, the group is unique to the vault server and no longer associated with the domain group.

■ In the Group Management dialog box, select an Active Directory group and then select Actions>Demote Domain Group. When the group is demoted, the domain name is removed from the group name. As a result, the demoted group might collide with an existing vault server group with the same name. If the vault server group name already exists, you are prompted to rename the demoted group. The vault server group retains the vault server group membership and permissions but is no longer associated with the Active Directory group.

# Update a domain group

If members have been added or removed from the Active Directory domain group, the vault server group can be updated to reflect the changes to the group.

1. In the Group Management dialog box, select a group.

2. Select Actions>Update Domain Group.

 One advantage to using groups is when you are adding users to a vault or vaults. First, create a group and add members to the group. Once members have been added to the group, assign a vault to the group.

# Exercise: Create and Edit Groups

In this exercise you will manage your groups by creating and editing them in the Group Management dialog box. Add roles, databases and members to the groups.

### Create a new group in Vault

1. Click Tools>Administration>Global Settings.

2. Go to the Security tab and click Groups.

3. The Group Management dialog box opens. Click the command New Group to open the Group dialog box.

4. Specify a name for your new group and enter it in the Group Name field.

5. Enter an email-address to the Email field to add contact data to this group.

6. Now choose the Roles from the Roles button to add them to the group.

7. Same with the Vaults and Groups.

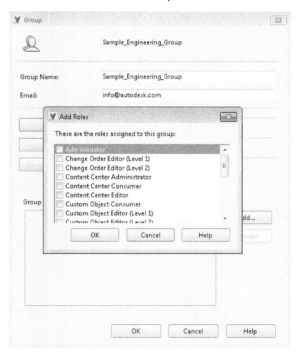

8. Finally add or remove Group Members to the group by clicking Add or Remove.

9. Confirm your settings with OK to save the new group in Vault.

### Edit the new group

1.  For editing an existing group, just select the group you want to edit and right click the cursor to open the context menu. You will find the Edit command on the top of context menu.

2.  Confirm your settings with OK to save the edited group in Vault.

# Exercise: Import User/Group via Active Directory

In this exercise you will import Users and Groups to use the Active Directory functionality in Vault.

## Import a User

1. Select Tools>Administration>Global Settings.
2. In the Global Settings dialog box, select the Security tab.
3. Click Users.

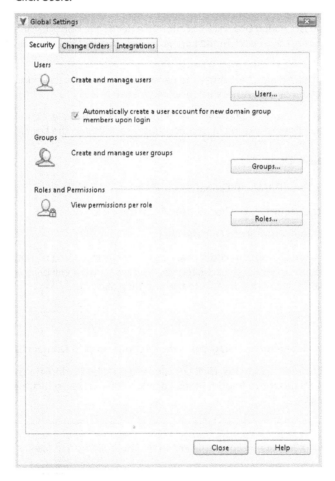

**4.**     In the User Management dialog box, select Actions>Import Domain User.

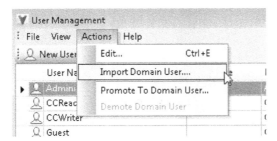

**5.**     In the Select Users dialog box, click Locations to specify the domain containing the Active Directory accounts to import. In the Locations dialog, select the domain to use and then click OK.

**6.**     In the Select Users dialog box, enter the names of the users to add from the Active Directory domain or click Advanced to search for the users.

**7.**     Once the users accounts have been specified, click OK in the Select Users dialog box. The selected Active Directory domain user accounts are added to the User Management list.

## Promote to a Domain User

**1.**     Select Tools>Administration>Global Settings.

**2.**     Then select the Security tab. Choose Users from the dialog box.

**3.**     Now click Actions>Promote to Domain User.

**4.**     In the Select Users dialog box, click Locations to specify the domain containing the Active Directory account to which the selected vault server account will be mapped. In the Locations dialog, select the domain to use and then click OK.

## Import a Group

**1.**     In the Group Management dialog box, select Actions>Import Domain Group.

**2.**     In the Select Groups dialog box, click Locations to specify the domain containing the Active Directory groups to import. In the Locations dialog box, select the domain to use and then click OK

 Only Security groups can be imported. Distribution groups cannot be imported.

**3.**     In the Select Groups dialog box, enter the names of the groups to add from the Active Directory domain or click Advanced to search for the groups.

**4.**     Once the groups have been specified, click OK in the Select Groups dialog box. The selected Active Directory domain groups are added to the Group Management list.

# Lesson: Project Sync

## Overview

The Project Sync feature provides file and folder synchronization between the Autodesk Vault and Autodesk Buzzsaw products. This capability enables Autodesk Vault users to automatically synchronize files from a folder in Autodesk Vault with a folder in Autodesk Buzzsaw. The synchronization works in both directions; files can be uploaded from Autodesk Vault to Autodesk Buzzsaw and vice versa, providing simple and reliable two-way communications between project team members.

### Objectives

After completing this lesson, you will be able to:

- Install Project Sync
- Configure the Project Sync utility.
- Understand the Project Sync settings.
- Understand the Project Sync commands.

# Configuration of the Project Sync Utility

The Project Sync utility can be configured to automatically perform synchronization in ways that best suit your needs. A synchronization can occur at a scheduled time each day, continuously, whenever a specified work event occurs, or on demand. For some, it might be required to synchronize each evening when the office is closed. For others, it might be required to set it such that when a user performs a change state on a file in Autodesk Vault, the file is automatically shared to Autodesk Buzzsaw and by all consumers.

Project Sync is installed from the Autodesk Vault Client installation media. In order to install and configure Project Sync, you must have the Autodesk Vault Professional software installed and must be a Vault Administrator. Since the Project Sync functionality depends on the Vault Job Processor to pull jobs from the Job Server queue, ensure that the Job Server is enabled. You must be an administrator in Vault to enable the Job Server.

To Install Project Sync:

1. Launch setup.exe for the Autodesk Vault Client.

2. Click Install.

3. Accept the License and Services Agreement.

4. Select Autodesk Vault Professional Project Sync on the Configure Installation screen.

5. Click Install.

After Project Sync is downloaded and installed, Autodesk Vault will have a Project Sync toolbar and a Project Sync Settings option in the Tools menu. The Settings dialog box enables the administrator to configure the site, username, project folder mapping, synchronization settings, and Proxy Settings.

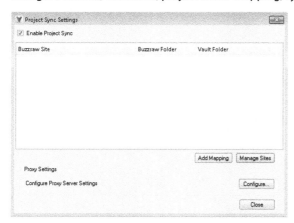

## Enable Project Sync

Enable and disable the Project Sync feature using this checkbox. This setting applies to the entire Autodesk Vault. When you enable it on your client, it is enabled for all users on the Vault.

## Site Configuration

Use Manage Sites to add, remove, and configure sites. You can also establish synchronization settings.

1.  Select Tools>Project Sync Settings to open the Project Sync Settings dialog box.

2.  Click Manage Sites on the Project Sync Settings dialog to open the Manage Sites dialog box.

3.  A list of sites displays. The list of sites can contain mapped and unmapped sites.

From here you can add, remove, and configure your sites.

-  Click Add Site to add a new site. Add the URL for the Autodesk Buzzsaw Site to which you are syncing. If you are using an Asia-Pacific Buzzsaw site, simply add the 'ap-' in the URL. The user name entered is the Buzzsaw user name and password, not the Vault user name and password. Each vault will use just one Buzzsaw username, so choose the Buzzsaw username and password carefully. The site, username, and password are all validated when you browse to the Buzzsaw folder for mapping.

 You can only create unique sites. The same site cannot be added twice.

4.  Click Define to configure your synchronization settings.

5.  Click OK.

6.  Click Edit on the right side of the site's row to make changes to the site. Click Delete on the right side of a site's row to delete that site. Deleting a site deletes all mappings for that site.

7.  Save your sites by clicking Close on the Manage Sites dialog box.

## Folder Mapping

The Project Sync feature enables one mapping from a Vault folder to a Buzzsaw folder. There might not be more than one mapping configured. These settings are per Vault basis. If you have more than one Vault, then each Vault can have its own mapping. Click Manage Mapping to configure your folder mappings. When the mapping is completed, the Vault and Buzzsaw folders are mapped to each other. The folder structure in these folders are replicated in the application as required.

### Add a Mapping

1.  Select Tools>Project Sync Settings to open the Project Sync Settings dialog box.

2.  Click Add Mapping.

3.  Select the Buzzsaw site containing the Buzzsaw folder that you want mapped.

 If the site that you want is not listed, click the plus sign to add a new site.

4.  Once the required site is selected, click the ellipses (...) button next to the Buzzsaw Folder and browse to the folder that you want to map on the Buzzsaw site. Click OK to return to the Add Mapping dialog.

**Important:** The folder must not already be mapped to another folder in a vault, nor can it contain folders that are already mapped. This is verified when you click OK on the Add Mapping dialog.

5.  Click the ellipses (…) button next to the Vault Folder and browse to the Vault folder to which you want the Buzzsaw folder mapped. Click OK to return to the Add Mapping dialog.

**Important:** The folder must not already be mapped to another folder in Buzzsaw, nor can it contain folders that are already mapped. This is verified when you click OK on the Add Mapping dialog.

6.  Click OK to verify the mapping. If all of the settings are valid, the mapping is saved. When the mapping is completed, the Vault and Buzzsaw folders are mapped to each other. The folder structure in these folders are replicated in the application as required.

## Synchronization

The synchronization settings enable you to configure how and when synchronization between the Autodesk Vault and Autodesk Buzzsaw folders take place.

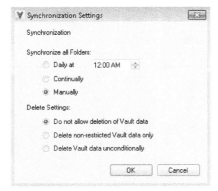

### Synchronize All Folders

Select the frequency for when synchronization between Autodesk Vault and Buzzsaw takes place.

- Daily at: Automatic synchronization between Vault and Buzzsaw will take place each day at the specified time.
- Continually: Automatic synchronization will take place every time the Job Processor executes jobs.
- Manually: Automatic synchronization is disabled with this setting. Synchronization will occur when you click Sync Now in the Vault stand-alone client. Choosing Sync Now will add the sync job to the Job Queue and will be processed the next time a processor runs.

### Delete Settings

Because administrators might not want to allow Autodesk Vault files to be deleted, they are able to configure what happens to files in the vault when files are deleted in Autodesk Buzzsaw.

- Do not allow deletion of Vault data: Files in the Vault will not be deleted if they are deleted in Buzzsaw.
- Delete non restricted Vault data only: Files in the Vault will be deleted if they are deleted on Buzzsaw, but only if an Administrator override is not required to delete the files.
- Delete Vault data unconditionally: Files in the Vault will be deleted if they are deleted on Buzzsaw, even if an Administrator override is required.

## Proxy Settings

The use of a proxy server can prevent the Vault server from synchronizing with the Buzzsaw server. If there is a proxy server in place, the administrators can configure the Project Sync tool to authenticate with the server.

1. Select Tools>Project Sync Settings to open the Project Sync Settings dialog box.
2. Click Configure.
3. In the Proxy Settings dialog box, check the box for Use a HTTP proxy server.
4. Fill in the HTTP proxy and Port data in the Proxy Server Settings field.
5. If authentication is required, input the authentication information in the Authentication Settings field. If not, leave them blank.
6. Choose OK.

The Project Sync tool will use this setting to synchronize data between Autodesk Vault and Autodesk Buzzsaw.

# Project Sync Commands

When Project Sync is installed, four new commands are added to the Vault client:

- Share to Buzzsaw
- Update from Buzzsaw
- Add from Buzzsaw
- Sync Now

Each command adds a job to the job queue. For the manual jobs, the job queue executes the command using the file(s) selected. For the Sync Now command, a job will be added to the queue that will synchronize the files between Vault and Buzzsaw databases.

## Share to Buzzsaw

The Share to Buzzsaw command enables you to upload the latest version of a vault file to the Buzzsaw server. Selected files are added from the Vault server to the Buzzsaw server based on the folder mapping configured on the Project Sync Settings dialog. If the file exists on the Buzzsaw server already, a new version is added.

1. In the Vault client, select the file or files that you would like to share to Buzzsaw.
2. Click Share to Buzzsaw
3. In the Share Options dialog, select one of the following options:
- Share the original selections only: Only the selected files are shared to Buzzsaw.
- Share the original selections and their dependencies: The selected files and all dependencies are shared to Buzzsaw. With this option, you can also select whether you want to share attachments and related documents as well.

If you choose to share attachments, any attachments to the dependencies are also shared.

For example, to share an Inventor assembly, a sub-assembly, child parts, and any related IDWs, select Share the original selections and their dependencies and choose the Also share related documents checkbox.

4.   Click OK.

A job for each selected file is added to the job queue and processed in the order in which it was added. These jobs are given a high priority and are processed before DWF publishing jobs.

## Update from Buzzsaw

The Update from Buzzsaw command enables you to update selected files from the Buzzsaw server to the Vault server. If there are no changes made to the files then no new version is created in the Vault.

1.   Select the file or files in Vault that you want to download from the Buzzsaw server.

2.   Click Update from Buzzsaw.

The updated files from Buzzsaw are compared against the Vault versions. If a file is unchanged then the file version is not changed. If there are changes in the file then a new version is created with the changes.

 The files must exist and be selected in Autodesk Vault for this command. Adding new files to the Vault can be done using the Add from Buzzsaw command.

A job for each selected file is added to the job queue and processed in the order in which it is added. These jobs are given a high priority and are processed before DWF publishing jobs.

## Add from Buzzsaw

Selected files are added from the Buzzsaw server to the Vault server. Any files that are not already in the Vault are added and any files that are already in the Vault are updated.

1.   Select the Add from Buzzsaw command.

2.   Navigate the Buzzsaw site and select the file or files that you would like to add to the Vault.

3.   Click Open.

## Sync Now

This command enables the user to synchronize all files in the mapped folders between the Vault server and the Buzzsaw server. If there are no changes made to the files then no new versions will be created in Vault or Buzzsaw.

1.   Click Sync Now to start synchronization.

During synchronization, any changes to the data in the Vault will be updated to Buzzsaw first. After changes have been updated from Vault to Buzzsaw, any remaining changes on Buzzsaw will be updated to the vault.

Once this command is selected, a sync job will be added to the job queue and will be processed in the order of priority and in which it was added. The job is given a high priority so it will be processed before jobs such as DWF publishing.

# Lesson: Replication

## Overview

Replication is the process of copying data from one server to another server usually located in two different physical locations. This process enables the setup of a Vault environment which has two different locations and users will not have to spend time downloading large CAD files across their Wide Area Network (WAN) connection. The replication solutions for Vault Professional include ADMS file store replication (multi-site, single workgroup configuration) for file store replication only, Full replication (connected workgroups configuration) for both file store and SQL database replication, and Autodesk Vault File Server (AVFS) which is an alternative file store replication solution.

### Objectives

After completing this lesson, you will be able to:

- Differentiate between an ADMS File Store Replication and a Full Replication
- Enable and Disable Workgroup Replication
- Add and Delete Workgroups
- Enable and Disable a Vault for a Multi-Site Environment
- Replicate a Vault, Files and Folders
- Export, Import and Configure Replication Priorities
- Schedule Replication for a Multi-Site Environment
- Describe benefits of Autodesk Vault File Server (AVFS)

# Replication Solutions Overview

Data replication is only available in a multi-site environment. A multi-site environment consists of multiple remote sites that can be configured to access the same vault data. A site is comprised of a dedicated Autodesk data management server and a file store. Each site accesses a shared AUTODESKVAULT SQL instance. The SQL database tracks which files and versions are at each site in a multi-site environment. Each site can be synchronized so that newer files and newer versions are shared across sites. Individual vaults can be replicated, or all of the enabled vaults on a site can be replicated. Replication can also be scheduled. By default, replication is set for 12:00 AM (midnight) each weekday when a vault is enabled. During the day, if a user finds that a file is not located on their site, they can replicate the file on demand. Companies which have multiple design organizations which work on the same projects need the ability to collaborate and share files.

Full replication, or Connected Workgroups, is an architecture suited for multiple sites that are distributed over great distances or poor networks. With this architecture, SQL databases are replicated across the multiple locations, as well as the file store.

The Autodesk Vault File Server (AVFS) is an alternative to the traditional ADMS file store replication solution.

### ADMS File Store Replication (Multi-site with single Workgroup)

You can replicate file stores from one site to another site. This process is managed by a Microsoft SQL database. The configuration used in the replication is known as a workgroup. The following illustration shows a typical workgroup configuration. All sites in a single workgroup share the same Microsoft SQL server.

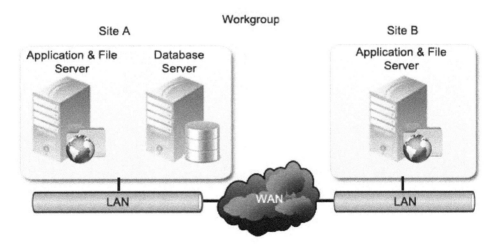

## Full Replication (Connected Workgroups)

To enable sites to have their own database server to increase SQL performance, the Autodesk Vault software uses connected workgroups. The following illustration shows a workgroup with two different sites connected to a second workgroup with a single site.

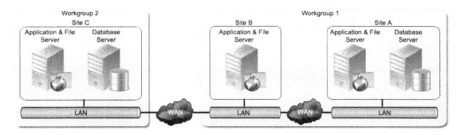

The connected workgroup feature, or full replication, supports the use of multiple database servers using Microsoft SQL Publisher/Subscriber technology. This technology enables the replication of the SQL database at multiple locations.

The terminology used for a Connected Workgroup (i.e., full replication) environment includes:

- **Site:** A location where the Vault server software is installed to which users connect using the client application.
- **Workgroup:** A group of sites connecting to the same SQL database.
- **Publisher:** The first SQL server configured in a full replicated environment.
- **Subscriber:** SQL servers replicating to the Publisher in a full replicated environment.

## Autodesk Vault File Server (AVFS)

AVFS offers a number of benefits over ADMS file store replication by providing a simpler install and configure solution, and an increase in the Autodesk Vault server connection performance. With an ADMS file store replication, each server has an installation of ADMS. This means that each user speaks to a local server, which then connects to the remote SQL server to execute SQL interactions. Due to the remote communications between ADMS and SQL, the client will experience a delay in response until the remote communications are complete. AVFS cuts out this intermediary step.

Users will still now log into a local AVFS server, which is configured to redirect the user's information requests. This means that the user communicates directly with the ADMS residing closest to the SQL, making it much faster to search and perform any database-related activity.

The file store still resides on the AVFS machine, so file retrieval is done locally and files are replicated the same as before. The only difference is that there is no ADMS installed on the server to process any SQL-bound requests.

# Manage Workgroup Replication

### Enable Workgroup Replication

To create a connected workgroup environment, workgroup replication must be enabled. Workgroup replication must be enabled from the publisher site before installing the subscriber sites.

1. Use Windows Explorer to create a network shared folder.

2. In the navigation pane, select Workgroups.

3. Right-click and select Enable Workgroup Replication.

4. Enter the path to the network shared folder.

5. Enter the user account setup to run replication. This account should have access to the network shared folder.

6. Enter and confirm the password for the replication account.

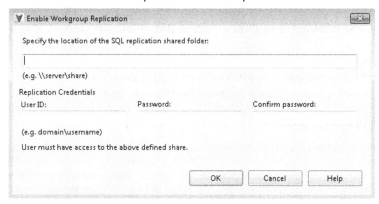

### Disable Workgroup Replication

To discontinue the use of a connected workgroup environment, workgroup replication must be disabled. Before disabling workgroup replication, all workgroups must be deleted.

1. In the navigation pane, select Workgroups.

2. Right-click and select Disable Workgroup Replication.

3. If the subscribing sites have not been deleted, check the box to delete the subscribing sites.

4. Click OK.

### Configure Workgroup Replication

Once a workgroup has been added to the Connected Workgroup environment, each vault in the new workgroup has to be configured to replicate. Only vaults selected to replicate from one workgroup will be accessible from a different workgroup.

1. In the navigation pane, select the workgroup of the Vault to be replicated.
2. In the right pane, right-click the Vault to replicate and select Manage Replication.
3. Use Add (>>) and Remove (<<) to select which workgroups to replicate the Vault.
4. Click OK.

# Adding and Deleting Workgroups

### Add a Workgroup

Before adding a subscribing Workgroup, a supported version of Microsoft SQL Server must be installed on the Subscribing server (the same version as is installed on the Publishing server). Vault does not support connected workgroups on Microsoft SQL Express.

 Do not install the Vault server on the subscribing server.

1. Install Microsoft SQL with an instance named AUTODESKVAULT on the subscribing server.
2. Launch the Vault server console from the publishing server.
3. Right-click on the workgroups node and select Add Workgroup.

4. In the Add Workgroup dialog, enter the required information.
5. Click OK.
- **Workgroup Name:** The name of the new workgroup.
- **Workgroup Label:** The unique name for the new workgroup. This name will be tied to all schemes created for this workgroup.
- **Subscriber Server Name:** The name of the server with SQL installed for the new workgroup.
- **Remote SQL Credentials:** The login credentials for the new SQL server being used for the new workgroup.
- **Remote Replication Credentials:** The credentials set up for replication when defined when configuring the publishing server.

### Delete a Workgroup

A workgroup that is no longer required can be deleted. A workgroup can be deleted using the server console from the publisher workgroup.

1. In the navigation pane, select Workgroups.

2. Right-click a workgroup in the list and select Delete Workgroup.

3. When prompted for confirmation to delete the workgroup, click yes.

4. If an error occurs where the subscriber database cannot be cleaned up, repeat the process but select Unconditional delete.

# Replicate a Vault

Use the following steps to replicate a vault from the Autodesk Data Management Server console.

1. In the navigation pane, expand the Workgroups node.

2. Expand the correct workgroup node.

3. Expand the correct site node.

4. Select a vault located on the current site from the list.

5. Right-click the site, and then select the replication option:

- Replicate Now: Synchronize all of the vaults on the current site immediately.

- Replicate Folders: Select which folders and files to replicate.

- Replication Schedule: Establish a synchronization schedule, or toggle off scheduled synchronization.

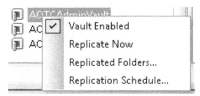

# Replicate Files and Folders

Folder and file replication can be accessed from the Autodesk Data Management Server console navigation pane.

 You can also replicate files and folders from the Replication Schedule dialog box by clicking Replicated Folders.

Use the following steps to access the folder and file replication dialog box from the Autodesk Data Management Server console.

1. In the navigation pane select, the workgroup of the vault to be replicated.

2. In the right pane, right-click the vault to replicate and select Replicated Folders.

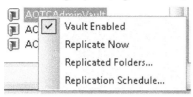

3. By default all folders will be checked. Uncheck any folders which do not need to be replicated. Check folders which need to be replicated.

 This feature only controls which files will be replicated from the file store and not the metadata about the files. Regardless of what is selected, all metadata is replicated to the subscriber sites. If you want to limit visibility of metadata, you need to apply the correct security on the folders and files.

# Enable or Disable a Vault for a Multi-Site Environment

### Enable a Vault

To make a vault accessible to other sites, it must be enabled. When a vault is enabled, it is available to all sites in a multi-site environment. Only vaults at the site from which the server console is running can be enabled. To enable a vault:

1. In the navigation pane, expand the Workgroups node.

2. Select the site to work with.

3. Select a vault located on the current site from the list.

4. Right-click on the vault name and then select Vault Enabled.

5. If the file store path for the selected vault is not set or is invalid, you are prompted to specify the file store path for the selected vault. Specify the location of the file store and then click OK.

6. You are prompted to select whether the vault data is synchronized now or at the next scheduled replication. By default, replication is set for 12:00 AM (midnight) each weekday.

### Disable a Vault

To restrict any other site from accessing a vault, it must be disabled. When a vault is disabled, it is no longer available to any other site in a multi-site environment. A disabled vault is available only to the site where the vault is located. Only vaults at the site from which the server console is running can be disabled. To disable a vault:

1. In the navigation pane, select Sites.

2. Select the line containing the current site and the vault to enable at this site.

3. Right-click on the vault name and then toggle off Vault Enabled.

### View Site Details

To view site details:

1.  In the ADMS console navigation pane, select Workgroups.

2.  Select the Site that you want to manage.

Each site is listed along with a summary of site statistics, including:

| | |
|---|---|
| Server Name | Replication Type |
| Description | Last Replication |
| Location of File Store | Next Replication |
| Vault Name | Site Status |
| Vault Status | |

# Replication Priorities

Replication Priority (Site Affinity) enables administrators to gain control of how multi-site and database replication files are handled from site to site. Replication Priority enables you to set up a preferred list of Sites or a selected Site for file replication. With Replication priority, you can prioritize Sites in the preferred Sites list. Once Replication Priority has been set up for a Site, any subsequent file replication (both on-demand and scheduled) uses the preferred list of Sites. Replication Priorities for all Sites can be exported to an XML file which can then be edited in a text editor and imported back into Vault.

## Configure Replication Priority

1.  On the Server Console, select a Site by expanding the Workgroups node and then expand the Site's workgroup.

2.  Right-click on the site and select Manage Replication Priority.

3.  On the Manage Replication Priority dialog, add Sites to the Prioritized section by using Add.

4.  Prioritize Sites in the Prioritized section by using Move Up and Move Down.

5.  Click OK to save your changes.

## Export Replication Priorities

1.  In the Server Console, right-click on the Workgroups node and select Export Replication Priorities.

2. Select a location, enter a name in the Save dialog box, and click Save.

3. Click OK on the confirmation dialog.

4. Open the XML file in a text editor.

5. Set up Replication Priority by editing the XML file and saving your changes.

### Import Replication Priorities

1. In the Server Console, right-click on the Workgroup node and select Import Replication Priorities.

2. Browse to where the XML file with the Replication Priority is located.

3. Select the file and click Open.

4. Click OK on the confirmation dialog.

5. Validate the import by selecting each Site under the Workgroup node and viewing the Site's Replication Priority table.

# Schedule Replication for a Multi-Site Environment

Data replication can be scheduled to occur daily, or at a specified intervals. By default, replication is set for 12:00 AM (midnight) each weekday when a vault is enabled.

1. In the navigation pane, expand the workgroup node.

2. Select the workgroup you want to work with.

3. Select the appropriate site.

4. Right-click on the Vault, and then select Replication Schedule.

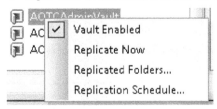

5. In the Scheduled Replication dialog box, select the Enable scheduled replication checkbox.

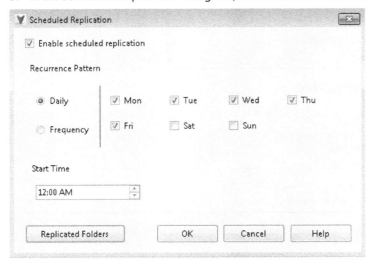

6. Choose either a daily schedule or a replication frequency.

- **Daily:** The default daily replication schedule is weekdays at midnight. Specify a start time and select which days to perform the replication.

- **Frequency:** Specify a start time and then select how often the replication is performed.

7. Click OK.

# Autodesk Vault File Server (AVFS) Configuration

Once the Vault File Server is installed, you need to launch and configure the server settings before you can begin using the Vault File Server.

1. Launch the Vault File Server Console

2. On the Server Configuration dialog, enter the server where your Vault Server is located. The Vault File Server cannot be installed on the same machine as the Vault Server.

 The default port is 80. You must manually insert a different port if required. For example: RTH5Server:90.

3. Perform one of the following tasks:

- Select the Windows Authentication checkbox to log into the Vault File Server using your Microsoft Windows user account credentials

- Enter the user name and password assigned to you by your system administrator

4. Click OK to complete the configuration and begin using the Vault File Server

# Chapter Summary

The high flexible configuration and administration functionality in Autodesk Vault Professional makes it easy and possible to manage users, groups and their rights and rules. Same with the backend and security of Vault. Backup and Restore becomes an easy job and reflects the powerful functionality of Autodesk Vault. The Project Sync utility provides powerful synchronization capabilities to facilitate sharing of project data between the Autodesk Vault and Autodesk Buzzsaw products. The Autodesk Vault Professional software has multiple replication solutions available to suit your organization's needs, such as the ADMS file store replication (multi-site, single workgroup configuration) for file store replication only, Full replication (connected workgroups configuration) for both file store and SQL database replication, and Autodesk Vault File Server (AVFS), an alternative file store replication solution.

Having completed this chapter, you can:

- Manage User accounts regarding the Active Directory.
- Manage Groups in Autodesk Vault.
- Use the Project Sync utility to synchronize files and folders between Autodesk Vault and Autodesk Buzzsaw products.
- Differentiate between an ADMS File Store Replication and a Full Replication.
- Enable and Disable Workgroup Replication.
- Add and Delete Workgroups.
- Enable and Disable a Vault for a Multi-Site Environment.
- Replicate a Vault, Files and Folders.
- Export, Import and Configure Replication Priorities.
- Schedule Replication for a Multi-Site Environment.
- Describe benefits of Autodesk Vault File Server (AVFS).

# Additional Resources

A variety of resources are available to help you get the most from your Autodesk® software. Whether you prefer instructor-led, self-paced, or online training, Autodesk has you covered.

For additional information, please refer to the disc that accompanies this learning guide.

- Learning Tools from Autodesk
- Autodesk Certification
- Autodesk Authorized Training Centers (ATC®)
- Autodesk Subscription
- Autodesk Communities

## Learning Tools from Autodesk

Use your Autodesk software to its full potential. Whether you are a novice or an advanced user, Autodesk offers a robust portfolio of learning tools to help you perform ahead of the curve.

- Get hands-on experience with job-related exercises based on industry scenarios from Autodesk Official Training Guides, e-books, self-paced learning, and training videos.
- All materials are developed by Autodesk subject matter experts.
- Get exactly the training you need with learning tools designed to fit a wide range of skill levels and subject matter—from basic essentials to specialized in-depth training on the capabilities of the latest Autodesk products.
- Access the most comprehensive set of Autodesk learning tools available anywhere: from your authorized partner, online, or at your local bookstore.
- To find out more, visit http://www.autodesk.com/learning.

## Autodesk Certification

Demonstrate your experience with Autodesk software. Autodesk certifications are a reliable validation of your skills and knowledge. Demonstrate your software skills to prospective employers, accelerate your professional development, and enhance your reputation in your field.

## Certification Benefits

- Rapid diagnostic feedback to assess your strengths and identify areas for improvement.
- An electronic certificate with a unique serial number.
- The right to use an official Autodesk Certification logo.
- The option to display your certification status in the Autodesk Certified Professionals database.

## For more information:

Visit www.autodesk.com/certification to learn more and to take the next steps to get certified.

## Autodesk Authorized Training Centers

Enhance your productivity and learn how to realize your ideas faster with Autodesk software. Get trained at an Autodesk Authorized Training Center (ATC) with hands-on, instructor-led classes to help you get the most from your Autodesk products. Autodesk has a global network of Authorized Training Centers that are carefully selected and monitored to ensure you receive high-quality results- oriented learning. ATCs provide the best way for beginners and experts alike to get up to speed. The training helps you get the greatest return on your investment, faster, by building your knowledge in the areas you need the most. Many organizations provide training on our software, but only the educational institutions and private training providers recognized as ATC sites have met Autodesk's rigorous standards of excellence.

## Find an Authorized Training Center

With over 2,000 ATCs in more than 90 countries around the world, there is probably one close to you. Visit the ATC locator at www.autodesk.com/atc to find an Autodesk Authorized Training Center near you. Look for ATC courses offered at www.autodesk.com/atcevents.

Many ATCs also offer end-user Certification testing. Locate a testing center near you at www.autodesk.starttest.com.

## Autodesk Subscription

Autodesk® Subscription helps you minimize costs, increase productivity, and make the most of your Autodesk software investment. With monthly, quarterly, annual, and multi-year options, you can get the exact software you require for as long as you need it. For a fee based on the term length, you receive upgrades released during your contract term. Subscribers can also get licensed software that they can use on their home computer.

- For more information, visit www.autodesk.com/subscription.

## Autodesk User Communities

Autodesk customers can take advantage of free Autodesk software, self-paced tutorials, worldwide discussion groups and forums, job postings, and more. Become a member of an Autodesk Community today!

 Free products are subject to the terms and conditions of the end-user license agreement that accompanies download of the software.

## Feedback

Autodesk understands the importance of offering you the best learning experience possible. If you have comments, suggestions, or general inquiries about Autodesk Learning, please contact us at learningtools@autodesk.com.

As a result of the feedback we receive from you, we hope to validate and append to our current research on how to create a better learning experience for our customers.

## Useful Links

Learning Tools

www.autodesk.com/learning

Certification

www.autodesk.com/certification

Find an Authorized Training Center

www.autodesk.com/atc

Find an Authorized Training Center Course

www.autodesk.com/atcevents

Autodesk Store

store.autodesk.com

Communities

www.autodesk.com/community

Student Community

students.autodesk.com

Blogs

www.autodesk.com/blogs

Discussion Groups

forums.autodesk.com